W9-CLH-721

The
Jutland Scandal

The
Jutland Scandal

The Truth about the First World War's Greatest Sea Battle

**Rear Admiral J.E.T. Harper CB, MVO
and
Admiral Sir Reginald Bacon KCB, KCVO, DSO**

Skyhorse Publishing

First Skyhorse Publishing 2016
Copyright © 2016 by Frontline Books, an imprint of Pen & Sword Books Ltd

Part I first published as The Truth About Jutland, by Rear Admiral J.E.T. Harper CB, MVO in 1927 by John Murray Ltd., London. Part II first published as The Jutland Scandal, by Admiral Sir Reginald Bacon KCB, KCVO, DSO in 1933 by Hutchinson & Co Ltd, London.

Skyhorse Publishing books may be purchased in bulk at special discounts for sales promotion, corporate gifts, fund-raising, or educational purposes. Special editions can also be created to specifications. For details, contact the Special Sales Department, Skyhorse Publishing, 307 West 36th Street, 11th Floor, New York, NY 10018 or info@skyhorsepublishing.com.

Visit our website at www.skyhorsepublishing.com.

10 9 8 7 6 5 4 3 2 1

Jacket design: Dave Cassan
Jacket images: Pen & Sword Books; Historic Military Press

Library of Congress Cataloging-in-Publication Data is available on file.

Print ISBN: 978-1-5107-0871-6
Ebook ISBN: 978-1-5107-0859-4

Printed in the United States of America

Contents

List of Illustrations in Plate Section

1: The 1st Earl Beatty (17 January 1871 – 11 March 1936) whilst a Vice Admiral.

2: Admiral John Jellicoe (5 December 1859 – 20 November 1935), pictured wearing the uniform of Admiral of the Fleet, the rank he attained in 1919.

3: The British Grand Fleet on its way to meet the warships of Imperial German Navy's High Seas Fleet in the North Sea on 31 May 1916.

4: The bow and stern of HMS *Invincible* sticking out of the water as the battlecruiser sinks. The destroyer HMS *Badger* is desperately searching for survivors. *Invincible*'s remains were first located in 1919 and she was found to have been blown in half by the explosion. Pieces of the wreckage rest on a sandy bottom near each other, the stern right-side up and the bow upside-down. The roof of the aft 12-inch turret is missing, the guns still loaded.

5: Damage caused to a British light cruiser at Jutland. Unfortunately, it is not known which of the light cruisers damaged this is. Two, HMS *Black Prince* and HMS *Tipperary*, were sunk, whilst HMS *Southampton* was the light cruiser hit the most times – with eighteen shells striking her.

6: Taken from the deck of HMS *Inflexible*, the next ship astern, this picture shows the massive plume of smoke caused when HMS *Invincible* exploded during the Battle of Jutland after she was hit five times by shells from the German battlecruisers *Derfflinger* and *Lützow*. The last hit blew the roof off 'Q' Turret and set fire to the cordite propellant. The flash soon spread to the magazine and *Invincible* was ripped in two by the explosion. She sank with the loss of all but six of her crew of 1,021 (though the number of survivors varies from account to account). One of the survivors, Gunnery Officer Hubert Dannreuther, was the godson of the composer Richard Wagner. Admiral Hood was among the dead.

7: HMS *Royal Oak*, HMS *Acasta*, HMS *Benbow*, HMS *Superb* and HMS *Canada* in action during the battle. The latter had originally been built for the Chilean Navy, but was purchased by the British on the outbreak of war in 1914. During the Battle of Jutland, HMS *Canada* fired forty-two rounds from her 14-inch guns and 109 6-inch shells. She suffered no hits or casualties. Amongst the targets engaged was the cruiser *Wiesbaden*.

8: The Royal Navy's battlecruiser HMS *Indomitable* pictured in port. She damaged the German battlecruisers *Seydlitz* and *Derfflinger* during the Battle of Jutland.

9: Damage to SMS *Derfflinger* pictured after the Battle of Jutland. During the course of the engagement, *Derfflinger* was hit seventeen times by heavy calibre shells and nine times by secondary guns. She was in dock for repairs until 15 October 1916. *Derfflinger* fired 385 shells from her main battery, another 235 rounds from her secondary guns, and one torpedo.

10: The funeral pyre of HMS *Queen Mary* during the Battle of Jutland. After a German salvo had hit this battlecruiser amidships, her bows plunged down and her stern rose high in the air. A few minutes later there was nothing to be seen but this pillar of smoke rising hundreds of feet into the air. All but nine of her 1,266 crew were lost – two of the survivors were picked up by German ships.

11: HMS *Lion* leading the battlecruisers during the Battle of Jutland. At one point in the battle, a heavy shell struck HMS *Lion*'s Q-turret, entered the gun-house, burst over the left gun, and killed nearly the whole of the guns' crews. It was only the actions of Major F.J.W. Harvey, RMLI that saved the flagship from sudden destruction; in spite of both his legs being shot off he was able to pass the word down to close the magazine doors and flood the magazines. Harvey thus prevented the fire which had started from reaching the ammunition, an action for which he was posthumously awarded the Victoria Cross.

12: The German battlecruiser SMS *Seydlitz* on fire during the fighting on 31 May 1916.

13: A chunk of armour knocked from HMS *New Zealand*'s 'X' Turret during the Battle of Jutland. It can be seen on display at the Torpedo Bay Navy Museum in Auckland.

14: The German battleship SMS *Schleswig-Holstein* fires a salvo during the Battle of Jutland.

15: The Revenge-class battleship HMS *Royal Oak*. Completed in 1916, *Royal Oak* first saw action at the Battle of Jutland.

16: British and German sailors buried side by side in Frederikshavn Cemetery. Pictured here during the 1920s, the British memorial is on the left; the German one nearest the camera. Frederikshavn is a port in northern Jutland, about twenty-five miles from the northernmost point of Denmark. Buried there are four First World War casualties, all naval ratings killed in the Battle of Jutland.

17: A surprising relic from Jutland – the last surviving warship that participated in the battle which is still afloat. HMS *Caroline*, a C-class light cruiser, was built by Cammell Laird at Birkenhead, and launched in December 1914. Along with her sister ships of the Fourth Light Cruiser Squadron, HMS *Caroline* formed part of the anti-submarine screen for the Royal Navy battleships as they rushed south towards the German battlecruisers. During the main battle she took part in the destroyer clash between the main fleets; towards the end of this main action, her squadron caught sight of a group of German capital ships, believed to be their battlecruisers and pre-dreadnaught battleships, and fired two torpedoes at them.

Foreword

For most British people brought up to believe in the invincibility of the Royal Navy, Jutland was probably the most disappointing battle fought during the Great War. The heaviest British losses occurred during the first phase of the battle when a force of six battlecruisers and four modern battleships, commanded by Vice Admiral Sir David Beatty, lost two battlecruisers and two destroyers while engaging a German squadron of five battlecruisers which lost just two destroyers. Once the main action was joined, the ratio of capital ships was seven to five in favour of the Royal Navy. The latter lost one battlecruiser, three old armoured cruisers and six destroyers while the Germans lost one battlecruiser, one pre-dreadnought battleship, four cruisers and three destroyers. Furthermore, the High Seas Fleet suffered far more damage than it inflicted in terms hits on surviving ships. Consequently, once Scheer encountered the full might of the Grand Fleet he had only one aim: to avoid further combat by getting back to base under the cover of darkness.

Thus, while it is clear that the Germans secured a tactical victory in the initial battlecruiser duel, it is also clear that they were defeated once the Jellicoe's battleships joined the fray. It is also obvious that despite sinking more British ships and causing more fatalities, the Germans suffered a strategic defeat from which they never recovered. That being the case, why was the outcome of the battle so controversial and divisive?

In one respect, Jutland assisted the Royal Navy by shattering the over-confidence in materiel and training but the spectacle of seeing four large British warships explode must have had an effect on all who witnessed it. A 'Trafalgar' on 31 May 1916 would have, in all probability, restored British naval supremacy for decades. Instead, the failure to annihilate the High Seas Fleet meant that the Royal Navy began to lose its moral ascendency after Jutland. Thus, with the passage of time it became less and less likely that those manning the fleets of, for example, Japan and the United States of America, would be overawed by the force of British naval tradition.

Controversy about Jutland was inevitable because poor visibility meant that no two British commanders had the same view of the battle. Consequently, there were never more than three or four German capital ships in sight from any part of Jellicoe's battlefleet, despite the presence of over 250 ships in the area. Unfortunately, the failure to convert the tactically indecisive Jutland into a 'Trafalgar', despite the public expectation of such an outcome, had a corrosive effect on the Royal Navy leading to the growth of Jellicoe and Beatty factions within its officer corps.

However, the Jutland controversy was more than a personal dispute between Jellicoe and Beatty and their respective supporters. Instead, it should be viewed as part of the British response to the Great War and their subsequent feelings of failure, futility and revulsion at the whole bloody business.

Dr. Richard Osborne
Nailsea, July 2015

Introduction

For more than 100 years Britain's position as the world's leading naval power was never seriously challenged. Yet, between the Battle of Trafalgar and the start of the First World War, almost every aspect of naval warfare had changed. Over the course of the intervening century, iron and then steel had replaced wood, and the standard 32-pounder cannon of Nelson's day that was designed for close range fighting had been superseded by the 15-inch breech-loading gun that fired a shell weighing 1,938lbs a distance of more than nineteen miles. Possibly the most significant change, however, was from sail to steam. No longer was the movement of ships dictated by the vagaries of the wind.

All of these changes meant that much of the Royal Navy's sailing and gunnery expertise, passed down from generation to generation, had been lost. Britain, though, had invested heavily in its navy, ensuring that in terms of both technology and scale, it remained far in advance of any other country. The new and energetic state of Germany, nevertheless, sought to rival Britain and an enormously expensive arms race between the two nations began towards the end of the nineteenth century, backed by wide-spread public support. This reached its peak with the introduction of the Dreadnought-class of battleships which were far superior to any that had preceded it, so superior in fact that all earlier classes of battleships were immediately rendered obsolescent. It seemed that whoever had the most Dreadnoughts, not the most warships, would win the next battle. So, once again, the advantages that the Royal Navy had over its rivals was in danger of being lost. Britain might well have by far the largest and most powerful navy, but if Germany could build more Dreadnoughts it might well win a war at sea.

When war broke out in the summer of 1914 Britain still retained a numerical advantage over Germany, having built twenty-nine Dreadnoughts to Germany's seventeen, but the Battle of Tsushima, fought between Japan and Russia in 1905, indicated that having more battleships did not necessarily ensure victory.

In that battle the Russians had twice as many battleships as the Japanese, but the latter had an enormous advantage in the number of cruisers and destroyers. The Russian fleet was all but destroyed and the remnants compelled to surrender at sea. This was the only large-scale engagement with modern vessels prior to the First World War and it indicated that there were other factors to consider beyond having the most ships with the biggest guns. No-one knew, therefore, how the Royal Navy would fare in a major fleet action with the latest warships.

So, when after almost two years of cat-and-mouse antics in the North Sea the British Grand Fleet and the *Kaiserliche Marine*'s High Seas Fleet met on 31 May 1916 off Denmark's Jutland Peninsula, it was the climax of years of preparation and anticipation.

As is well-known, the result of the Battle of Jutland was indecisive, despite the Royal Navy's huge numerical advantage in every category of warship involved. As the commander of the Grand Fleet, it was Admiral Sir John Jellicoe who was considered to have failed in destroying the enemy and this view was propagated by the ambitious Vice Admiral Sir David Beatty, who led the Battle Cruiser Fleet. As a result Jellicoe was moved from an active sea command to become First Sea Lord. Beatty replaced him as commander of the Grand Fleet.

The British public demanded to know the truth about Jutland and an official account of the battle was eagerly awaited. The new First Sea Lord, Admiral of the Fleet Rosslyn Erskine Wemyss who had superseded Jellicoe, instructed Captain John Ernest Troyte Harper to "prepare a record, with plans, showing in chronological order what actually occurred in the battle". The account was to be based solely on the written records available at the Admiralty, without commentary on the merits of what had taken place. Its official title was *The Record of the Battle of Jutland* and became known as the *Harper Record*.

Harper duly completed his investigation into the battle and submitted his report. Though he had endeavored to be impartial, his research indicated that the actions of Beatty, and who had been seen as the hero of the Battle of Jutland, were not as glorious as had been portrayed. Harper later wrote that: "We find that on the British side Beatty had under his command 4 battleships and 6 battle-cruisers against Hipper's 5 battle-cruisers. In light cruisers and destroyers Beatty was also numerically superior. In spite of this overwhelming preponderance of power, we lost two battle-cruisers, sunk by gunfire, while the enemy lost none. Considerably more damage was caused to our ships than they inflicted on the enemy. It *is* unpalatable – extremely unpalatable – but nevertheless an indisputable fact that, in this first phase of the battle, a British squadron, greatly superior in numbers and gun-power, not only failed to defeat a weaker enemy who made no effort to avoid action, but, in the space of 50 minutes, suffered what can only be described as a partial defeat."

Harper also showed Beatty's own ship, HMS *Lion*, puzzlingly performing a complete circular turn. Beatty claimed that he had not turned a full circle but instead that it had manoeuvred through two 180 degree turns in an 's' shape.

As Harper had drawn his evidence exclusively from the written records, it meant that he did not interview any of the participants in the battle and was, consequently, not subject to the influence of any individual or group. This meant that his account was factual and unbiased.

The first draft of Harper's report, which was completed on 2 October 1919, was passed around the Admiralty and a number of corrections and alterations were suggested. Over the succeeding months this led to two further revisions and a third proof was produced.

Amongst those who inspected Harper's account was of course Beatty, the rising star of the Royal Navy, who objected to elements of the account. He claimed that the the logs kept during battle were inaccurate, and he succeeded in blocking its publication. At the beginning of 1919 Beatty was promoted to full Admiral and before the end of the year had replaced Wemyss as First Sea Lord. Beatty was now in a position to ensure that the *Harper Record* never saw the light of day. The general public, though, still demanded answers and, as it was known that Harper had completed his account, the clamour for its release grew. There were even repeated questions raised in Parliament and equally repeated promises that Harper's account would be published, but those promises remained unfulfilled.

The longer that *Harper Record* was delayed, the more people began to question the reasons for its non-publication. In the end Beatty decided that the only way to "clear up the supposed mystery" was to publish Harper's original record. However, no copies of this could be found at the Admiralty. Finally, it was agreed that the third proof would be the one that would be published. Even then, it was proposed to include the caveat that "this is not regarded as an official report". However, this had to be dropped when it was pointed out that this would imply that work undertaken on behalf of the Admiralty had been "unsupervised and undirected".

It was thought advisable that an explanatory Foreword would be included with the *Harper Record* and Sir Julian Corbett, who was in the process of compiling the third volume of the *Official History of the Great War – Naval Operations*, was approached. Sir Julian's publishers, Longman, Green and Co., were very unhappy with this because the volume they were about to release was the one that dealt with Jutland. This meant that two "official" reports on the same battle were about to be published at the same time!

C.J. Longman wrote to Sir Julian, asking him: "Will not this seriously interfere with your account of the Battle of Jutland? If, as may be the case, you differ from Captain Harper will it be possible to reconcile two 'official' accounts?"

Longman was also believed that his company would suffer "loss and injury" as his book would be competing for sales with the *Harper Record*. "Under the agreement between H.M. Stationery Office and ourselves, the exclusive right of publication of the 'Official' Naval History of the War is vested in us," Longman informed the Admiralty, with the underlying threat of legal action. Their Lordships, therefore had little choice but to shelve the *Harper Record*.

More fuel was added to the fire in 1924 when Filson Young, author of *With the Battlecruisers*, published an article in *The Sunday Express* in which he attacked Jellicoe's cautious approach to the battle. This partisan and inaccurate attack provoked a furious response from Admiral Sir Reginald Bacon and prompted him to produce his own account of the battle, which he called *The Jutland Scandal* in 1925. He wrote the book to set the record straight, particularly to counter the growing "blind hero-worship" that led to "the belief that the surest way of belauding Lord Beatty lay in belittling Lord Jellicoe". It contained a complete reproduction of *The Sunday Express* article and a point-by-point demolition of Young's arguments.

Inevitably, the hiatus in producing an official account led to others taking up their pens, including Winston Churchill. The former First Lord of the Admiralty supported Beatty, placing the blame for the escape of the High Seas Fleet squarely on Jellicoe's shoulders. 'Praiseworthy caution had induced a defensive habit of mind and scheme of tactics which hampered the Grand Fleet', wrote Churchill in *The World Crisis*, adding to this by describing Jellicoe as being 'ponderous'.

Harper's original report into the battle was never published – though a small number of copies of the *Harper Record* was printed and one of these can now be viewed at the British Library. As a result, John Harper took it upon himself to set before the public his account of the battle and *The Truth About Jutland* was published in 1927.

The great irony is that the *Harper Record* was a clinical study of the movements and actions of the ships involved. It drew no conclusions and made no attempt at ascribing blame, whereas in *The Truth About Jutland*, being an unofficial document, Harper was able to put his own interpretation of events. The consequence of this being that Beatty was given far harsher treatment. Had Beatty permitted the *Harper Record* to be published it would have raised few eyebrows. But by suppressing this entirely factual report he compelled Bacon and Harper to act, and in doing so undoubtedly tarnished Beatty's reputation.

This is evidenced by the fact that the *Harper Record* included a considerable number of plans and diagrams and it was decided by the Admiralty that these could be made available for the public to view. There is no record of anyone ever bothering to look at those diagrams.

It is interesting to read that when Harper chose to publish his own book he applied to the Admiralty for a copy of the *Record*. This was the secret

Admiralty view of this request: "An officer who has served at the Admiralty has no claim to be furnished with a copy of an official minute or memorandum of which he is the author." However, "to avoid any excuse for the blowing of another bubble over this matter", Their Lordships allowed Harper to have a copy which formed the basis of *The Truth About Jutland*.

What is presented here in this volume, published together for the first time to mark the 100th anniversary of the Battle of Jutland, is both Harper's account of the battle (Part I) and Reginald Bacon's *The Jutland Scandal* (Part II). Though originally published independently, the accounts are complementary – the blocking of one led to the production of the other. Their juxtaposition is further reinforced by the fact that Bacon revised his book after *The Truth About Jutland* had finally been revealed to the public, and it is that revised 1933 edition which is included here.

The original text of the two books has been retained with just a few minor corrections to obvious errors. The notes and references have been modified to equate more closely with modern convention and an index covering both volumes has been added.

Rarely has a battle prompted such prolonged bitterness between the leading individuals on the same side. Beatty initially emerged the victor from the contest between the two British admirals, but time has allowed a more balanced verdict – thanks to the two most important early accounts of the largest naval battle in history *The Jutland Scandal* and *The Truth About Jutland*.

John Grehan
Shoreham-by-Sea, May 2015

PART I

THE TRUTH ABOUT JUTLAND
Rear-Admiral J.E.T. Harper CB, MVO

Introduction

I want to make it quite clear that this is *not* the so-called *Harper Record*, so frequently demanded in the House of Commons. The Official Record of the Battle of Jutland, which I was originally directed, by Admiral-of-the-Fleet Lord Wester Wemyss, to prepare and which was completed in October 1919,[1] was simply a plain, straightforward narrative of the sequence of events, together with track charts showing the movements of every ship present on both sides. It was, in fact, "the truth about Jutland", from start to finish, in the form of an unvarnished statement based solely on documentary evidence and free from comment or criticism. By Lord Wester Wemyss' direction, all statements made in the Record were to have been in accordance with evidence obtainable from Official documents, and no oral evidence was to be accepted. These instructions were faithfully followed by me, as stated by Lord Wester Wemyss in a letter to the Press published on 16th December 1920.

Had the Record been published, in its original form, it would have been of no great interest to the reader looking for something sensational, but it would have prevented the flood of misconceptions and misrepresentations with which the public has been misled for some seven years past. It would also have prevented the controversy, largely of a personal nature, so virulently waged in the Press.

On the other hand, it is a very good thing that in its ultimate form it never did see the light of day. The whole story of the deletions, alterations and additions – or in Parliamentary language "the necessary revision of the material"[2] – demanded by those in authority cannot be told in these pages. The vicissitudes which the original Record underwent must, however, be patent to anyone who followed the series of tortuous manoeuvres and official prevarications in Parliament whenever it was asked for. In this connection a somewhat lengthy précis of a very few of the many Answers on the subject, in chronological order, will now be given. Space does not permit of quoting these in full.[3] The italics are mine.

1

1919

19th March "Steps are already being taken to draw up a narrative showing the actual sequence of events ..." The question of publication *"will be, considered"*.

26th March "Captain J.E.T. Harper has been attached to the War Staff for the purpose ..." Publication *"will be considered"*.

9th July It is anticipated that Captain Harper's investigation will be completed at the "end of September and *publication will be considered"*.

25th July "The Official Record is now being compiled ..."

A DEFINITE PROMISE

29th October "No 'inquiry' has been held, nor is one in contemplation. A narrative of events *has been completed* and *will be published when printed."*

3rd December "It is hoped to *publish shortly."*

1920

18th February "The Official narrative of the Battle of Jutland will, I hope, be *published shortly* ..." A report by Admiral Scheer *will be published "as an appendix to the Official narrative*. This report *has been utilized* to check the information available from our own records ..."

14th April "Technicalities connected with production make it improbable that *publication can take place in much less than* 3 *months from now."*

23rd June "Regret date (of publication) cannot be given. Difficulties arising, among other things, from the *provision of paper for the charts, are stated to be likely to cause delay* ..."

4th August "Fresh evidence has recently come to light which must be considered before the Official Report, *which had almost reached completion,*[4] can be published ... shall certainly ensure that he (Lord Jellicoe) will see the final form before publication."

THE PROMISE IS NOW RESCINDED

27th October. *"It is not now proposed to publish an Official account* ... any record based on *British official evidence only* would inevitably present a one-sided version ... Moreover, Sir Julian Corbett's 'Naval History of the War' ... includes Jutland, is likely to be published in the course of next year, and the *publishers have made representations that they would have strong reason to complain* of the simultaneous publication by the Admiralty of any such narrative. However, all the material prepared by the Admiralty will be placed at Sir Julian Corbett's disposal."

"Both gallant Admirals (Jellicoe and Beatty) *have seen the report.*"

1st November. The Prime Minister would not promise that the Official Record would be included in the 'Naval History of the War' as it stands, *without any amendment, alteration, or omissions.* His reasons for the Admiralty having gone back on their decisions to publish was, that it was a "highly controversial topic" and possibly not "desirable that there should be a separate account". He further stated that the publishers had *"absolutely no right"* to object to the Official publication of a separate Admiralty account.

4th November.The Prime Minister stated: "In view of the general wish expressed on Monday for the immediate publication of documents relating to the Battle of Jutland, a Parliamentary Paper will be issued at an early date containing *all these documents* whether reports, despatches or signals."

This reply was taken to mean that my Official Record would be published, as evidenced by a letter from Viscount Curzon published in *The Times* on 5th November 1920, in which he said: "I cannot help writing these few lines with reference to the announcement by the Prime Minister that the Official Report of the Battle of Jutland is to be published. ... The non-publication of this Report represented the worst possible results of the policy of Hush ... I maintain that the country has a right to know the truth."

Further evidence as to the accepted meaning of the Prime Minister's promise is contained in a Question and Answer in the House of Commons on:

15th November In reply to the question: "When the *Official Record of the Battle of Jutland will be published?*" it was stated: "It is hoped that *publication will be possible within a month.*"

Several other questions were asked during November 1920, the replies to which at length made it clear to the House that the promised publication was not the Official Record. This led to the following Answers being given in reply to further demands for that Record:

22nd November "The reason for not publishing Captain Harper's summary of events was ... that a record based on *British Official evidence only* would inevitably present a one-sided version."

1st December "Captain Harper's diagrams will not be included."

8th December Viscount Curzon pressed for a reconsideration of the decision not to publish the "Harper diagrams", but he was informed that: "Facts were asked for and the facts at the disposal of the Admiralty … will be published."

Rear-Admiral Adair then remarked that "the Official despatches will be so much Greek to the general public and to most of the Members of this House, and that it is only such a report as Captain Harper's that anything intelligible can be made out of them." He was then told that "that was the *attitude the Admiralty took up in the first instance*, but the demand of the House for immediate publication of the Official documents was granted by the Prime Minister … The Admiralty was rather turned down as to the procedure which they proposed to take."

The despatches, signals and other documents referring to the battle were, in December 1920, published as a Blue Book (*Battle of Jutland, Official Despatches with Appendices*, Cmd. 1068). This publication not unnaturally led to several more questions being asked in the House and to objections in the Press, because the issue of this mass of undigested documents only confused public opinion more than ever.

Further requests were made in the House of Commons on 23rd December 1920, 11th April 1923, 27th February 1925 and 14th March 1927, and in the House of Lords on 8th March 1921, for the publication of the Official Record and the charts which accompanied it; but all requests were met with a refusal. On 11th April 1923, in reply to a Question, it was stated that the Record was "*only completed some months after he* (Lord Wester Wemyss) *had left the Board.* By the time it was completed further information had become accessible *which necessitated revision of the material.*"

The nation and the Press have, not unnaturally, sensed a "mystery" about Jutland. Actually there is not, and never has been, any mystery about the details of the battle, but the public has every reason to be suspicious and dissatisfied with the Admiralty's attitude towards the subject.

The present small work is not intended to be a comprehensive account of the battle. Such an account is to be found in the *Official History of the War – Naval Operations – Vol. III.* Its author, that gifted and honest historian, the late Sir Julian Corbett, had all the secret and other records, including the *Harper Record,* at his disposal,[5] and all the essential facts are truly and comprehensively stated in his account; but, like all Official publications, any comments it contains are explanatory and not critical. It is very curious, however, that even this straightforward account, published under the auspices of the Committee of Imperial Defence, at the public expense, should have been specifically repudiated by the Board of Admiralty in a note on the fly-leaf.

In the chapters which follow I have only attempted to outline the salient features of the Battle of Jutland, and in doing so I have made use of no information which is not available to the public; but it has been my endeavour to show just where, and how, the public has been so badly misled on many important points. For sake of brevity the full titles of the Admirals mentioned are, in most cases, omitted, and they are alluded to, with all respect, by their surnames only.

The Official Record, prepared under my supervision, would not have dotted the "Is" and crossed the "Ts" of its narrative as I have been able to do, to a certain extent, herein. My readers may also be able to draw their own conclusions as to the real reasons why that Record was not published.

It only remains to recall that Admiral-of-the-Fleet Lord Wester Wemyss was the First Sea Lord who originally issued the orders for an Official Record of Jutland to be prepared, in a form in which it could be published should such a demand arise. He perused it on its completion and, on 16th December 1920, wrote to the Press as follows: "The report was only finished just before I left the Admiralty … I regret that the Admiralty should withhold from the public a paper which was designed for their information, and which would materially have assisted them in forming an opinion upon a somewhat involved subject."

Admiral Sir Francis Bridgeman, another one-time First Sea Lord, wrote to *The Times* on 3rd January 1921 referring to Lord Wester Wemyss' letter. He said: "Lord Jellicoe has asked no less strongly, and still asks, that it should be published. What is standing in the way? As a former First Sea Lord, may I add my voice to that of Lord Wester Wemyss and Lord Jellicoe, in the interests of the Service."

We have, therefore, three ex-First Sea Lords, two of whom, Lord Wester Wemyss and Lord Jellicoe, had seen the Record, and all of whom desired the publication of all the facts connected with the battle. On 1st November 1919 Lord Wester Wemyss left the Board of Admiralty, and the position of First Sea Lord has, since that date, been held by Lord Beatty.

AUTHOR'S NOTE TO FIRST EDITION

Since this book went to press, in reply to a question asked in the House on 4th May 1927, it was officially stated that "it had been decided to issue what was known as the Official Record of the Battle of Jutland". In response to a further question as to whether this would be "in the same terms as were *originally laid before* the Board of Admiralty," it was stated that it would be "the Harper Report" and that "it would be in the same terms as were *approved by* the Board of Admiralty".

As explained in the Introduction, Admiral Harper's original work was completed in 1919; it was a *Record* and not a Report. Since then, all essential facts about the Battle have been made public in the British and German official Histories.

The object with which this book was written was not to controvert these facts, but to show how the public has been misled by their being distorted.

FURTHER NOTE TO THIRD IMPRESSION

On 25th May 1927, the day before the First Edition of this book was published, it was officially stated in the House of Commons that Admiral Harper's Record would be published "as originally compiled, without any amendment."

The publication of an eight-year-old Record can add nothing to our present knowledge of the *facts*.

Chapter 1
Weather Conditions

It is of the first importance for the student and critic of the Battle of Jutland to keep in mind the conditions of visibility during the various stages of the battle. The weather had an important bearing on the issues; in fact, it is not too much to say that if it had been clear the tactics used on both sides might have been very different to what they were. Clear weather would have been unfavourable to the fleet which wished to avoid action, and would, therefore, have been to our advantage.

During the early stages of the battle-cruiser action the visibility was comparatively good; but, by 4.15 p.m., the visibility to the eastward had become considerably reduced, and favoured the enemy. By 5 p.m. these conditions became worse and, as Beatty states: "Our ships being silhouetted against a clear horizon to the westward, while the enemy were for the most part obscured by mist, only showing up clearly at intervals."

By the time the battle fleet came into action these conditions had become still worse; the sky was overcast, the sea calm, the wind light and, owing to the combination of atmospheric conditions and the smoke from the ships, the visibility was very bad, and great difficulty was experienced in distinguishing ships.

Extracts from the published reports of Flag Officers and Captains show that it was quite impossible, after 6 p.m., to state the range of visibility with any degree of accuracy. The visibility varied in different directions and in different localities. It seems that at no time, after 6 p.m., was the general average visibility more than 12,000 yards, or 6 nautical miles, and as a rule it was less. In exceptional cases, in certain directions, objects could be seen for a short time up to 16,000 yards, but in other directions they could be seen only 2,000 or 3,000 yards away. It is safe to say that, at no time after 6 p.m., were more than three or four of the enemy capital ships seen at one and the same time from any one of our capital ships.

These facts have not, previously, been given sufficient prominence. Jellicoe was unaware throughout the action of the strength, or composition, of the German Fleet, and he could not ascertain it from the occasional glimpses obtained of a few ships through the mist and smoke.

On the morning of 1st June Jellicoe inquired by signal as to the whereabouts of the *Indefatigable*, and other ships, thereby indicating that he was actually unaware of our own losses on the previous day.

It will bear repeating that the average visibility should be constantly in the mind of anyone who is considering the tactics at Jutland, and more especially when studying, or even glancing at, any diagram showing the positions of the ships.

If, when studying a diagram, the student and critic would draw a rough circle with its centre at the *Iron Duke*, and with a radius of 5 to 6 miles, he would realize, approximately, how much of the depicted situation was seen by Jellicoe at the time. Always remembering, also, that many portions of the area inside this circle were shut out by smoke from intervening ships. It is not, however, equitable to judge the tactics employed entirely by what could be seen from the *Iron Duke*. Such a method would ignore the presence of other ships and other Admirals, who, although they had equally bad visibility, were viewing the situation from different positions in the line. Diagrams which are shaded to indicate what Jellicoe could see are, therefore, nearly as misleading as ordinary diagrams. In fact, the only method to arrive at a fair and just appreciation is to remember, *and to keep on remembering*, that our Admirals were *not* sitting up aloft, in a balloon, with a clear bird's-eye view of the fleets, conducting the battle as on a tactical board.

Chapter 2

The Influence of Under-Water Attack on the Tactics at Jutland

In the hundred years and more which intervened between Trafalgar and Jutland not only had steam and long-range guns completely changed the character of naval warfare, but the advent of under-water weapons and the submarine had profoundly influenced tactics.

It is quite impossible for anybody to begin to understand the Battle of Jutland, much less to form a just or reasoned opinion about it, without thoroughly grasping the nature of the various forms of under-water attack and the measures necessary to counter them. The former may be tabulated as follows:

1. Torpedo attacks from heavy ships in the line.
2. Torpedo attacks by light surface craft.
   (a) By day.
   (b) By night.
3. Torpedo attacks by submarines.
4. Mines dropped by retreating ships in the path of their pursuers.
5. Mines laid in the form of a minefield.

Let us consider each of these in turn, and see how they influenced the movements of the rival fleets.

1. TORPEDO ATTACKS FROM HEAVY SHIPS IN THE LINE:
Battleships and battle-cruisers on both sides were so heavily gunned and such conspicuous targets at anything inside torpedo range, so long as daylight held, that a torpedo duel, naturally, did not commend itself to either side. On the other hand, the torpedo armaments of the capital ships, taken *en masse*, were formidable and could not be ignored. A few lucky hits underwater might have much reduced the speed of one or two battleships, even though they did not sink them, as actually happened in the case of the *Marlborough*, although at first the damage did not greatly impede her.

Lame ducks are a serious embarrassment to a Commander-in-Chief. He must either reduce the speed of the whole fleet to their speed, which may force him into a position of great tactical disadvantage, or he must detach ships to protect the laggards, or he must leave them to look after themselves.

The net result of this particular menace, so far as Jutland was concerned, was that neither side tried to get within torpedo range of the opposing battle line, and it was definitely to the advantage of the British Fleet with superior gun power to keep outside that range if possible.

2. TORPEDO ATTACKS BY LIGHT SURFACE CRAFT:

(a) By day:

Destroyers, and to a lesser degree light cruisers, can appreciably influence the tactics of the battle fleet if, by using their speed, they can mass in a position from which to launch a torpedo attack. A day attack may be made from a bow bearing, at comparatively long range, the torpedoes having less distance to run because their quarry is coming to meet them. The light surface craft can also close very rapidly, and this, coupled with the fact that they are not conspicuous targets, makes it very hard for the battleships' guns to hit them before they release their torpedoes.

In this connection, the non-technical reader should realize that a destroyer flotilla may launch an attack at a distance of 20,000 yards, but may be away and out of sight long before the torpedoes reach their objective.

There are three methods of parrying these daytime attacks: the first is for the battle fleet to hold the enemy craft at arm's length with their gunfire; the second is to intercept them with our own flotillas and light cruisers before they are able to release their torpedoes with any prospect of hitting; the third is to swing the individual ships of the threatened battle line off their original course and either let the enemy torpedoes expend themselves short, or pass through the intervals between the ships.

It is clearly advantageous to prevent an attack being launched, but this is not always possible with a determined enemy, especially in misty weather. Once torpedoes are running, it is, obviously, stupid for the ships attacked to stand on and offer themselves as a sitting target, so to speak, and the question of turning towards or away from an attack is a highly technical one; but it is sufficient to say here that under the conditions prevailing at the time of the massed German torpedo attack, to cover the second retreat of the High Sea Fleet, it was the accepted principle and invariable practice by the Admirals on both sides to swing their ships away, and there was one occasion when Jellicoe resorted to this manoeuvre.

(b) By night:

Conditions of low visibility may improve the chances of surface torpedo-craft, for surprise is necessarily a great factor in their success; but the less the range of vision the greater their difficulty in finding their quarry, in manoeuvring into a favourable position to attack and in distinguishing friend from foe.

At night, too, the surprise may be mutual, and the guns of a battleship on the alert may make short work of a destroyer sighted at almost point-blank range. At night, too, the interval between firing a torpedo and it reaching its mark is so small that it gives little time for evasive manoeuvres on either side.

The night after Jutland found two huge fleets, each knowing the other was in the vicinity, but neither wishing to risk a meeting. At first sight this would seem to have afforded an ideal opportunity for using torpedo craft. Actually, both Commanders-in-Chief were disinclined to lose their flotillas into the uncertainty of darkness on the "hit or miss principle"; both kept them in company with the battle fleets, although the British flotillas were well clear astern.

A flotilla might easily have spent much precious fuel and achieved nothing; there might easily have been "regrettable incidents" with friends, and, at daylight, when destroyers became vitally necessary for a renewed general engagement, they would probably have been widely scattered and not available at the psychological moment.

3. TORPEDO ATTACKS BY SUBMARINES:

The submarine differs from the destroyer in that it is very much slower, and has much less range of vision; but it is far less conspicuous and it can disappear instantly after firing a torpedo. It is more difficult, therefore, for an under-water craft to attain a favourable position to launch its attack, especially in a fleet action with ships moving at high speed; it has rather to await the opportunity afforded by an unsuspecting quarry coming towards it. Limitation of vision prohibits long-range attacks, while the fact that sub-merged craft cannot manoeuvre *en masse* like destroyers, lessens the chances of hitting on the principle of "browning the covey".

On the other hand, the extreme difficulty of detecting a small object like a periscope, which at the time Jutland was fought was the sole means of locating a submarine's presence, made them objects of constant alarm to surface ships, especially the deep-draught battle-ship and battle-cruiser. Experience had not yet shown that a mass of ships moving in company at high speed present a very difficult target to a submarine, which, under such conditions, is wont to be more concerned with her own safety than with a carefully planned attack.

Precautions against submarine attack on our side took the form of an anti-submarine screen of destroyers scouting on the bows of the battle fleet and battle-cruisers. This undoubtedly tended to tie certain of the British flotillas to this duty when they might, otherwise, have been free to take up a more aggressive role; but it must be remembered that, whereas the

11

Germans could count on the fact that the British fleet had come too far and too fast to have submarines in company, our command had to bear in mind that we were meeting the enemy more or less in his own waters and within easy range of his submarine bases.

It is easy to be wise after the event and to say that it is now known that there were no submarines in the vicinity at all, and that it should have been obvious that there never could have been any, but it should be noted that there was every reason, before the action, to believe they would be used by the enemy, and this belief was strengthened during the action by categorical reports of submarines sighted continually being made to Jellicoe.[6]

Measures to counter submarine attack can take the form of a detour, so that it is never in position to fire a torpedo; this necessitates ample warning; alternatively, and more normally, the safest line of action is to charge straight for the submarine and compel it to dive for its own safety.

In actual fact the false reports of submarines, disconcerting as they were, had little influence on the course of events at Jutland, except, as already mentioned, a tendency to keep part of our destroyer flotillas acting on the defensive.

4. Mines Dropped by Retreating Ships:

The possibility of running into mines dropped by a retreating enemy fleet had been taken into very full consideration by the British high command, both afloat and at the Admiralty before Jutland. This menace coupled with the torpedo advantage enjoyed by ships ahead over ships astern was regarded as being so serious as to make direct pursuit prohibitive.

Under-water weapons had, therefore, introduced an entirely new element which under such circumstances did much to neutralize the advantages which the more powerful fleet might have secured in olden days.

"Nothing but ample time and superior speed can be an answer, and this means that, unless the meeting of the fleets takes place fairly early in the day, it is most difficult to fight to a finish," wrote Jellicoe before Jutland. "Time" and "light", however, were the two things denied him, nor did he have more than a couple of knots superiority in speed, battle fleet for battle fleet.

Again, it is easy to say that the enemy did not, in fact, drop mines to cover his retreat. All that was known at the time was that certain of the enemy capital ships were fitted for mine laying and that he had practised it since the outbreak of war.

5. Mines Laid in the Form of a Minefield:

German minefields were extensive and were fairly accurately known to our command. They limited the exits and re-entries of the High Sea Fleet to certain channels which were kept swept, and this had a considerable bearing on Jellicoe's strategy as we shall see in due course. They also precluded our fleet from following the enemy to the German coast the morning after Jutland.

With this brief survey of two vital factors, – weather and under-water attack – to give us a right perspective, we may now proceed to examine the course of the battle and to trace the parts played by the chief personalities.

Chapter 3
Preliminary Movements

A question that is often asked is: "How did the Battle of Jutland come to be fought?" To answer this it is necessary to have some acquaintance with the motives underlying the movements of the opposing fleets before the battle to enable a correct appreciation to be formed of the battle itself.

In naval actions it is rarely, if ever, the case that both sides wish to fight. Rival fleets do not proceed to sea in battle formation with a mutual intention of seeking a pitched battle in the open. It may be that one of the combatant nations has an object to attain, through the medium of its navy, but in order to attain that object fully it may be desirable to avoid a fleet action with its consequent certain weakening, or annihilation, of the fleet itself. In such a case the opposing forces would endeavour to force a fleet action as the best method of preventing the enemy attaining his object.

During the Great War it was the wish of everyone in the Grand Fleet to come to grips with the High Seas Fleet, in a naval action, but for nearly two years our battle fleet had to exercise patience and "serve by waiting". The time was not, however, wasted, neither did the efficiency of the fleet suffer. Frequent cruises were made into the North Sea and the time in harbour was occupied in rigorous training and exercises in gunnery and torpedo work.

It is no easy matter to keep a fleet in a high state of efficiency when all, both officers and men, are straining at the leash to get at the enemy. Admiral Jellicoe, as Commander-in-Chief, was personally responsible for the state of efficiency of the fleet, and it was he, more than any other, who built up that efficiency, not only by virtue of his position, and his ability, but also because he was beloved and trusted by everyone in his great command.

While the Grand Fleet was periodically sweeping the sea, the German Battle Fleet remained impassive in protected harbours. The enemy battle-cruisers made periodical "tip-and-run" raids on our coast and were, more than once, brought to action, with indecisive results, by our battle-cruisers.

The use of force by our ships to attack the enemy ships in his protected harbours, or to draw them into the open sea, could only have resulted in failure, owing to the presence of minefields, submarines and shore batteries. It would have been madness to have embarked on a forlorn hope of this nature, with the almost certain loss of a large proportion of our fleet, on which the allied cause and the future of the British Empire depended.

The German Fleet did not want a general action and, provided they remained in harbour or cruised only in the limited waters of the Heligoland Bight or of the Southern Baltic, there seemed no way in which they could be drawn into one.

Admiral Scheer had for long been an opponent of the policy of deliberate inactivity for the High Seas Fleet. He was an advocate of submarine warfare on merchant vessels, but saw no reason why the German Navy should confine itself to this form of warfare, when it had a fleet in being.

SCHEER'S PLAN

He assumed command of the High Seas Fleet early in 1916, at a time when our blockade of Germany's ports was being tightened up, with the result that its effects were more universally felt in that country. Scheer realized that it was becoming increasingly necessary for the High Seas Fleet to make some demonstration to justify its existence. An opportunity soon occurred when, owing to the feelings of neutral nations being aroused by the attack on the cross-channel ferry *Sussex*, many submarines were temporarily withdrawn from the trade routes. These submarines, therefore, were available for other services, and enabled plans, for offensive action, to be drawn up.

Scheer had no wish to encounter our Grand Fleet at full strength, so he sought a method whereby he might possibly succeed in bringing his whole available force against a portion of our fleet and thus cause some diminution of our power.

His plan was as follows: The majority of his available submarines were to be stationed off the Pentland Firth, Moray Firth and Firth of Forth, our three main Grand Fleet bases; some were also to be stationed off the Humber. He then intended to send his battle-cruisers to bombard Sunderland. If, as was practically certain, the Rosyth force would emerge to attack the raiders, it was hoped that the submarines stationed off the Firth of Forth would account for some of these ships and that, if all went well, the remainder of this force would be led towards, and possibly brought to action by, the High Seas Fleet waiting well to the eastward. Meanwhile, the submarines off our other bases would not only be able to give him warning if the main fleet came out, but would also have an opportunity to attack.

Scheer was of course aware that Jellicoe with his whole fleet made frequent excursions into the North Sea, in many cases penetrating well south. As he had no desire to come to grips with the British main fleet he also provided for an efficient airship reconnaissance, which itself must of necessity depend on favourable weather.

In the event of the weather proving unfavourable for airships Scheer devised an alternative plan. The battle-cruisers, commanded by Admiral von Hipper, would be sent towards the Skagerrak so that, by showing themselves off the Norwegian Coast, they would draw some of our forces in that direction. Meanwhile, Scheer, with his battle fleet, would proceed up the coast of Denmark in support. By this means our forces would be drawn out over the waiting submarines and might also be placed at a disadvantage, especially if only a portion of our fleet emerged, or if the squadrons were divided.

By keeping in the eastern part of the North Sea, comparatively near to his own base, Scheer assumed that his advanced forces would guard him against surprise, if our whole fleet emerged. The submarines duly took up their positions off our bases, but the weather proved unfavourable for airships, and as the date approached when it would be necessary to withdraw the under-water craft, Scheer was forced to abandon the Sunderland scheme, or take the risk of meeting Jellicoe with his whole fleet. He therefore adopted the alternative scheme.

THE GRAND FLEET SAILS

Our Admiralty, with its nearly perfect system of intelligence, was not, however, ignorant of the movements of the enemy submarines, or of the fact that unusual activity was taking place in the German Fleet.

A telegram was accordingly sent to Jellicoe, on 30th May, informing him that the German Fleet intended some operation, and warning him to hold himself in readiness for eventualities. The Grand Fleet was, at this time, divided up among the three main northern bases as follows.

At Scapa Flow, Orkney Islands, under Admiral Sir John Jellicoe, Commander-in-Chief:[7]
  The First and Fourth Battle Squadrons.
  The Third Battle-Cruiser Squadron.
  The Second Cruiser Squadron.
  The Fourth Light Cruiser Squadron, and The Fourth; part of Eleventh; and Twelfth Flotillas of Torpedo-Boat Destroyers.

At Invergordon, under Vice-Admiral Sir Martyn Jerram:[8]
  The Second Battle Squadron.
  The First Cruiser Squadron and part of the Eleventh Flotilla of Torpedo-Boat Destroyers.

At Rosyth, under Vice-Admiral Sir David Beatty:[9]
  The Fifth Battle Squadron.

The First and Second Battle-Cruiser Squadrons.

The First, Second and Third Light Cruiser Squadrons.

Part of the First; Part of the Ninth; Part of the Tenth and Thirteenth Flotillas of Torpedo-Boat Destroyers.

At 5.40 p.m. on 30th May a further telegram sent from the Admiralty, which contained additional information and in which orders were conveyed to Jellicoe to concentrate his fleet to the eastward of the "Long Forties".[10] Jellicoe was also informed that eight enemy submarines were probably in the North Sea.

On receipt of the information Jellicoe sent the following instructions to the units of his fleet not stationed at Scapa Flow.

To Vice-Admiral Jerram, commanding the Second Battle Squadron at Invergordon:

"Leave as soon as ready. Pass through Lat. 58° 15′ N., Long. 2° 00′ E. Meet me 2 p.m. tomorrow 31st, Lat. 57° 45′ N., Long. 4° 15′ E. Several submarines known to be in North Sea (1930)."[11]

To Vice-Admiral Beatty, commanding the Battle-Cruiser Force at Rosyth:

"Available vessels, Battle-Cruiser Fleet, Fifth Battle Squadron and Destroyers, including Harwich Destroyers, proceed to approximate position Lat. 56° 40′ N., Long 5° E. Desirable to economize destroyers' fuel. Presume that you will be there about 2 p.m. tomorrow, Wednesday, 31st May. I shall be in about 57° 45′ N., 4° 15′ E., by 2 p.m. unless delayed by fog. Third Battle-Cruiser Squadron *Chester* and *Canterbury* will leave with me. I may send them on to your rendezvous. If no news by 2 p.m. stand towards me to get in visual communication. I will steer for Horns Reef from position Lat. 57° 45′ N., Long. 4° 15′ E. (1937)."

The Harwich Destroyers referred to in this message were part of the Ninth and part of the Tenth Flotillas – eight in all – which were temporarily stationed at Rosyth.

The distance between the positions in which the battle fleet and battle-cruiser fleet, respectively, were ordered to be by 2 p.m. was 69 miles, and in this connection Jellicoe, in his despatch, states:

"I felt no anxiety in regard to the advanced position of the force under Sir David Beatty, supported as it was by four ships of the Fifth Battle Squadron, as this force was far superior in gun-power to the First Scouting Group, and the speed of the slowest ships was such as to enable it to keep out of range of superior enemy forces."

It is probable, however, that Jellicoe would have been somewhat less easy in his mind if he had thought Beatty would divide his forces and go into action unsupported by these four powerful ships.

The various sections of the fleet left harbour, in accordance with prearranged plans, during the evening of 30th May.

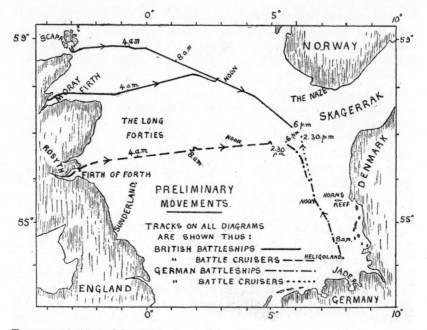

DIAGRAM 1: 10P.M. MAY 30 TO 6 P.M., MAY 31

THE BATTLE FLEET

By 10.30 p.m. the battle fleet at Scapa with its attendant cruisers and destroyers had cleared the harbour, and course was shaped for the arranged rendezvous.

Two reports were made by the *Trident* (a destroyer cruising off Rosyth), one at 9.20 p.m. and one at 9.45 p.m., that she had been attacked by a submarine; no damage was, however, done to her.

A number of neutral vessels and trawlers were met with by the battle fleet at intervals during the passage and were examined by the destroyers attached to the cruiser screen.

The squadron from Invergordon had also cleared the harbour shortly after 10 p.m. and, without incident, proceeded on its way to join the battle fleet from Scapa Flow. Junction between these two fleets was made at 11 a.m. on the following day. Wireless reports of enemy vessels having been sighted, by the light cruisers ahead of the battle-cruiser fleet, began to come through to the *Iron Duke* at about 2.30 p.m. Immediately the first report was received, Jellicoe ordered the speed of the battle fleet, and all other ships in his company, to be increased, and also ordered steam to be raised, immediately, for "full speed".

When in harbour, all ships of the Grand Fleet were kept complete with fuel in readiness for any eventuality. On leaving harbour for any operation it was very desirable, especially in the case of the destroyers, to economize fuel to the fullest extent compatible with efficiency. Any unnecessary expenditure of fuel in the preliminary stages of an operation, the extent of which could not be predicted with any certainty, might cause a shortage at a critical period of the operation; thereby resulting, possibly, in failure instead of success. The fleet would not, therefore, have steam for more than a knot, or two, in excess of the speed at which it was intended to proceed. With everything ready – and everything was always ready in the engine-room departments of our ships – steam for "full speed" could be raised with very little delay.

As the progressive reports of the action being fought by the battle-cruiser fleet to the southward were received the speed of the battle fleet was worked up by steps until at 3.13 p.m. the fleet was steaming 19 knots and at 3.58 p.m., 20 knots, the maximum speed at which the battle fleet as a whole could keep station.

At 3.13 p.m., on May 31st, the columns of battleships were opened to manoeuvring distance in readiness for instant deployment into line of battle, and the cruiser screen, stationed some miles ahead, was ordered to extend its distance. Owing, however, to the fact that the armoured cruisers of the First and Second Cruiser Squadrons, forming this screen, had little, if any, margin of speed over that at which the battle fleet was then steaming, in its endeavour to support our battle-cruisers, the cruiser screen was unable to increase its distance to the desired extent. The object of extending this distance was to ensure getting into visual touch with the battle-cruisers at the earliest possible moment.

Jellicoe's telegram of instructions to Beatty, it will be remembered, contained the following: "If no news by 2 p.m. stand towards me to get in visual communication."

This emphasized the well-known importance of having visual communication between the Commander-in-Chief and his advanced forces, but, as will be seen later, visual communication was not established until it was almost too late to be of use.

For the moment we may leave the battle fleet heading for the rendezvous and ready to form line of battle at any moment.

THE BATTLE-CRUISER FLEET

The Rosyth Force had cleared the harbour by 10.30 p.m. At 3.55 a.m. the light cruiser *Galatea* reported being fired at by a submarine, but nothing further of any interest occurred during the night.

Scheer's efforts to reduce the strength of our main fleet by submarine attacks, as it emerged from its bases, had failed. No capital ship had been attacked and no damage was done to any of our ships. It is doubtful also if these submarines rendered any valuable assistance to Scheer by the meagre information they were able to give him of the movements of our squadrons.

Such information as they afforded him did not, in any way, indicate that our whole fleet was out, and concentrating in his path.

At 8.19 a.m., when some 180 miles from Rosyth, the light cruiser *Yarmouth*, then a few miles ahead of the battle-cruisers, reported sighting a submarine and, on receipt of this report by Beatty, the whole force was immediately ordered to alter course 8 points, or 90 degrees to port.[12] This course was followed for eighteen minutes, during which time Beatty made further inquiries, of the *Yarmouth*, as to the position of the submarine which had been reported. Only the periscope had been seen from the *Yarmouth*, and nothing further was seen by any other ship in the vicinity. In any case this submarine, although it caused no actual damage to any of our ships, had more effect on the movements of our fleet than had any of those stationed nearer the coast, as it delayed our battle-cruisers reaching their rendezvous – the big alteration made in the course having the effect of adding some 6 miles to the distance to be travelled.

BEATTY'S FATAL ERROR

Beatty now made a decision which was to cost us dearly a few hours later. At 10.10 a.m., on May 31st, the Fifth Battle Squadron was ordered to take station on a compass bearing N.W. and distant 5 miles from his flagship, the *Lion*.

It is incomprehensible why such a position was selected for this powerful force. In Jellicoe's battle plans[13] this squadron was "given the functions of a free wing squadron, which, not forming part of the main line of battle, could be used at any opportune moment in an action for bringing a concentration to bear on part of the enemy fleet, or otherwise by independent attack to modify the rigidity of the old single line ahead formation."

It may be that Beatty also desired to give this squadron a freedom of action instead of keeping them rigidly in the same line as the battle-cruisers. It was, however, most improbable that the enemy, if met with at all, would be sighted from the north-westward or westward. The most probable directions for first sighting him was obviously easterly or southerly. That this was Beatty's own opinion at the time can be seen by a glance at Diagram No.2, which shows the disposition of his advanced cruiser screen. The diagram indicates, approximately, the arc guarded by the screen and, therefore, the arc in which he anticipated that the enemy would most probably be first seen.

In the event of an enemy being sighted to the north-eastward or eastward, it would be Beatty's endeavour to cut them off from their base to the south-eastward. This he actually did when they were sighted, his action being fully approved of by Jellicoe.

The position was, therefore, that Beatty expected and had prepared his outposts for a meeting with the enemy to the south-eastward, yet he had stationed the heaviest and slowest ships of his force 5 miles to the north-

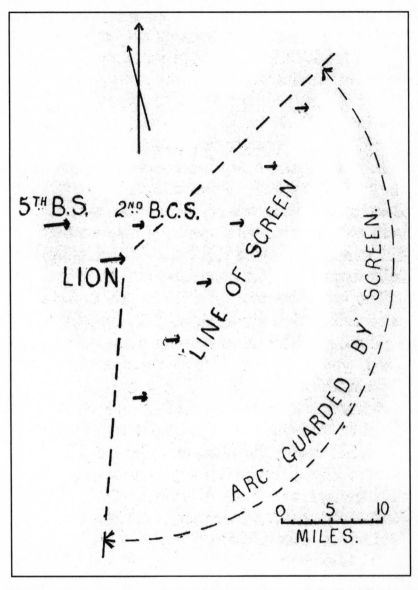

DIAGRAM 2: STATIONING OF FIFTH BATTLE SQUADRON, 10.10 A.M., MAY 31

westward, where they would almost certainly be delayed coming into action. In other words, he made the fatal and elementary mistake of dividing his forces, so that he could only engage with part of them. This, as will be seen later, produced results which can only be termed disastrous.

21

At 1.30 p.m. the line of direction of the cruiser screen was altered to E.N.E. and the Fifth Battle Squadron was stationed N.N.W. 5 miles from the *Lion*.

THE HIGH SEAS FLEET

The High Seas Fleet left the Jade between 2 a.m. and 2.30 a.m. 31st May, the battle fleet being preceded by the cruisers and battle-cruisers. The battle-cruisers drew rapidly ahead for the purpose of reaching the vicinity of the Norwegian coast before dark, it having been arranged that the battle fleet would join them the next morning.

By 2.30 p.m. the German battle fleet had passed Horns Reef, the battle-cruisers being then some 50 miles ahead. An hour or two before this five reconnaissance airships had been sent out, but they saw nothing of our fleet and rendered no assistance to Scheer. The German Admiral had at this time no suspicion that the Grand Fleet was at sea, steaming to meet him. Jellicoe's dispositions were, however, well calculated to bring the German fleet to action with the whole Grand Fleet.

Chapter 3

Battle-Cruiser Action

Having arrived at the position ordered and no news having been received of the enemy, our battle-cruiser fleet, in accordance with the instructions of the Commander-in-Chief, altered course to the northward to close our battle fleet. At 2.15 p.m., as this alteration was being made, the light cruiser *Galatea*, 17 miles distant from the *Lion*, sighted a steamer, apparently stopped and blowing off steam, some 10 miles to the eastward.

The presence of this neutral merchant steamer undoubtedly precipitated the action which followed. It is impossible to conjecture what the result would have been if this vessel had not unintentionally blundered into sight of the rival fleets, but the presence of an enemy would not have been known to either side until the rival battle-cruisers had proceeded some considerable distance farther to the northward. The enemy battle-cruisers would by then have extended their distance from the supporting High Seas Fleet and our battle-cruiser force would have been more favourably placed for receiving support from our battle fleet. In fact, the situation, when contact was eventually made, would have been to our greater advantage. Conjecture is, however, useless – to return to facts.

THE BATTLE OPENS

Immediately on sighting the steamer, the *Galatea* steamed towards her at full speed, and quickly made out the masts and funnels of a warship in her vicinity. It was soon seen that the steamer had been stopped by two German destroyers, and that there was a squadron of cruisers a little to the north-eastward. A wireless report of sighting the enemy was made without delay by the *Galatea*, and fire was opened on the two destroyers by the *Galatea* and *Phaeton* at 2.28 p.m. Four minutes after this the enemy cruiser *Elbing* opened fire on the *Galatea* and *Phaeton*, the range being about 15,000 yards.

Our light cruisers were outranged, so course was altered in an endeavour to lead the enemy in the direction of our battle fleet, without losing touch but keeping just out of gun range. At 2.35 p.m. the *Galatea* reported that she had sighted a large amount of smoke, as though from a fleet, bearing E.N.E. These ships were the German battle-cruisers, which were coming to the westward, at high speed, to give support to the light cruisers.

Beatty's battle-cruisers, at this time, had just altered course to the south-eastward, the signal to do so having been made by flags as the turn was being made. The flags could not be distinguished by the battleship *Barham*, flagship of the Fifth Battle Squadron, at the distance she had been stationed, and it was not repeated to her by other means at the *Lion's* disposal. It was some minutes, therefore, before Evan-Thomas realized that the battle-cruisers had altered course. As they had also increased speed to 22 knots the Fifth Battle Squadron was soon left over ten miles astern, and was for some time actually out of sight.

This failure, in the *Lion*, to convey the executive order to turn to the *Barham* still further delayed the time at which those powerful battleships could come into action to support the battle-cruisers. A preparatory signal for altering course had been made by the *Lion* about five minutes earlier, and if at the same time the signal "Close" had been sent to the Fifth Battle Squadron the distance between the two squadrons would have been rapidly diminishing, instead of increasing, at the time the *Lion* made the executive signal.

The latest report from the *Galatea* made it clear that the enemy would not be able to escape by the Horns Reef passage before being brought to action. Beatty, therefore, subsequently altered course to the east and north-east to close the enemy.

The seaplane-carrier *Engadine*, which was attached to the battle-cruiser fleet, was at 2.45 p.m. ordered to send up her machine. The seaplane took the air at 3.8 p.m., but, owing to poor visibility, could see little of the enemy ships. Three reports were made by signal, but these did not reach the *Lion*. After about half an hour the seaplane had to descend on account of engine trouble. With this exception, no British air-craft took any part in the action.[14]

At 3.34 p.m. the ships reported by the *Galatea* were identified as five German battle-cruisers, with cruisers and destroyers in company.

Although the presence of the enemy battle-cruisers was now known to both Jellicoe and Beatty, there was no reason for either of them to suppose this indicated that the enemy battle fleet was also at sea. The warning telegrams sent from the Admiralty on 30th May indicated that the enemy intended an operation, probably on a large scale. About noon on the 31st, however, a message was sent from the Admiralty to inform Jellicoe that directional wireless placed the flagship of the High Seas Fleet in the Jade River at 11.10 a.m.[15]

All messages made by wireless from the Admiralty to the Commander-in-Chief would, according to normal procedure, also be received by Beatty in the *Lion*. It was only natural, therefore, that both Jellicoe and Beatty should think the operation being undertaken by the enemy was one in which his battle fleet was not taking an active part.

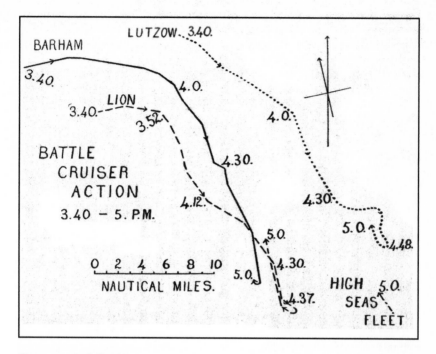

DIAGRAM 3: MAY 31

A RUNNING FIGHT TO THE SOUTH

As soon as the presence of our battle-cruisers became known to Hipper he turned his squadron to the southward for the purpose of falling back on the support of his battle fleet, and also for the purpose of drawing our battle-cruisers to within their reach.

Jellicoe, in his despatch, states: "When Sir David Beatty sighted the enemy battle-cruisers he adopted the correct and only possible course in engaging and endeavouring to keep between the enemy and his base. Whether the First Scouting Group was unsupported or not, his duty would be to engage and keep touch with the enemy vessels of similar class to his own, so long as he was not in manifestly inferior force. In this case he had a great superiority, and there could be no question as to his action."

Fire was opened at 3.45 p.m. from both sides practically simultaneously. The battle-cruiser *Lutzow,* the flagship of the German First Scouting Group, fired the first shot. The opening range was, in reality, about 16,000 yards, but as accurate range-finding was impossible owing to bad light, our battle-cruisers miscalculated the range, making it considerably greater. This was all to Hipper's advantage, as the guns of our battle-cruisers could outrange those of his ships. By withholding fire until the range had closed to one at which the German guns would be equally effective to our own, the superior gun-power of our battle-cruisers was not exploited to its fullest extent.

A running fight now took place between the respective battle-cruisers, the superiority in Beatty's favour being 6 to 5; but this first phase of the action went decidedly in favour of the enemy. At about 4 p.m. the *Lion* was very badly hit, a shell striking 'Q' turret and putting it out of action. Several fatal casualties were caused and the ship would, without doubt, have been lost save for the presence of mind of Major Harvey, Royal Marines, who, although fatally wounded, realized the danger and gave the necessary orders to close and flood the magazines. This action on his part, which won him a posthumous Victoria Cross, saved the ship.

At two minutes past four, the range having then closed to 14,600 yards, the battle-cruiser *Indefatigable* was hit by three shell, falling together, which were fired by the German battle-cruiser, *Von der Tann*. An explosion followed and she fell out of the line, sinking by the stern. After being hit once again she turned over and sank.

Six minutes after this, at 4.8 p.m., the Fifth Battle Squadron was able to open fire at a range of 20,000 yards and, although the fire from these ships' 15-inch guns could not have been as effective at this range as it would have been at the closer range at which the battle-cruisers were engaged, the effect was felt at once. In this connection, Beatty states his despatch: "The enemy's fire now appeared to slacken."

The battle-cruiser *Queen Mary* was the next victim. At 4.26 p.m. this ship was struck by a salvo and, almost instantaneously, there was a terrific upheaval and a dense cloud of smoke rose high in the air.

The battle-cruiser *Tiger* was following next astern of the *Queen Mary*, and as she passed through the cloud of smoke, about 30 seconds after the explosion, there was a heavy fall of debris on her decks, but, according to her report,[16] no sign of the *Queen Mary*. Seventeen survivors were subsequently picked up by destroyers.

Faulty distribution of fire in our battle-cruiser squadron resulted in the German battle-cruiser *Derfflinger* being unfired at for some time. That ship was, therefore, able to carry out a form of target practice, using one of our battle-cruisers as the target. She had the opportunity of inflicting as much damage as she could without interruption from our ships.

This regrettable omission undoubtedly went some way towards accounting for our losses; but the chief cause was the failure to co-ordinate the movements of the Fifth Battle Squadron to those of the battle-cruisers. Had the former been kept closed up or, better still, been stationed on a bearing where the enemy was most, and not least, likely to be met, the enemy would have been subjected to an overwhelming fire and would have been far less able to inflict on us such terrible losses. The value of the Fifth Battle Squadron was such that when they did open fire, even at extreme range, the enemy's fire "appeared to slacken".

In the meantime the flotillas had not been idle. At about 4.25 p.m. twelve of our destroyers made an attack; almost simultaneously the enemy destroyers moved out, but were forced to withdraw before their attack had been pressed home. They fired twelve torpedoes before retiring, however, which were avoided by the Fifth Battle Squadron by turning away two points, or 22°, for a few minutes. The enemy battle-cruisers were also forced to turn away to avoid the torpedoes fired by our destroyers, and the German battle-cruiser *Seydlitz* was hit, but was able to remain in the line.

In these attacks the enemy lost the destroyers *V.27* and *V.29* and we lost the destroyers *Nomad* and *Nestor*, which, after being severely damaged, subsequently came under the fire of the enemy battle fleet and were sunk.

GERMAN BATTLE FLEET SIGHTED

The light cruiser *Southampton*, flagship of the Second Light Cruiser Squadron, sighted and reported the enemy battle fleet at 4.38 p.m., and at about the same time it was sighted from the *Lion*.

The definite news that the enemy battle fleet was at sea, and in a position to support its battle-cruisers, must have come as somewhat of a surprise to Jellicoe and Beatty in view of the message previously received from the Admiralty. If the enemy battle fleet was in the Jade River at 11.10 a.m., how did it arrive in its present position, about 180 miles from the Jade, by half-past four? The information derived from directional wireless sent from the Admiralty was in this case obviously incorrect.

The Admirals afloat would have had no idea how this incorrect information came to be transmitted, but the mere fact that it was now proved beyond doubt to be incorrect would naturally lessen their subsequent reliance on information obtained by directional wireless, transmitted from the Admiralty.

On sighting the enemy battle fleet Beatty made a general signal, by flags, to turn 16 points – 180° – in succession. The effect of the recent torpedo attack, which was the cause of the enemy battle-cruisers turning away, was now evident, as this turn of 16 points was made without any of our ships receiving damage by gunfire. The signal to turn, having been made by flags, was again not clear to the Fifth Battle Squadron, some miles astern. This squadron being, therefore, still on a southerly course rapidly approached our battle-cruisers, now steering to the northward.

The signal to turn was repeated, and immediately the *Lion* had passed, on her northerly course, the Fifth Battle Squadron turned up astern of the battle-cruisers. During this turn the Fifth Battle Squadron came under fire from the leading ships of the High Seas Battle Fleet, and some salvoes fell close to them. No ship was, however, hit during the turn, although the *Barham* was hit more than once a few minutes after turning. The German battle-cruisers turned to the northward a few minutes after our battle-cruisers.

The *Southampton*, meanwhile, had pressed on to within 13,000 or 14,000 yards of the head of the enemy line for the purpose of obtaining as accurate information as possible of the composition and disposition of the enemy battle fleet. This action shows that Commodore Goodenough was one of those who realized fully that the most important duty of the advanced cruisers is to obtain and transmit accurate information of the enemy battle fleet to the Commander-in-Chief. It will be seen that he kept this duty in mind throughout the entire battle.

THE RUN NORTH

Intermittent firing on a northerly course now took place. Our battle-cruisers lost sight of the enemy, and consequently ceased firing, at 5.12 p.m.

The Fifth Battle Squadron, following about 2 miles astern of the *Lion*, however, continued to be hotly engaged with both enemy battle-cruisers and battleships. The *Barham* and *Valiant*, the two leading battleships, fired at the battle-cruisers at ranges of about 18,000 to 20,000 yards. The two rear ships, *Malaya* and *Warspite*, joined action with the head of the enemy battle fleet.

The superior gunnery of the Fifth Battle Squadron now began to show its effect. It is abundantly clear from German evidence that before this time little damage had been received by the enemy from the gunfire of the British battle-cruisers, except from that of *Queen Mary*, which ship appears to have obtained more hits than her consorts in the short time available before her regrettable loss. During this period, however, although the *Barham*, *Valiant* and *Malaya* received several hits, they inflicted damage on the German battle-cruisers and battleships. Our battle-cruisers opened fire again, for a few minutes, at 5.40 p.m., but, owing to decreasing visibility, the firing was only intermittent, at a range of about 17,000 yards.

While these actions were taking place the Third Battle Cruiser Squadron, which left Scapa Flow with the battle fleet, was, at 4.5 p.m., ordered by Jellicoe to proceed with the light cruisers *Chester* and *Canterbury* to support Beatty. Course was subsequently altered as necessary to close the *Lion*, but, owing to the uncertainty of the position of our battle-cruisers, the *Invincible* led the squadron too far to the eastward.

At 5.36 p.m. the *Chester* sighted some enemy light cruisers of the Second Scouting Group and fire was opened on both sides. The *Chester* received severe damage from this superior force, and, after being under fire for nineteen minutes, was saved from further damage by Admiral Hood leading the Third Battle-Cruiser Squadron between the *Chester* and the enemy.

At about 5.50 p.m. the *Lion* sighted the cruiser screen ahead of our battle fleet, and a few minutes later sighted the leading ships of the British battle fleet. This must have been a welcome sight to a sorely damaged squadron.

AN UNPALATABLE RESULT

Thus ended the battle-cruiser fleet action and, as Jellicoe said in his despatch, the "result cannot be other than unpalatable".

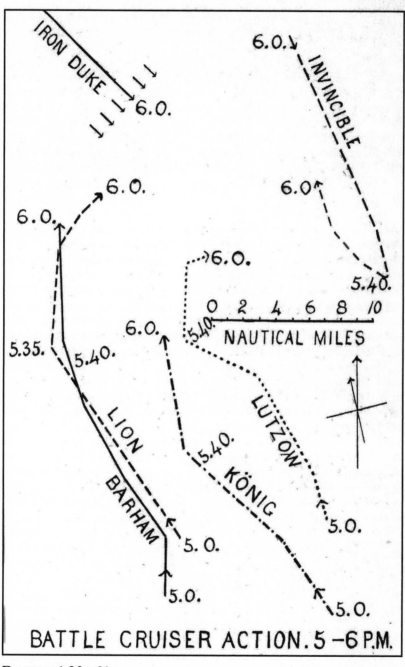

IRON DUKE
6.0.

6.0. INVINCIBLE

6.0.

6.0.

6.0.

6.0.

6.0.

5.40.

5.35.
5.40.

6.0.

5.40.

NAUTICAL MILES
0 2 4 6 8 10

LION

LUTZOW

BARHAM

5.40.
KÖNIG

5.0.

5.0.

5.0.

5.0.

5.0.

BATTLE CRUISER ACTION. 5 – 6 P.M.

DIAGRAM 4: MAY 31

Let us consider the first phase of this action, between the time of opening fire and the time of sighting the enemy battle fleet. We find that on the British side Beatty had under his command 4 battleships and 6 battle-cruisers against Hipper's 5 battle-cruisers. In light cruisers and destroyers Beatty was also numerically superior. In spite of this overwhelming preponderance of power, we lost two battle-cruisers, sunk by gunfire, while the enemy lost none. Considerably more damage was caused to our ships than they inflicted on the enemy. It *is* unpalatable – extremely unpalatable – but nevertheless an indisputable fact that, in this first phase of the battle, a British squadron, greatly superior in numbers and gun-power, not only failed to defeat a weaker enemy who made no effort to avoid action, but, in the space of 50 minutes, suffered what can only be described as a partial defeat.

This regrettable result cannot be entirely explained away by the lack of armour protection of our battle-cruisers, the poor quality of the British shells, and the disadvantage under which, it is stated, our ships suffered after the first quarter of an hour in regard to light. The first of these factors certainly had considerable bearing on the total loss of our two ships, but does not account for the comparatively minor damage inflicted on the enemy. For this we must find other reasons, which were, without doubt, firstly, the delay in bringing the Fifth Battle Squadron into action, and, secondly, the inaccurate shooting of our battle-cruisers; which has been specially remarked on by the Germans.

The battle-cruisers and Fifth Battle Squadron had now, in spite of their difficulties and losses, gallantly led the enemy to within striking distance of the Grand Fleet. To those in the Battle-Cruiser Fleet it might, at the time, have seemed that nothing now remained but for Jellicoe to strike an annihilating blow.

Defeat was not, however, to be changed to victory as easily as it appeared. In naval warfare a sweeping victory is the exception and inconclusive actions the general rule. For a sweeping victory time and clear weather are essentials; but the atmospheric conditions alone would have prevented anything in the nature of a sweeping victory, and the late hour of meeting was all in favour of an enemy fleet bent on avoiding action.

Chapter 5

The Meeting of the Fleets

In Chapter III we left the British Battle Fleet steaming to the south-eastward at high speed, in their endeavour to support our battle-cruisers at the earliest possible moment, and ready to form into line of battle directly the advanced cruisers made contact.

It was of the utmost importance for Jellicoe to know, as accurately as possible, the position of the enemy battle fleet relative to his own position. It was also important for him to know from time to time the direction in which the enemy was steering. With this knowledge he would have been able, with some certainty, to forecast the bearing on which he would sight the enemy.

To form the battle fleet into line of battle – or in other words, to deploy – before reliable information of the enemy's position was obtained would have been the negation of sound tactics. An early deployment on insufficient information obviates any chance of tactical advantage in deployment. An early deployment on reliable information is sound.

After deployment, provided deployment is judged correctly, the battle fleet should be steaming in a single line, in such a direction that all the guns of the main armament can be brought to bear on the enemy, with a good margin of training in reserve to allow for unavoidable minor miscalculations of the actual bearing of the enemy. It is also important that the deployment should be carried out as expeditiously as possible. To enable this to be done, it is an accepted axiom of tactics that the fleet should be formed into divisions, or columns, the bearing of the leaders of each column from one another being kept as nearly as possible at right angles to the bearing on which it is expected to sight the enemy. If this is done, the utmost flexibility is obtained and the actual deployment can be made in either direction without any unnecessary waste of time.

It is obvious, therefore, that, if possible, the deployment should be made in time for the whole battle fleet to be in line of battle shortly before the enemy is actually within gun range; which, in these days of long range, means shortly before the enemy is sighted.

31

It has long been considered that tactical advantage is gained by deploying outside the maximum range of the torpedoes of the enemy battleships. The effective range of the German torpedoes was about 15,000 yards, and the enemy battleships were superior to ours in torpedo armament.

Our gun armament, on the other hand, was superior to that of the enemy.

THE COMMANDER-IN-CHIEF'S NEED OF INFORMATION

If, therefore, Jellicoe was to get the best use out of his superior gun armament, and obviate any disadvantage due to the enemy's superior torpedo armament, it was desirable to deploy outside a range of 15,000 yards from the enemy battle fleet. To enable him to do this, timely and accurate information of the position and course of the enemy was all important; but, unfortunately, this was the very thing denied to the Commander-in-Chief.

A ship in visual touch with the enemy, but out of sight of her Fleet Flagship, must, in reporting the enemy's position, also give her own geographical position (by latitude and longitude); the accuracy with which the Commander-in-Chief can then determine the relative bearing and distance from him of the enemy will depend upon the accuracy with which the geographical positions of his flagship and the ship making the report are known. In the cloudy weather usually prevailing in the North Sea, especially when course and speed have to be continually altered in the presence of the enemy, it is too much to expect that any ship would know her geographical position with absolute accuracy. Small errors, some one way and some another, are usually cancelled if several reports are received. Hence the necessity of continuous and reliable reports.

The first definite information of the presence of the enemy battle fleet which reached Jellicoe was that sent by the *Southampton* at 4.38., which read: "Have sighted enemy battle fleet bearing approximately S.E. Course of enemy North. My position Lat. 56° 34' N., Long. 6° 20' E. (1638)."

Several reports had, however, previously been received in the *Iron Duke* giving the position of the enemy battle-cruisers. Owing, however, to signalling, or ciphering errors, and also owing to the unavoidable errors in the dead-reckoning of the ships concerned, the position of the enemy relative to the *Iron Duke* must have been, to say the least, conjectural.[17]

Between the time of sighting the enemy battle fleet and the time visual contact was made between our advanced forces and our battle fleet Jellicoe received four messages from the *Southampton*; one message from the *Champion*, which contained information that was obviously inaccurate; and one message from the *Lion*, which was sent at 4.45. p.m. This one message sent from the *Lion* was, unfortunately, mutilated in transmission. It should have read, "Have sighted enemy's battle fleet, bearing S.E. ..."

Owing to the *Lion*'s wireless having been shot away, the message had to

32

be passed through the battle-cruiser *Princess Royal*, which caused some delay, and when it was received by Jellicoe, twenty minutes later, it read: "26 to 30 battleships probably hostile bearing S.S.E. Steering S.E."

During the hour preceding the time at which visual contact was made, a period during which it was all-important for Jellicoe to receive accurate information, no ship of the advanced forces, except the *Southampton*, sent any message. This was partly due to the battle-cruisers having lost touch with the enemy battle fleet during the run North. The Fifth Battle Squadron was, however, still in touch. In fact, two of these battleships were engaged in a gunnery duel with the leading German battleships, and authentic reports of the position of the enemy could have been sent at regular intervals, but no report was sent from this source. The vital importance of sending continuous information appears to have been appreciated only by the *Southampton*.

Under the circumstance, therefore, it is not surprising that Jellicoe was uncertain as to the bearing on which the enemy would be sighted. In his despatch he states: "It was apparent on meeting that the reckoning of the Battle-Cruiser Fleet was about 12 miles to the Eastward of *Iron Duke*'s reckoning. In consequence of this the enemy were sighted on the Starboard bow instead of ahead, and some twenty minutes earlier than was anticipated …"

The difference in reckoning, on meeting, between the *Iron Duke* and the *Lion* was, in reality, about 10 miles. The *Iron Duke* was some 4 miles to the south-eastward of her reckoning and the *Lion* about 6 miles to the westward. Jellicoe would not, however, have formed his opinion entirely on the only message received by wireless from the *Lion*, after the enemy battle fleet was sighted. In the messages sent from the *Southampton*, in which her position is given, that sent at 4.38 p.m. was 13 miles to the eastward of her correct position and those at 4.45 p.m. and 4.48 p.m. 6 and 9 miles respectively. These errors, if due to dead reckoning, should have been nearly constant. It is probable, therefore, that they were partly due to the other causes mentioned.

Jellicoe continues: "Owing to the uncertainty as to the position of the enemy battle fleet, it had not been possible to redispose the guides of columns on any different bearing. Consequently the deployment was carried out under some disadvantage, and, indeed, it was not easy to determine the correct direction of deployment until the battle fleets were almost in contact."

We see, therefore, that although the rival battle fleets were rapidly closing one another and, although not in sight, were getting close to gun range, Jellicoe had no reliable information on which to deploy. If he deployed on such scanty information, he might give the enemy a great advantage; and again, if he waited for more news, he might find himself within gun and torpedo range without his fleet being deployed. In an endeavour to obtain

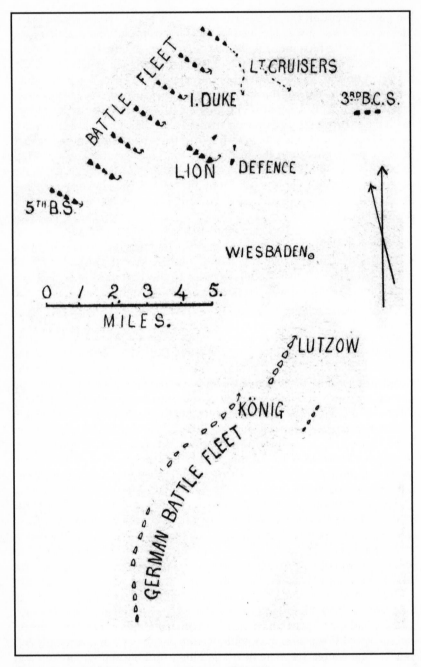

DIAGRAM 5: THE SITUATION AT 6.14 P.M., MAY 31

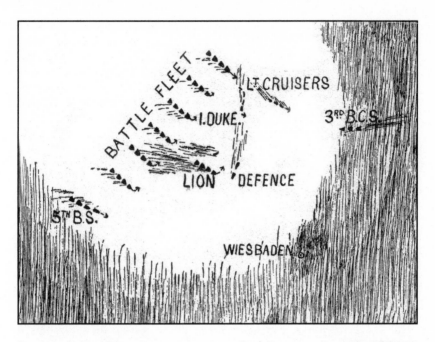

DIAGRAM 6: THE SITUATION AT 6.14 P.M., AS SEEN FROM THE *IRON DUKE* MAY 31

some reliable information as to the whereabouts of the enemy Jellicoe made a visual signal to Beatty at 6.1 p.m.: "Where is enemy's battle fleet?"

After waiting for some minutes without receiving any reply, a repetition of the signal was made at 6.10 p.m., and at 6.14 p.m. the reply was received: "Have sighted enemy's battle fleet bearing S.S.W."

JELLICOE'S DEPLOYMENT

There was now not a moment to spare, and Jellicoe still had no definite news of the course the enemy was steering, but an immediate decision on his part was imperatively necessary. He decided to deploy on his port wing column, which was being led by the *King George V*. The signal ordering this movement was made at 6.15 p.m., one minute after the receipt of the signal from the *Lion*.

By way of comparison, it is interesting to note that at the Battle of Trafalgar there was a total of 71 ships engaged – at Jutland 260. At Trafalgar the main fleets were in sight of one another for several hours before the light wind enabled them to close to effective range at the speed of 2 to 3 miles an hour. At Jutland the fleets were closing at some 40 miles an hour.

Considerable uninformed criticism has been directed at the method of deployment adopted by Jellicoe. It has been described, incorrectly, by some critics as a deployment "away from the enemy". Suggestions have been made that deployment should have been made on the starboard wing column or, by a somewhat complicated manoeuvre which might have been misunderstood in the fleet, on a centre column. What, however, is the use of conjecture as to the relative advantages of other means of deployment when we must admit that the manoeuvre, as ordered, was understood by the whole fleet; that it enabled our fleet to cross, the enemy's "T", and placed our main force between the enemy and his base? A deployment which achieved these results is above adverse criticism. It is difficult to understand how any other method of deployment could have attained a better result.

While the battle fleet was forming line of battle, the battle-cruisers were proceeding at full speed to take up their assigned station at the head of the battle fleet. Their smoke seriously hampered the view from many of the battleships, especially those at the head of the line. This, unfortunate though it was, was unavoidable, as no other action was possible.

At the time the signal for deployment was made it is unlikely that the enemy battle fleet, or any portion of it, had been sighted from our battle fleet. It is true that in some of the reports sent in by the Commanding Officers mention is made of enemy battleships having been sighted before this time, but it is considered most probable that, owing to the mist and smoke-haze, friends were mistaken for enemy, or cruisers for battleships. It is certain, however, that neither Scheer, in the enemy battle fleet, or von Hipper, in his battle-cruisers, had sighted or located our battle fleet at this time.

In fact, Scheer had only recently suspected our battle fleet was anywhere in the vicinity. Scheer's appreciation of the situation, shortly after this, was that our battle fleet was in single line, heading to the south-eastward and stretched well to the southward across his course. The misty weather had, obviously, misled him and a glimpse of the *Invincible*, leading the Third Battle-Cruiser Squadron, had been mistaken for the van of our battle fleet. This led him to believe that our battle fleet was a good deal farther advanced than it really was.

Chapter 6
General Fleet Action

The action between the battle fleets commenced immediately the signal for deployment had been hauled down, but firing was not general, mainly owing to the mist and smoke and partly owing to the masking of the enemy by our own ships. The reports from Flag and Commanding Officers, in several cases, make mention of the difficulty in obtaining a clear range, and a close study of these reports shows a considerable amount of masking occurred. This would appear to have been unavoidable, considering that all our detached and outlying squadrons were at this time converging on the battle fleet; and that the battle-cruisers were passing between our fleet and the enemy as they strained to get to the head of the line.

The Sixth Division – the rear division of the battle line – was the first to come into action. As the battleship *Hercules* started to turn into line of battle she was straddled, that is to say, shots of a salvo from the enemy fell, some short of, and some over, her; but she was not hit. Splashes from salvoes like these reached as high as the foretop. The enemy's shells were also falling close to the battleships *Vanguard* and *Revenge*.

At this time the German light cruiser *Wiesbaden*, which had been severely damaged when in action with the battle-cruiser *Invincible*, was lying, apparently stopped, and on fire, in a favourable position as a target for any of our battleships which could not, at the moment, see any enemy capital ship to open fire on. She was engaged, and hit, by several of our ships, and, as the reports mention that shots which apparently came from the enemy ships were also falling close to the *Wiesbaden*, it is probable that this unfortunate ship was being fired on by her friends as well as her foes. She was also hit by a torpedo fired by the destroyer *Onslow*, and finally sank.

As our battle fleet started to deploy, the *Defence* and *Warrior*, which had been engaging enemy light cruisers, crossed so close ahead of the *Lion* that the battle-cruisers' course had to be altered to clear them. These two armoured cruisers then found themselves within comparatively close range of the heavy ships of the enemy. They were immediately subjected to a very heavy concentrated fire, which in a minute or two was the cause of the *Defence* being blown up and sunk. The *Warrior* also received severe damage, but was able to withdraw from the battle. She would probably have suffered the same fate as the *Defence* but for the battleship *Warspite*, which, owing to her helm having jammed, described an involuntary circle between the *Warrior* and the enemy, thereby receiving many of the hits which were intended for the other ship. The *Warrior* was subsequently taken in tow by the seaplane carrier *Engadine*, but sank before reaching home, while the *Warspite* took no further part in the battle and was eventually ordered back to harbour.

The *Marlborough*, flying the flag of Admiral Burney, second-in-command of the Grand Fleet, leading the Sixth Division of Battleships, opened fire at 6.17 p.m., followed after a few minutes by the *Revenge*, and as the range cleared the ships ahead were able to come into action. The enemy battle fleet was at this time steering to the north-eastward.

BATTLE FLEETS IN ACTION

The situation at 6.26 p.m., a few minutes after the deployment commenced, is seen in Diagram No.7. This shows our battle fleet, in one line, leading round to the south-eastward. Our battle-cruisers are trying to get to the head of the line and the Third Battle-Cruiser Squadron is in action with the enemy battle-cruisers. It became necessary to reduce the speed of the battle fleet in order to allow the battle-cruisers to get clear, and thus give a better chance to the battleships to obtain a clear range.

As the battle-cruisers drew ahead the general situation became somewhat plainer to Jellicoe, although it was yet far from clear. He realized, however, that the moment had come when he could probably inflict severe damage on the enemy, and, at 6.29 p.m., he signalled for the course to be altered, by sub-divisions, to S.S.E., to bear down on the enemy. But this signal had to be cancelled for two reasons.

Firstly, there was some bunching up of our ships in the rear divisions, caused by the enforced reduction of speed to allow the battle-cruisers to draw ahead, and consequently the rearmost ships had not yet turned to the new course. Secondly, because the battle-cruisers were rapidly converging on the head of our line, which would have prevented the *King George V*, the leading battleship, from closing the enemy. This passage across the front of the battle fleet, to which Beatty was unavoidably committed, marred to some extent a very promising opening of the general action, and prevented full advantage being taken by Jellicoe of his position. At the moment of deployment, when the rear divisions were nearest the enemy, they were being masked by the battle-cruisers, and later on, as the head of our line came into a suitable position to inflict damage, it was prevented from doing so.

By 6.30 p.m. all the divisions of the battle fleet, except the First Division, had come into action. The view from the First Division was still obscure.

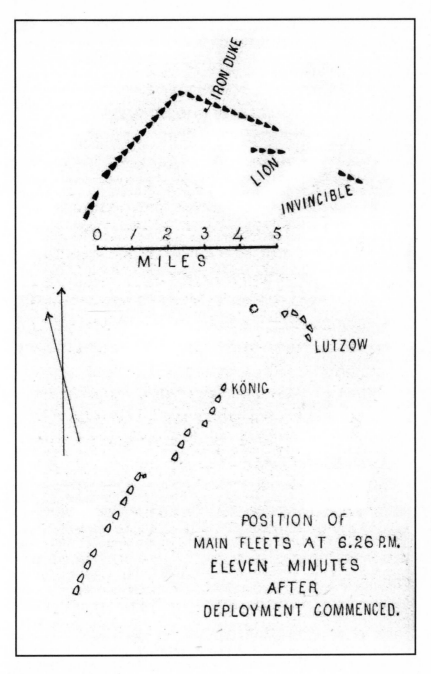

IRON DUKE

LION

INVINCIBLE

0 1 2 3 4 5
MILES

LUTZOW

KÖNIG

POSITION OF
MAIN FLEETS AT 6.26 P.M.
ELEVEN MINUTES
AFTER
DEPLOYMENT COMMENCED.

DIAGRAM 7: MAY 31

At the head of the line the *Invincible*, leading the Third Battle-Cruiser Squadron, had just turned to take station ahead of the First Battle Cruiser Squadron, and was heavily engaged with the enemy, when, at 6.34 p.m., she was badly hit, blew up and sank.[18]

Owing to the concentrated fire of many of our battleships, assisted by that of the battle-cruisers, the enemy suffered appreciable damage at this time. The enemy battle-cruisers suffered most, in fact, the *Lutzow* was so badly damaged that von Hipper was compelled to shift his flag. His first attempt was to board the *Seydlitz*, but as this ship was also badly damaged he went to the *Moltke*. The major portion of the damage incurred by them was, undoubtedly, inflicted after our battle fleet came into action. The fact that little damage was done to these ships before this explains, to a certain extent, the severe losses incurred in the sinking of the *Indefatigable* and the *Queen Mary*, and the considerable damage done to the *Lion*, which nearly resulted in her loss. The shooting of the enemy during this early stage was good, but it fell off later, and it was an established fact that the German gunnery efficiency showed a rapid decline as soon as our ships established hitting.

Several of the enemy battleships also suffered damage at this time. The *Konig*, at the head of the line, probably received greater damage from gunfire than any other enemy battleship.

THE FIRST GERMAN RETREAT

Scheer, to whom the situation was still obscure, now found himself becoming enveloped by our fleet. The British battle-cruisers, having reached the head of the line, were fine on his starboard bow and a great line of ships stretched across his track.

Owing to Jellicoe's well-directed deployment, his "T" was practically crossed and his position was a desperate one. To escape from this predicament he made the famous "Battle turn away", of the Germans, with his whole fleet. This manoeuvre was designed to enable his weaker fleet to get out of a tight corner. To gain time, and to enable the "turn away" to be made without considerable risk, a smoke-screen was put up by the enemy destroyers and, it is stated, a torpedo attack was also launched against our battle line. It seems more probable that the enemy destroyer flotilla was making an endeavour to reach the damaged *Wiesbaden* to rescue her crew, but on encountering the heavy fire directed on them by our battleships they were forced to retire. Six torpedoes were discharged at the rear of our battle line, but none hit, nor did this attack cause Jellicoe to deflect from his course.

Although the smoke-screen had prevented Jellicoe from seeing the enemy's movements, it very soon became apparent to him that they must have turned away. There is no direct answer to the "Battle turn away" except a stern chase on the part of the stronger fleet, and a stern chase under

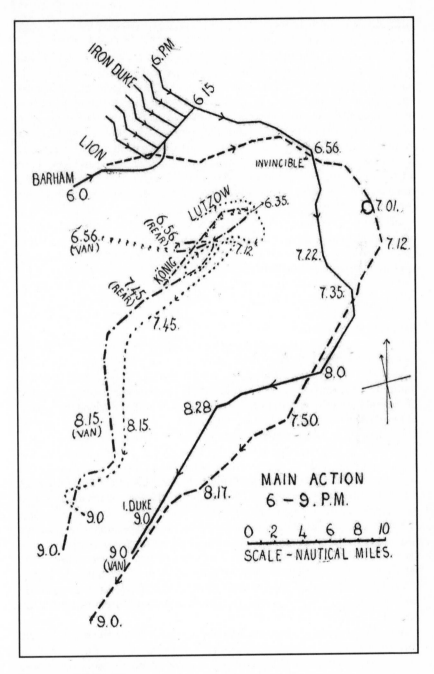

DIAGRAM 8: MAY 31

such conditions would have been accompanied by risks which no prudent admiral could accept.

As we saw in Chapter II, a turn to follow the enemy directly would have placed our battle fleet in a position of great tactical disadvantage. It would have laid our ships open to attacks by torpedo from the German battleships, and also their destroyers, both of which would have been in the best possible position for this purpose. The menace of floating mines, dropped from the German battleships, would also have had to be accepted, as also would the possible danger from submarines. Our battle fleet had very slight superiority in speed over the enemy. A chase, therefore, would have been a long chase, with little hope of overtaking the enemy before dark, and some probability of losing the advantage, already gained, of being between the enemy and his base.

In clear weather the difficulty might have been met by dividing our fleet and despatching fast squadrons to harass his flanks; but, even so, the day was somewhat too far advanced to render this desirable. In the misty weather prevailing, and with so few hours of daylight remaining, such tactics had little to commend them owing to the difficulty of co-ordination between squadrons separated from one another.

BEATTY FAILS TO REGAIN TOUCH

Since there was nothing to indicate to Jellicoe, within a wide arc, the direction in which the enemy had retired, he took the only action possible which, at this time, might lead to ultimate victory. At 6.44 he turned the battle fleet to south-east, this being the best course to ensure getting fair between the enemy and his base, and at the same time to close the enemy obliquely for the purpose of renewing the action. Our battle-cruisers, whose main duty now was reconnaissance, also altered course to south-east and later to S.S.E. These alterations did not again bring the German ships into view, but Beatty did not turn farther in their direction.

In his despatch he states: "Caution forbade me to close the range too much with my inferior force." This statement does not refer definitely to any particular time, so may be assumed to be his general policy. Beatty's "reconnaissance force" was now six battle-cruisers against the enemy's four; in this respect, therefore, Beatty had superior force. He also had ample superiority in speed to regain touch with the enemy and to ensure a safe retreat on our battle fleet without undue risk to his command.

Owing to the turn away of the enemy battle fleet, fire between the opposing capital ships ceased for a while. Ten minutes after altering course to the South-east the course of our battle fleet was again altered to starboard, to South, to close the supposed position of the enemy more directly.

At 6.54 p.m. the *Marlborough* was struck by a torpedo, which was probably fired by the damaged *Weisbaden*. She was able, however, to keep her place in the line for several hours, although her maximum speed was considerably reduced. At about this time our battle fleet passed the wreck of the *Invincible*, the Third and Fourth Divisions passing her one on either hand, the wreck being clearly visible with the bow and stern standing up out of the water, showing that the ship had been broken in two by the explosion, the midship parts resting on the bottom.[19]

SCHEER BLUNDERS INTO OUR BATTLE FLEET

Scheer, having extricated himself from his perilous position by his precipitate retreat and by standing to the westward for some minutes, turned again to the eastward. For all his protestations, it is unbelievable that he did this for the purpose of renewing the action. What is probable is that he had been misled, owing to the mist and smoke, as to the actual position of our battle fleet at about 6.35 p.m., and thought they were farther to the southward than was the case.

It seems probable, too, that he was of opinion that if he now turned back to the eastward he might succeed in crossing astern of our fleet, thereby not only getting into a more favourable position as regards his own base, but, in the event of a renewal of the action, getting the advantage of light towards sunset. No other explanation of Scheer's tactics, at this time, appears reasonable. A capable leader and skilled tactician, as Scheer undoubtedly was, would not purposely have headed his fleet directly towards the centre of the arc formed by our battle fleet, thus bringing his leading squadrons under the concentrated fire of practically all our battleships, which is what happened.

At 6.54 p.m. Jellicoe, having had no report of the position of the enemy from his van ships, realized that the enemy battle fleet could not yet be heading for home, so he turned his fleet to south.

Commodore Goodenough, in the *Southampton*, who had previously sent so many reports of the position of the enemy battle fleet, made yet another effort to locate it. At about 7 p.m. he turned his squadron to the southward from his position near the rear of our battle line, and again located and reported the enemy, coming under heavy fire as he did so.

No firing was now taking place between the main fleets, the enemy being out of sight of all our battleships, and also of our battle-cruisers, which were at this time some 6 miles on the port bow of the *Iron Duke*, and farther from the enemy than the Fleet Flagship. Beatty had gone on at high speed and lost touch with what was happening.

Owing to the decreasing visibility, he would not have seen the battle fleet hauling round towards the enemy, but all signals for alteration of course, made from the *Iron Duke*, were sent out by wireless, so would have reached the battle-cruisers. He now reduced speed to 18 knots and began to circle to starboard to close the battle fleet. A complete circle was made by the *Lion*, the *Princess Royal*, *Tiger* and *New Zealand* following her round. Immediately after the completion of this turn the battle-cruisers *Inflexible* and *Indomitable*, which had been keeping ahead of the *Lion*, took station in line astern.[20]

THE SECOND GERMAN RETREAT

At 7.10 p.m. the head of the enemy fleet again came into sight from some of our battleships, and fire was immediately opened on the head of his battleship line by the *Marlborough* and her division, and on the enemy battle-cruisers by the Fifth Division. At this time the range was as low as 9,000 yards in some cases.

In a very short time practically the whole of our battle fleet was engaged, at ranges varying from 11,000 to 14,000 yards; but owing to the poor visibility organized concentration of fire was impossible. The enemy, especially his battle-cruisers, again received severe damage from our battleships. Some of our battle-cruisers also came into action again for a few minutes, but at a somewhat greater range.

Jellicoe had again secured a position of immense tactical advantage, having fairly crossed the enemy's "T", and only the poor visibility saved the German fleet from suffering an overwhelming defeat there and then.

As soon as the action was resumed Scheer realized that his position was an impossible one, and that his passage to the eastward was barred. Only one chance was his, and he took it. His flotillas were ordered to attack and put up smoke-screens. His battle-cruisers were ordered to, "Charge the enemy. Ram. Without regard to consequences", and his battle fleet was again ordered to make the "Battle turn away". The manoeuvre was successfully accomplished and the whole enemy fleet once more retired from the scene of action. This move on the part of the enemy was, again, not clear to Jellicoe, owing to the smoke screen.

ENEMY TORPEDOES ELUDED

At 7.22 p.m. the Eleventh Half-Flotilla of German Destroyers was observed to fire torpedoes and three minutes later the Seventeenth Half-Flotilla – twenty-one enemy torpedoes were fired in all. Immediately after launching this attack the enemy destroyers turned away and disappeared in a smoke-screen. Ten minutes later a further attack was made by the Third and Fifth Flotillas of the enemy. This attack, however, was largely frustrated by a counter-attack on the part of our Fourth Light Cruiser Squadron.

When the torpedoes were fired, Jellicoe, at 7.22 p.m., in accordance with established custom, turned the battle fleet away 2 points, by sub-divisions; and after an interval of three minutes, when calculations showed that this turn would not be sufficient to avoid the torpedoes, he ordered a further turn of 2 points. The result of this manoeuvre was that, although several torpedoes were seen by our battleships, not one hit.

In his despatch Jellicoe states: "The torpedo attacks launched by the enemy were countered in the manner previously intended and practised during exercises."

The torpedo attack, as an attack, failed; but the smoke-screen developed by the enemy destroyers was so far effective that it prevented Jellicoe from knowing the extent of the turn away of the enemy battle fleet.

Having avoided the torpedoes, he therefore turned our battle fleet to S. by W., 5 points towards the enemy. Without knowing the position of the enemy it would have been unwise to turn more than this, as he might have lost his position between the enemy and his base.

At 7.45 p.m. our battle fleet was again turned, to south-west towards the enemy, and at 8 p.m. to west. During this time, while course was being gradually altered to the westward, the enemy battle fleet was out of sight of our battle fleet. The signals received by Jellicoe during this time are not easy to understand.

The "Follow Me" Incident

At 7.40 p.m. our battle-cruisers, having drawn ahead, had again lost touch with our battle fleet. The *Lion* was actually only 5¼ miles distant from the leading battleship, but, owing to poor visibility, was not in sight of her. Beatty, however, at this time remarks that the visibility had improved to the westward, and he signalled by wireless to Jellicoe to say: "Enemy bears from me N.W. by W. distant 10 to 11 miles." The visibility must, therefore, have been very variable.

Again, at 7.45 p.m. Beatty signalled: "Leading enemy battleship bears N.W. by W. Course about S.W." This makes it appear that the visibility to the north-westward was sufficiently good to judge the approximate course of a ship at a distance of about 11 miles.

Owing, however, to the *Lion* not being in sight of our battle fleet, which was now only 6 miles to the northward, this visual signal had to be passed through an intermediate ship, the armoured cruiser *Minotaur*. No mention is found in the reports from the other battle-cruisers that the enemy was in sight at this time, and in the report from the Captain of the *Lion* we find, under 7.32 p.m.: "The enemy was still not sufficiently visible to open fire, and this continued until 8.21 p.m."

At 7.50 p.m. Beatty made the following signal by wireless to the Commander-in-Chief: "Submit van of battleships follow battle-cruisers. We can then cut off whole of enemy's battle fleet."

Considerable prominence has been given to this signal in the Press; more especially was this the case immediately after the publication of the official despatches. It may, therefore, be equitable to refer to it in some detail.

As our battle fleet was not in sight from the *Lion*, it is not clear how Beatty could know in what direction it was then steering. This could have been quickly ascertained by a visual signal to one of the ships bridging the gap.

Such a signal was made by Beatty at 8.15 p.m., so why not at 7.50 p.m. also? Again, it is not clear what "cutting off" is referred to. There is no suggestion that part of the enemy could be cut off from the main force, but that the whole battle fleet could be cut off. Presumably, therefore, it refers to cutting the enemy off from his base. The position, course and speed of our battle fleet could not have been improved upon for this purpose. As a fact, at the time the signal originated the van of the battle fleet was steering the same course as the *Lion*; was practically following the battle-cruisers – if anything, the van was a little on the *Lion*'s starboard quarter – and it was also nearer the enemy than was the *Lion*. An alteration in the course, to follow the battle-cruisers, at the moment the signal was made would, therefore, have caused the van to converge less on the enemy's course than it was actually doing.

The message sent was, therefore, quite unnecessary, and likely to mislead the Commander-in-Chief.

This cipher message, which was timed 7.50 p.m., was received in the *Iron Duke* at 7.54 p.m., and must have led Jellicoe, who would not have seen it until it had been deciphered some minutes later, to conclude that the battle-cruisers, which he could not see, were steering a very different course to that of the battle fleet. Jellicoe at once signalled to the *King George V*, the van ship, to follow the battle-cruisers, and this order was received by Admiral Jerram at 8.7 p.m.

Meanwhile, at 8 p.m., the battle fleet had altered course to west, 4 more points towards the enemy. The signal for this alteration was made by flags, and also by wireless, so it would be received without delay by all ships. The battle-cruisers did not, however, turn at once but, for the next quarter of an hour, continued on a south-west course. They then altered course to west, towards the enemy, conforming to the movement of the battle fleet. The receipt of the signal to follow the battle-cruisers must have puzzled Jerram, because they were not in sight from the *King George V*. They could not be on his starboard side, because our battle fleet was in that direction, and any alteration to port would have led the First Division of the battle fleet farther from the enemy. Jerram, therefore, did the best thing possible and continued on his course.

CONTACT REGAINED, BUT THE ENEMY RETREATS AT ONCE

At 8 p.m. Beatty ordered the First and Third Light Cruiser Squadrons to sweep to the westward and locate the head of the enemy's line before dark. The Third Light Cruiser Squadron, after being in action with some enemy cruisers, located the enemy battle-cruisers and, at 8.46 p.m., reported their position. Before, however, this report was made, our battle-cruisers had, almost immediately after turning to west, sighted what appeared to be two battle-cruisers and some battleships, and at 8.23 p.m. fire was opened on them. At this time the enemy's main battle fleet, led by the battleship

Westfalen, was steering a southerly course, with their battle-cruisers on the port bow and the Second Squadron of pre-Dreadnought battleships on the starboard bow.

Immediately our battle-cruisers opened fire the enemy battle-cruisers turned away to the westward; but the Second Squadron of old battleships, which now came into action for the first time, held on their course. The action lasted only for a few minutes before this squadron also turned away.

At 8.28 p.m. the course of our battle fleet was altered to south-west. The enemy at this time was bearing about west from the *Iron Duke*, and it was necessary for our battle fleet to alter course to port to prevent the enemy from passing ahead, and thus attaining an improved strategical position. By 8.40 p.m. the enemy had completely disappeared from sight from our battle-cruisers and was not seen again by them.

It is of interest that, at 8.40 p.m., all our battle-cruisers and some of the ships of the First and Third Light Cruiser Squadrons report feeling a shock, as if struck by a mine or torpedo. The reports are so definite that it is undeniable that some severe explosion occurred at this time. No satisfactory explanation of the cause of a shock of such magnitude can be given. The only explosion reported as having been seen at this time was seen from the light cruiser *Calliope*. It is possible that this was the enemy battleship *Markgraf* being hit by a torpedo, but *Markgraf* was some 8 miles from our battle-cruisers. It is practically certain that no submarine was in the vicinity.

Jellicoe received information of the whereabouts of the enemy, at about 8.40 p.m., from the light cruiser *Comus*, and shortly after this from the *Falmouth* and also from the *Southampton*.

This information, confirmed by a message sent from the *Lion* at 8.40 p.m. and received in the *Iron Duke* at 8.59 p.m., made the situation plain enough for Jellicoe to decide on his movements during the night. It was now getting dark, as sunset was at 8.7 p.m. and there was no moonlight during the dark hours.

The Problem Of The Night

Although darkness was now approaching, the problem of Jutland was by no means completed. It was, in fact, only beginning. With no more than three hours of daylight remaining after the main fleets met, it would have required more than a genius to ensure a decisive victory, against an enemy who was persistently endeavouring to avoid action, in the conditions of visibility then prevailing.

The actions before dark on 31st May must be considered, therefore, to be in the nature of preliminary skirmishes, of necessity curtailed owing to the late hour in the day at which the fleets met.

The real problem which then faced Jellicoe was, how to make as certain as human brain could make it that the enemy main fleet would be brought to action as early as possible after daylight the following morning.

The proceedings, and incidents, during the night cannot, therefore, be dismissed as subsidiary to the main problem, but should be as carefully and fully studied as any of the actions during daylight on 31st May.

Chapter 7
The Night

At 9.1 p.m. the battle fleet was turned to south and subsequently assumed night-cruising formation. At 9.27 the destroyer flotillas were ordered to take station 5 miles astern of the battle fleet.

The course of the battle fleet was signalled to Beatty, and at 9.30 p.m. the battle-cruisers, then about 12 miles on the starboard bow of the *Iron Duke*, also altered course to south. The *Marlborough*, being now unable to maintain the speed of the fleet, 17 knots, owing to her damage, had dropped somewhat astern with her sub-division.

Jellicoe, in his despatch, states: "I rejected at once the idea of a night action between the heavy ships as leading to possible disaster owing, first, to the presence of torpedo craft in such large numbers, and, secondly, to the impossibility of distinguishing between our own and enemy vessels. Further, the result of a night action under modern conditions must always be very largely a matter of pure chance. ... I therefore decided to steer to the southward, where I should be in position to renew the engagement at daylight, and should also be favourably placed to intercept the enemy should he make for his base by steering for Heligoland or towards the Ems and thence along the North German coast"

Beatty, in his despatch, states: "I assumed that the enemy were to the north-westward, and that we had established ourselves between him and his base. ... In view of the gathering darkness and for other reasons, viz. (a) our distance from the battle fleet; (b) the damaged condition of the battle-cruisers; (c) the enemy being concentrated; (d) the enemy being accompanied by numerous destroyers; (e) our strategical position being such that it appeared certain that we should locate the enemy at daylight under most favourable circumstances, I did not consider it proper or desirable to close the enemy battle fleet during the dark hours."

JELLICOE'S STRATEGY
We see that both Jellicoe and Beatty decided against a night action between

49

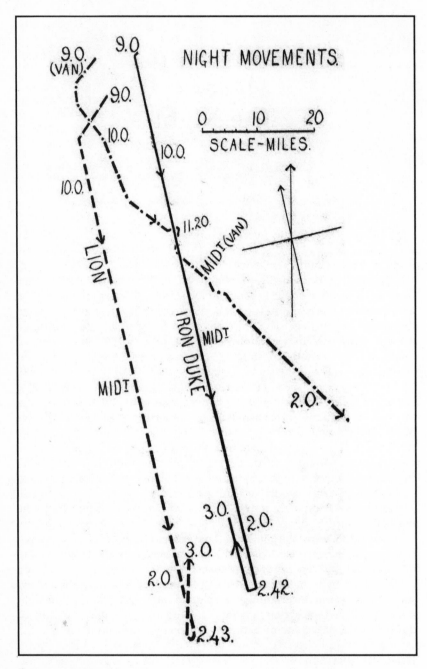

NIGHT MOVEMENTS.

9.0. (VAN).
9.0.
9.0.
10.0.
10.0.
10.0.
11.20.
MID^T (VAN)
LION
IRON DUKE
MID^T
MID^T
2.0.
3.0.
2.0.
3.0.
2.0
2.42.
2.43.

0   10   20
SCALE–MILES.

Diagram 9: May 31 to June 1

capital ships and also that they both considered the position strategically good for intercepting the enemy.

There were three routes which had to be considered: the northern one by Horns Reef; the southern one near the Frisian Coast and an intermediate one approaching Heligoland from the westward.

Beatty placed his battle-cruisers well ahead to ensure that the enemy could not pass round the southern flank of the battle fleet, which it would have to do if either of the southern channels was to be used.

The destroyer flotillas, being stationed astern, not only acted as a security for the battle fleet against attack by light craft from astern, but also as a menace to the enemy battle fleet if it attempted to cross astern. By massing them astern, Jellicoe also minimized the chance of "regrettable incidents" with our own battleships; likewise they were in a convenient position for rejoining when the fleet turned to the northward at daylight.

All the three routes could not be guarded against with any certainty. The disposition certainly made the two southern routes as secure as possible, but even with the destroyers astern, the three submarines which had left Harwich on the evening of 30th May in position near the Horns Reef Passage before daylight on 1st June,[21] and the additional precaution of sending the *Abdiel* to lay mines in that passage, there was an off chance that the enemy might cross astern without being detected and brought to action by our battle fleet at daylight. The chance was a small one, but it existed.[22]

The remote possibility of the enemy turning to the northward after dark, and making for the Skagerrak, does not appear to have been considered, neither does Scheer mention this possible alternative. Such a course could only have been successful if the movement was undetected until too late to allow our ships to overtake him.

SCHEER EDGES TOWARDS HOME

The enemy battle fleet, which had altered course to the southward at about 8 p.m., began hauling over to the westward at about 8.30 p.m., when attacked by the Fourth Light Cruiser Squadron, resuming their southerly course at about 8.50 p.m.

This general direction was maintained until about 9.40 p.m., except on two occasions when they hauled to the westward, for a few minutes, owing to having sighted our ships.

After 9.30 p.m. the German battle squadrons proceeded in the order: First Squadron, Fleet Flagship, Third Squadron, Second Squadron, the *Westfalen* leading the line.[23] Before this time the Second Squadron was in the van.

At about 9.5 p.m. some ships believed to be enemy battle-cruisers were sighted by the light cruisers *Royalist* and *Caroline*, and also by the *Castor* and some of the Eleventh Flotilla. Some doubt existed as to the identity of these vessels.

The Vice-Admiral commanding Second Battle Squadron, in his report, states: "About 9 p.m. I negatived an attack with whitehead torpedoes ordered by *Caroline* as I was certain that the vessels seen on our starboard beam were our own battle-cruisers ... shortly afterwards I told *Caroline* to attack if he was quite certain they were enemy ships as he was in a better position to see them than I was, but I do not know whether an attack was made. If they were enemy ships and no attack was made, the fault is mine, and not that of *Caroline*."

This incident, occurring as it did at dusk, but before darkness had actually set in, indicates that Jellicoe was correct in saying it would be impossible to distinguish our own ships from the enemy ships during the night. Another incident further emphasizes this point.

At about 10 p.m., when on the starboard quarter of the battle fleet, three or more cruisers were sighted on the starboard bow of the *Castor*. These ships belonged to the Second Scouting Group. According to the report from the *Castor*, these ships challenged her by making the first two signs of the secret challenge of the day. When about 2,500 yards away the two leading ships switched on searchlights and opened fire on the *Castor*, who returned the fire. Two of the eight destroyers following the *Castor* fired torpedoes, but others believed that, in spite of the gunfire, the ships opposed to them were our own ships, so they decided not to fire their torpedoes.

The *Castor*'s report continues: "It is unfortunate that this element of doubt existed in the minds of the Captains of the destroyers as to whether the ships were enemy, as a good opportunity of firing torpedoes was lost."

INDISCREET SIGNALLING

In regard to this element of doubt, which would naturally be caused if a strange ship was seen to make the secret challenge of the day, or even part of it, correctly, the *Castor*'s report states: "I would mention that some ship ahead of the Second Battle Squadron at about 9 p.m. made the signal by searchlight: 'Please give me the Challenges and Replies for the day, as I have lost mine.' I did not see a reply made, but evidently the signal was taken in by one of our ships, and the Captain of the *Manners* informs me he saw the reply being made. It is possible that this was one of the enemy's ships asking, and may account for *Castor* being challenged by at any rate part of the correct challenge for the day."

No enemy ship was "ahead" of the Second Battle Squadron between 9 p.m. and 10 p.m., but a possible explanation of this matter can be found by a perusal of the signals given in Appendix II of the *Official Despatches*. We find, at 9.32 p.m., some time before the *Castor* was challenged, the following signal made by flashing-lamp from the Vice-Admiral commanding Battle-Cruiser Fleet to the *Princess Royal*: "Please give me challenge and reply now in force as they have been lost." And appended to this is the note: "(Challenge and reply passed as requested)."

At the time this visual signal was made from the *Lion* to the *Princess Royal* the *Lion* had just turned to a south course; the *Princess Royal* was astern of *Lion*; the enemy was bearing about north, the Second Squadron being about 4 miles away and the other enemy battle squadrons about 6 or 7 miles. The *Castor* was also about 7 miles distant from *Lion,* and if this was the signal read by the *Manners* there is no reason why it should not have been read by the enemy.

At 10.20 p.m. the Second Light Cruiser Squadron came into action with enemy ships, and the German light cruiser *Frauenlob* was sunk. As usual the *Southampton* sent a report of the enemy's position to the Commander-in-Chief, but, owing to her wireless having been shot away, the information did not reach Jellicoe until about an hour later. The flashes of the guns were seen in the *Iron Duke,* but were taken to mean that an enemy destroyer attack was being driven off. Shortly after this the *Castor* and the Eleventh Flotilla were again in action for a few minutes, and at 11 p.m. the Fourth Flotilla was in action with enemy cruisers.

BRITISH DESTROYER ATTACKS

The best example of the difficulty of distinguishing ships in the dark, however, occurred during this action when the destroyer *Spitfire,* after firing two torpedoes, one of which probably hit the enemy light cruiser *Elbing,* turned to the westward, firing on the enemy ships to distract their concentration of fire on the *Tipperary,* already badly damaged.

The *Spitfire* then attempted to return to the *Tipperary,* and observing what she thought to be a cruiser with her searchlights trained on the *Tipperary,* opened fire on her. This enemy ship was not a cruiser but the *Westfalen* leading the enemy battle fleet line. The *Spitfire* then cut through the enemy line astern of the *Westfalen.*

In the *Spitfire's* report it now states: "I then closed *Tipperary* but immediately came in sight of two enemy cruisers close to, steering to south-eastward. The nearer or more southern one altered course to ram me apparently, I therefore put my helm hard-a-port and the two ships rammed each other, port bow to port bow."

It was no cruiser, however, that the *Spitfire* rammed but the dreadnought battleship *Nassau.* At the moment of impact the *Nassau* fired at the *Spitfire,* but owing to the proximity of the ships the guns could not be depressed sufficiently, and all but two of the shots passed over her. The *Spitfire* was telescoped for a considerable portion of her length; her bridge, searchlight platform and upper works being demolished. She succeeded, however, in reaching home.

At 11.25 p.m. the Fourth Destroyer Flotilla came into action with the enemy. A large ship, probably the *Westfalen,* was sighted from the flotilla leader *Broke.* Fire was immediately opened on the *Broke* as she was turning away under full helm. A shell struck her lower bridge, killing all hands there and jamming the helm. In consequence, the *Broke* continued to turn, and struck the *Sparrowhawk*, her next astern. The *Sparrowhawk* while still locked with *Broke* was rammed, right aft, by another destroyer, and 5 feet of her stern was cut off.

WHY THE ENEMY ESCAPED

It is desirable now to deal, in some detail, with the information, or lack of information, received by Jellicoe. It has been often assumed, and, in fact, stated, that Jellicoe should have known that the enemy would return by the Horns Reef, and the mere fact that a large enemy fleet was able to cross astern of our battle fleet, and escape into protected waters, without being brought to action by our capital ships, certainly requires explanation and cannot be dismissed as being merely "the fortunes of war".

No report of the whereabouts of the enemy fleet having reached Jellicoe since nightfall, at 10.46 p.m. he signalled asking the *Castor* if she was engaging enemy destroyers, and a message from the *Castor*, which crossed his signal, informed him that enemy cruisers were being engaged. The message reporting the *Southampton*'s action did not reach Jellicoe until 11.38 p.m.

Messages received from the Admiralty did not make the situation any clearer. One of these, received in the *Iron Duke* at 10.23 p.m., gave the geographical position of the enemy battle fleet at 9 p.m., but this position was obviously incorrect, and Jellicoe had to ignore it. At 10.41 p.m. a further message sent from the Admiralty informed him that the enemy was believed to be returning to its base, as its course was S.S.E.¾E. This message was not received in the *Iron Duke* until after 11 p.m., and the information did not fit in with that of the *Southampton*'s message received at 11.38 p.m., or with one from the *Birmingham* received at 11.30 p.m. Both these latter messages made it look as if the enemy was still to the westward, making to the southward.

Actually the message sent from the Admiralty, at 10.41 p.m., was a summary of two or three enemy messages, which had been intercepted. One of these, which was made by Scheer shortly after 9 p.m., asked for an airship reconnaissance near Horns Reef at daylight. Here was a definite indication of Scheer's intended route home.

Such information, if given to Jellicoe, must have entirely altered his plans during the night; but this vital information, which could have reached him before 9.30 p.m., was withheld. Apparently it was deemed sufficient to send him a brief summary, about one and a half hours later, stating the course and speed of the enemy, but omitting all reference to the all-important fact, a plain indication that Scheer intended returning by the Horns Reef Passage.

Information received direct from a ship actually sighting the enemy would obviously carry more weight than intercepted messages, forwarded from the Admiralty after a considerable time had elapsed. Further, implicit reliance would not, in 1916, have been placed on the accuracy of positions obtained by directional wireless, then in its infancy. In any case, there was no information as yet to justify any change in the belief that the actions taking place were only between light forces.[24]

In the heat and turmoil of night actions, while destroyers are under heavy fire, being separated from their leaders, experiencing collisions and other distracting incidents, it is to be expected that individual Captains of destroyers would have little time to think of sending messages reporting the enemy. It would naturally appear to them that what they saw, their leaders also saw. We have noted also that, even the destroyers, in some cases, mistook battleships for cruisers. It does, however, appear that one of the leaders of the flotillas should have sent some information to Jellicoe. It was done by the leader of the Twelfth Flotilla later, as we shall see, under equally difficult circumstances. In this connection, in referring to the sighting of some ships by the Thirteenth Flotilla at 2.35 a.m., Beatty, in his report, states:

"Some of the strange vessels were sighted by *Champion* and *Obdurate*, who took them to be some of our own light cruisers. This is impossible, and it is very much to be regretted that *Champion* did not take steps to identify them. If, as is probable, they were the enemy, an excellent opportunity was missed for an attack in the early morning light. More important still, a portion of the enemy might have been definitely located."

A Bad Failure

What applies to destroyers does not, however, apply to battleships. We have seen before that when reports came in by wireless, to the Commander-in-Chief, the geographical position of the ship making the report could not be implicitly relied on.

Jellicoe could not, himself, visualize the position, relative to the *Iron Duke*, of the *Birmingham* when that ship made an important signal, at 11.30 p.m., giving information of enemy battle-cruisers. The position given by the *Birmingham*, in this message, was not correct and, if treated as even approximately correct, would have led Jellicoe to suppose that the enemy was well to the westward, which agreed with his appreciation. The *Birmingham*, which had lost touch with her squadron, was, in fact, close to the Fifth Battle Squadron, on their starboard quarter, but Jellicoe could not know this. The Fifth Battle Squadron – now consisting of three ships[25] – was some miles astern of the main fleet, and the damaged *Marlborough*, with her subdivision, was 3 miles to the eastward of the *Barham* – that is, farther from the enemy.

Jellicoe had not yet been informed that the *Marlborough* had dropped a long way astern. He was also unaware of the exact position of the Fifth Battle Squadron relative to the *Iron Duke*, but he could visualize, with approximate accuracy, the position, relative to the *Iron Duke*, of this squadron; and any information from this authoritative source would have been invaluable to him.

Referring to the published reports of the Commanding Officers, we find that from the *Valiant* states: "At 10.39 p.m. observed heavy firing on starboard quarter … this appeared to be a night attack by one of our light cruisers and four of our destroyers on a column of enemy ships."

Again, at 11.35 p.m., the report continues: "Observed heavy night action on starboard quarter. From the evidence we surmised that there appeared on this occasion to be two German cruisers with at least two funnels and a crane amidships, apparently steering to the eastward at high speed."

The only German ships which answered to this description were the *Westfalen* class of battleships, and this fact would, or should, have been known to all those concerned.

In the report from the *Malaya*, the rear ship of the Fifth Battle Squadron, we find: "11.40 p.m. 3 points abaft starboard beam observed what appeared to be an attack by our destroyers on some enemy big ships steering the same way as ours, two of which used searchlights. One of our destroyers with three funnels (appearance of *Termagant* class) was set on fire, but not before she had hit the second ship. This was seen by the column of smoke, and also the explosion was distinctly heard and felt. The leading ship of the enemy, which was seen by the flash of the explosion, had two masts, two funnels, and a conspicuous crane (apparently *Westfalen* class)."

At this time the *Malaya* was just under 4 miles distant from the van of the enemy battle fleet. The *Valiant* was in the line ahead of the *Malaya*, and ahead of the *Valiant* was the *Barham* leading her squadron.

It will be noticed that no mention is made, in the written report from the *Valiant*, of actually distinguishing a battleship. No mention is made of these occurrences in the *Barham*'s letter of proceedings, beyond the statement that "during the night there appeared to be constant attacks by torpedo craft on ships".

It is obvious, from the written reports of the *Malaya* and *Valiant*, that the van of the enemy battle fleet was actually seen, at this time, from these ships. The wealth of detail contained in the *Malaya*'s report removes all doubt on this point, and it is a matter of some surprise that so little is noted as having been seen from the *Barham*.

WHAT OUR ADMIRALS KNEW

Information that enemy battleships had been sighted at this time, and in this position, must have made Jellicoe alter his appreciation of the general situation. The invaluable information was, however, not sent, and we therefore lost the opportunity to secure the immediate fruits of victory, for which all had striven. Had definite reports of sighting enemy battleships been sent from the *Malaya* and *Valiant*, there can be little question that the German fleet would have been brought to action at daylight.

Beatty's criticism, already quoted – in regard to the failure of the *Champion* to identify strange vessels and thus definitely locate a portion of the enemy – applies with additional force to the present case, in which enemy vessels were identified, and located, but to no purpose, as no action was taken.

It is clear, from the evidence available, that firing was heard, and flashes of guns were seen, in the *Iron Duke*, and other battleships; but, as Jellicoe says in his despatch, what was seen made it "evident that our destroyer flotillas and light cruiser squadrons were in action". There was nothing to indicate to Jellicoe that the enemy battleships or battle-cruisers were in action.

The Vice-Admiral commanding the First Battle Squadron in the *Marlborough* – which ship was only 7 miles from the van of the enemy fleet at 11.40 p.m., whereas the *Iron Duke* was 11 miles distant from it – in his report makes no mention of the probability of capital ships being engaged. His appreciation was, therefore, presumably similar to that of Jellicoe.

But more important still: the appreciation made by the Rear-Admiral commanding the Fifth Battle Squadron in the *Barham* was also the same. He says: "Destroyers appeared to be attacking the cruisers."

No mention is made in any of the reports from the battle-cruisers that any firing was heard, or flashes seen, from those ships. This is peculiar, because at about 10.30 p.m. the battle-cruisers were no farther from the action then being waged, than was the *Iron Duke*, and in the signal log of the *Princess Royal* the following remark is inserted under 10.5 p.m.: "Opened fire on cruisers on S. beam. 10.20 p.m. ceased fire."[26] This can only refer to other ships firing, because none of our battle-cruisers had fired a gun for nearly two hours. By 11.40 p.m. the battle-cruisers were some miles farther off than the *Iron Duke*.

In the absence of any information from any of his light forces, some 10 miles astern, or from the Fifth Battle Squadron, known to be astern, Jellicoe could not have known, or even suspected, that the enemy battle fleet was crossing astern. It would have appeared to him next to impossible that such a movement could take place without someone in the ships astern detecting it. If detected, he would naturally expect to be given information.

We see, therefore, that, up to midnight, Jellicoe had no reason whatever to suppose that the enemy was crossing astern of our battle fleet.

What The German C.-In-C. Knew

Scheer, however, was perhaps not equally ignorant as to the position of our battle fleet. The German Admiralty had intercepted Jellicoe's wireless message, made at 9.15 p.m., ordering destroyer flotillas to take station 5 miles astern of our battle fleet. There is some doubt whether this information was transmitted to Scheer by his Admiralty. The *Official History* states that it was transmitted, but the Germans deny this.

If Scheer had the information, he would have realized that when his light cruisers and the van of his battle fleet ran foul of our destroyers, our battle fleet would be some miles to the southward.

He could not know, though, that our Fifth Battle Squadron and the *Marlborough's* sub-division were so far astern of the main fleet. It is believed that Scheer never wavered from his original intention of steering direct for Horns Reef, as soon as darkness set in.

At 0.10 a.m. the armoured cruiser *Black Prince*, which had lost touch with the main fleet some hours before, was steaming to the southward to again get into touch, when she closed the rear of the First Squadron of the enemy battle fleet and was sunk at point-blank range. Ten minutes before this occurrence the *Marlborough* and her sub-division had crossed ahead of the enemy at a distance of only 4 miles from the leading ship, the *Westfalen*. If the enemy battle fleet had not been delayed by our destroyer attacks or if, owing to her damage, the *Marlborough's* speed had been reduced a little more than it was, the enemy battle fleet would have fairly met the *Marlborough's* sub-division at about midnight. There would have been terrible losses, but, we hope, not before reliable information had reached Jellicoe.

At 1.48 a.m. Jellicoe received information that enemy submarines were being sent out from German ports. At 1.55 a.m., owing to the *Marlborough's* speed being still further reduced, the Vice-Admiral commanding the First Battle Squadron decided to shift his flag to the *Revenge*. This was accomplished at 2.30 a.m.

Last Contact

At 1.43 a.m. the *Obedient*, belonging to the Twelfth Destroyer Flotilla, sighted six enemy battleships to the south-westward. These proved to be the Second Squadron of the enemy battle fleet, and immediately the British destroyers were sighted they turned away.

On receiving the report from the *Obedient*, *Faulknor*, leading the flotilla, ordered an attack, and proceeded to a favourable position for delivering it. At 2.6 a.m. the *Faulknor* followed by three destroyers commenced to deliver her attack, under heavy fire from the enemy. The *Onslaught* was badly hit, receiving severe damage and many casualties, including her Captain and First Lieutenant. All destroyers fired their torpedoes, and the German battleship *Pommern* was hit and sunk.

During this time two reports were made by the *Faulknor* to the Commander-in-Chief. At 1.52 a.m.: "Enemy's battleships in sight. My position 10 miles astern of First Battle squadron." And again at 2.12 a.m.: "Course of enemy S.S.W."

Both these signals were made by wireless, but they were not received in the *Iron Duke*, neither did any other ship except the *Marksman*, who was in close proximity to the *Faulknor*, intercept this important information. There was a great deal of interference, at this time, from German wireless, but it is most improbable that this interference would have prevented any other ship receiving the *Faulknor*'s message if her wireless had been in perfect adjustment. It can only be concluded, therefore, that her wireless had been thrown out of adjustment in the action.

Thus the only messages which were sufficiently reliable, and definite, to justify Jellicoe in altering his appreciation failed to reach him. If these messages, which gave a definite relative position, instead of a geographical position of doubtful accuracy, had reached him and no delay, however small, had occurred in deciphering them, considering them and acting on the information, it would have been just possible, if the speed of the enemy battle fleet was not increased, for the Grand Fleet, by proceeding at full speed, to bring Scheer to action before he reached his protected waters. There would, however, not have been time to collect all our scattered destroyer flotillas or, possibly, some of the light cruisers. The battle-cruisers also, being farther to the south-west, might have been unable to arrive in time to take up station in advance of the battle fleet.

On the other hand, we know that the enemy battle-cruisers were unfit for action on the morning of 1st June, as a result of the fighting the day before.

Chapter 8
After Daylight, 1 June

Being still without news of the enemy, the last reports having reached him at 11.30 p.m., Jellicoe decided, at 2 a.m., that if he heard nothing further during the next half-hour he would turn to the northward. When the time came for the battle fleet to turn, a report was received from the *Colossus* to the effect that the *Marlborough* and her sub-division had dropped far astern. This was the first intimation that Jellicoe had that he would be four battleships short if he encountered the enemy before the three undamaged ships of the *Marlborough*'s division had rejoined.

An exaggerated importance appears to have been attached by certain Commanding Officers to keeping the position of our battle fleet concealed during the night at all costs. During the early hours of darkness Scheer must have known, approximately, the whereabouts of our fleet; he must have known it was somewhere between him and his base. Wireless silence was not, therefore, as important as before the fleets met, and it would have been to our advantage to break wireless silence rather than to leave Jellicoe ignorant of the movements, or whereabouts, of portions of his own fleet and of the enemy. In several cases important information could have been passed to the *Iron Duke*, visually, by shaded flashing-lamp, but even this comparatively safe method appears to have been sacrificed at the expense of secrecy.

This unnecessary caution is apparent when we find from the official despatches that between 9.17 p.m., when the *Iron Duke* made the last flag signal before nightfall, until 2.20 a.m., when it was again light enough to distinguish flag signals, no less than 42 wireless and 85 flashing-lamp signals are recorded, many of which are of a comparatively trivial nature.

Sunrise on 1st June was at 3.9 a.m., so by 2.30 a.m. it would be daylight, and if the enemy was still to the westward, in a position to be brought to action, he would in all probability shortly be sighted by our battle fleet, or battle-cruisers. At 2.30 a.m., therefore, Jellicoe made a signal ordering the battle fleet to alter course to north, and he informed Beatty, and all squadrons not in touch with him, to this effect.

In his despatch Jellicoe states: "The weather was very misty at daylight, visibility being only 3 to 4 miles, and I deemed it advisable to disregard the danger from submarines due to a long line of ships, and to form line of battle, at once, in case of meeting the enemy battle fleet before I had been able to get into touch with my cruisers and destroyers."

This extract clearly shows that Jellicoe was still ignorant of the fact that the German battle fleet had passed astern of our fleet during the night.

JELLICOE DISILLUSIONED

All doubt as to the enemy's whereabouts, and all hope of being able to renew the action, was, however, finally dispersed when, at 3.55 a.m., a message was received in the *Iron Duke*, from the Admiralty, which read: "At 2.30 a.m. German Main Fleet in lat. 55° 33' N., long. 6° 50' E., course S.E. by S., 16 knots" (0329). This position was only 17 miles from Horns Reef, whereas our fleet was still double that distance away, so it was useless to attempt to overtake the enemy.

The chance of action at daylight, for which Jellicoe had hoped and for which his night dispositions had been made, was lost for two reasons, neither of which were within his control. First, the failure on the part of the Admiralty to forward the information that Scheer intended to return by Horns Reef; and, second, the failure of the ships astern of our main fleet to inform him that the enemy battle fleet was crossing astern.

We have already reviewed the meagre information which was available to Jellicoe, and the definite information which should have, but did not, reach him during the night. In this connection it is interesting to note that, with the exception of the firing heard astern, after 11 p.m. similar information was available to Beatty, in the battle-cruisers.

All messages sent by wireless from the Admiralty, or from ships when reporting the enemy, would, normally, be taken in by both the *Iron Duke* and the *Lion*. In the present instance, owing to the *Lion*'s wireless having been shot away, the messages were received in the *New Zealand* and should have been passed on, by visual signal, with no appreciable delay.[27] This is merely in accordance with the ordinary signalling arrangements in force in the fleet, and the procedure was well understood by all concerned. The only difference, therefore, would be that, as these messages had to be passed to the *Lion* from another ship, Beatty could not see them until a few minutes later than would be the case if the *Lion*'s wireless had been in order.

WHAT BEATTY THOUGHT

The appreciation of the situation made in the *Lion* should, therefore, have been made on the same information as the appreciation made in the *Iron Duke*. Let us now see what Beatty's appreciation was.

At 3.50 a.m. Beatty signalled to Jellicoe: "When last seen enemy was to the west, steering S.W., and proceeding slowly. Zeppelin has passed astern of me steering west. Submit I may sweep S.W. to locate enemy."

At 4.7 a.m. Beatty ordered his light cruisers to "spread well to the westward to locate enemy".

At 4.30 a.m. he signalled to his battle cruisers: "Damage yesterday was heavy on both sides. We hope today to cut off and annihilate the whole German fleet. Every man must do his utmost. *Lutzow* is sinking and another German battle-cruiser expected to have sunk."

The above signals can only mean that Beatty's appreciation of the situation at daylight was the same as Jellicoe's, for he clearly believed that the enemy was still to the westward and in a position which would enable our fleet to bring it to action. This belief appears to have been maintained by Beatty after Jellicoe had reluctantly altered his views. Beatty's 4.30 a.m. signal to his battle-cruisers must have been made before he himself saw the information contained in the 0329 message from the Admiralty, which would have been received by the *New Zealand*, on behalf of the *Lion*, at 3.55 a.m., the same time as it was received in the *Iron Duke*.

There is no reason to suppose that any of the Admiralty messages failed to reach the *Lion*. They should not have failed. Beatty's reference to *Lutzow* sinking, in his 4.30 a.m. signal to the battle-cruisers, indicates that the 1.48 a.m. message was received; without this message, which gave the position of the damaged *Lutzow*, it is not clear how it would be known that she was sinking. As this message was, apparently, received it can only be assumed the others were received also.

Any doubts Beatty may have had as to the accuracy of the information contained in the Admiralty message, or of the position of the enemy, were laid at rest at 4.40 a.m., when he received a signal from Jellicoe, saying, "Enemy fleet has returned to harbour. Try to locate *Lutzow*." As a fact, the *Lutzow* sank at about 1.45 a.m., though this was not known at the time.

THE GERMAN FLEET RETIRES INTO PORT
The German fleet passed Horns Reef at about 3.20 a.m. and reached their protected waters shortly afterwards, but not before the battleship *Ostfriesland* had struck a mine, in a minefield laid by the *Abdiel* a month before. The fleet passed just clear of the mines laid by the *Abdiel* at 2 a.m.

With the knowledge we now have, it is safe to say that Scheer had decided before dark to make his way as quickly, and as directly, as possible to Horns Reef. He was frequently delayed by his line being thrown into disorder by our destroyer attacks, but he succeeded in avoiding a renewed general action and attained his object, not, however, without losses. His "breakthrough" cost him a battleship, three light cruisers and two destroyers, no small tribute to Jellicoe's disposition of our forces and the gallantry of our own light cruisers and destroyers during these few crucial hours of darkness.

Our fleet now cruised about, searching for damaged ships and picking up survivors, until noon, when, having swept out the area south of the scene of action without obtaining any further sight of the enemy, a course was shaped for home. The battle fleet arrived at Scapa Flow during the forenoon of 2nd June, and at 9.45 p.m. on the same day Jellicoe telegraphed to the Admiralty: "Battle fleet at four hours' notice and ready for action."

Chapter 9

Accounts and Their Authors

A few trustworthy and reliable accounts of the Battle of Jutland have already been published. Chief amongst these is that, already alluded to, contained in the *Official History of the War – Naval Operations*, Vol. III, the work of the late Sir Julian Corbett. Two others of merit are the account in the latest (1926) additional volumes of the *Encyclopaedia Britannica*, written by Captain E. Altham, C.B., R.N., and a short anonymous article published in the *Quarterly Review* of January 1924.

That portion of Admiral Sir Reginald Bacon's book, *The Jutland Scandal* [see Part II], which deals with the actual course of events during the battle provides a particularly clear and simple account, easily understandable by the layman. The statements of fact in all the foregoing accounts are accurate and no wrong conclusions are drawn through facts being misrepresented, or through the suppression of essential details.

On the other hand, there have appeared a number of accounts, written without adequate knowledge, historical or technical, some of which were, apparently, inspired by personal animus. These not infrequently give a totally false impression of the tactics employed by the various Commanders and the influences which governed them. It is to be feared too that an unduly large percentage of the public, which culls its naval knowledge solely from the newspapers, has been grievously misled on the subject of Jutland by articles which have from time to time appeared in certain sections of the daily, or weekly, Press.

It is extraordinary that newspapers of standing should accept the views and opinions of uninformed contributors on this and so many other professional matters connected with the Navy; for not only do they thereby admit to their pages articles which are full of errors, so palpable that they are ridiculous to the Service reader, but these papers do, unintentionally, a dis-service to the country by misleading the public on questions which are often of national importance.

In a short work of this kind it is not possible to refute each and every mis-statement, misconception, or misrepresentation which has been made about the Battle of Jutland; one can only select a few of the more glaring and persistent errors and deal with them.

Among those writers who have based much of their argument on the subject on false premises, the following are the most prolific: Mr. Filson Young, who before the battle was a temporary member of, the then, Sir David Beatty's staff in his flagship, the *Lion*; Mr. H.W. Wilson, author of a number of articles in the Press and of a work entitled *Battleships in Action*; Mr. A.H. Pollen, the writer of *The Navy in Battle*; Commander Carlyon Bellairs, M.P., who *wrote The Battle of Jutland – The Sowing and the Reaping*; and, more recently, The Right Honourable Winston S. Churchill, M.P.

Mr. Filson Young was the author of articles which, for inaccuracy and innuendo, it would be difficult to surpass. He has been very fully and capably criticized by Admiral Sir Reginald Bacon in his book, *The Jutland Scandal*, and it is not proposed to deal with his writings any further here.

The works of the other writers mentioned, however, require some detailed attention. To this end, it will be simplest to select successive phases of the battle and to show where their accounts, or observations, have gone particularly astray from realities. Before doing so, however, a few general remarks on the works of these writers will not be out of place.

At the outset it is necessary to remember that the conduct of war at sea is a highly technical art, to the study of which men devote their whole lives, and it is one which cannot be learned without practical experience in the handling of fleets. Of Mr. Wilson and Mr. Pollen it is kindest to say that in writing on this highly technical, and intricate, subject they attempted a task for which, by training, they were inadequately equipped. The former is a naval historian of some repute, but when he comes to dealing with the intricacies of modern naval warfare he is clearly out of his depth, or has been very badly advised. Mr. Pollen obviously wrote his book before he was even in a position to study the facts in detail. It teems with inaccuracies and loose generalities. Both these authors appear to have written with much bias, and to have "situated their appreciation" at the outset.

Commander Carlyon Bellairs' book is imbued throughout with a captious and carping spirit. Nothing that Admiral Jellicoe, or the battle fleet, did could be correct in the eyes of this omniscient and self-confident critic. His assertions, often made without any foundation or any evidence to support them, are presumptuous. He even attacked the proposed "Official Record of the Battle of Jutland" while it was still being considered by the Board of Admiralty, and before its contents were available to anyone outside those immediately concerned with its compilation.

Mr. Winston Churchill, who has lately given us his views on Jutland, must be suspect from the time when he claimed[28] to have "discovered"

Admiral Beatty and tried to impress on the public that the "decisions which I had the honour of taking (as First Lord of the Admiralty) in regard to him were most serviceable to the Royal Navy and to the British Arms".

One of the reasons given for forming such a high opinion of Beatty is that "he viewed questions of naval strategy and tactics in a different light to an average naval officer; he approached them, as it seemed to me, much more as a soldier would". Again, he says: "I had no doubts whatever when the command of the Battle-Cruiser Squadron fell vacant in the spring of 1913 in appointing him (Beatty) over the heads of all to this incomparable command."

He naively admits that his judgment of Beatty's qualifications was formed, not on the latter's service record or experience in high command, but owing to an impression conceived during conversations with him in a room at the Admiralty. This being so, we cannot expect to find Mr. Churchill indulging in criticism which might reflect gravely on his own judgment, but we do expect from a statesman of his eminence and a writer of his distinction impartial handling in his presentation of facts. Unhappily, as will be seen in due course, he fails us badly in this respect on more than one occasion.

There have been a number of less important articles and other publications on the subject of Jutland, but they too, for the most part, have been penned by those who can claim little or no personal knowledge of modern naval conditions, while many do not seem to have even possessed ability to follow actual events intelligently. This, however, can hardly be said of the account of the battle which appeared in the earlier (1922) edition of the *Encyclopaedia Britannica*. Captain A.C. Dewar, R.N., its author, had very exceptional facilities for checking his facts, and his early naval training (he retired from the Active List as a Lieutenant R.N. in 1910) should have been sufficient to have enabled him to draw correct conclusions. This he signally failed to do. It is only fair, though, to the publishers of that usually authoritative work to say that they were not long in realizing their mistake, and they have taken the first opportunity to expunge this article and replace it by that to which reference has already been made.

There remains one other publication to be noticed. This is the *Narrative of the Battle of Jutland*, published by H.M. Stationery Office in 1924. Nothing appears on the title-page, or elsewhere, in this book to indicate by what authority it had been compiled and published; it is only by turning to Appendix G, on page 106, that the uninitiated can discover the fact that it emanates from the Admiralty, and from Note 1, on the same page, that it is "official". No information is vouchsafed as to whether this *Narrative* is concurred in by the Board as a whole or not. The remarks in the Introduction may lead one to suppose that it is merely the *Harper Record* revised so far as German evidence is concerned. This is not the case.

It is probable that the compilation of material made for the "Official Record" was used when required, but of this I have no knowledge. It was unknown to me, except from hearsay, that a "narrative" was being prepared, and I had no part whatever in the production thereof.

We are told[29] that this publication is a "narrative" and not an "appreciation", and, again,[30] that "only statements of fact are included, inferences being omitted". Nevertheless, we find the word "probably" in connection with the movements of the British fleet, and such a phrase as "it is justifiable to assume". These should not occur in a narrative of *facts* only.

Again,[31] we read, "The *Lion* altered course at this time to N.N.E., apparently with the twofold intention ..." If there is evidence of intention the word "apparently" is redundant; if there was no such evidence it could easily have been obtained.

This "official" narrative is a curious, disjointed production. Important facts are often half-hidden in the form of footnotes, especially where they refer to our battle fleet, while Lord Jellicoe's dignified, and fully justified, criticisms of its errors and defects, published in the form of an Appendix, are answered by querulous interjections quite out of keeping with an official publication. The whole bears the imprint of many hands and much "chopping and piecing" to produce a desired impression. As an authentic record it can only be described as thoroughly unsatisfactory.

From the general we will now pass on to the particular.

Chapter 10
Some Misrepresentations and Misconceptions

1
THE DELAY IN BRINGING THE FIFTH BATTLE SQUADRON INTO ACTION.

Several publications, including the *Admiralty Narrative of the Battle of Jutland*, impute blame to Admiral Evan-Thomas, or misrepresent the reason, for the Fifth Battle Squadron not being in a position to support the battle-cruisers when the action opened at 3.45 p.m.

The *Admiralty Narrative* states: "When the action commenced it found itself seven miles on the *Lion*'s port quarter, and though the *Barham* and *Warspite* opened fire on the 2nd Scouting Group about 4 p.m. and drove them to the eastward, it was not till ten minutes later that they were able to range on the German battle-cruisers."[32]

Commander Carlyon Bellairs states: "The four fast battleships of the *Queen Elizabeth* class, armed with eight 15-inch guns each, were 10,000 yards, or 5 nautical miles, away and out of range."[33]

Mr. H.W. Wilson states: "The Battle-Cruiser Force was now steering north-east to close the Germans; unfortunately, during the alterations of course, the 5th Battle Squadron had fallen seriously out of station and were seven miles, instead of five (the distance ordered) from Beatty. It subsequently reduced this distance somewhat but was still dangerously out of station when contact with the German heavy ships was obtained."[34]

Again: "The aim of the whole British operation was to bring on a decisive battle. Beatty could only concentrate his force by falling back with his battle cruisers on the 5th Battle Squadron or by reducing speed in order to let the 5th Battle Squadron come up."[35]

Mr. Winston Churchill states: "At 2.32 the *Lion*, having already warned her consorts by signal of her intentions, turned about again, and increasing her speed to 22 knots set off in pursuit."[36]

This latter is a misrepresentation of the facts. The *Lion*, it is true, warned "her consorts" by a preparatory signal that she intended to turn to S.S.E., but turned herself without ensuring that the executive signal reached "her consorts" – the Fifth Battle Squadron. The preparatory signal is stated[37] to have been made by searchlight. The executive signal was, however, made by flags alone and failed on that account to be seen by *Barham* for several minutes.

The above misrepresentation, which appeared also in an extract published in *The Times* on 9th February 1927, very rightly brought forth a strong protest from Admiral Evan-Thomas in a letter to the same paper dated 13th February.

Mr. Churchill continues: "But the Fifth Battle Squadron, 4½ miles astern, continued to carry out the previous instructions, and for eight minutes steered in exactly the opposite direction … The result, however, of his (Admiral Evan-Thomas) eight minutes' delay in turning was inexorably to keep him and his tremendous guns out of action for the first most critical and most fatal half-hour, and even thereafter to keep him at extreme range."[38]

All the above extracts imply that the Fifth Battle Squadron was at fault in not coming into action against the heavy ships of the enemy as soon as possible. Mr. Churchill's somewhat severe criticism is, however, modified when he says, later: "It would, however, no doubt have been better if the original cruising formation of the battle-cruisers and the Fifth Battle Squadron had been more compact."[39]

With this one exception none of these publications contain one word of criticism of Beatty, the Admiral commanding the advanced forces, for having definitely stationed the Fifth Battle Squadron 5 miles away from the *Lion*, and in such a direction that it would certainly be delayed in joining action if our battle-cruisers were the first to meet the enemy. It was this decision, combined with the omission to order "Close" when the preparatory signal was made and failure on the part of the signal staff of the *Lion* to pass the executive signal without delay to "her consorts", which lost Beatty the services of these powerful ships during the "most critical and most fatal half-hour".

It is, at all times, the duty of the senior officer so to dispose his forces that if a concentration of these forces is desirable it can be effected without delay. The disposition ordered by Beatty was the fundamental cause of the delay in concentration, and it is unjust to blame Admiral Evan-Thomas for this.

In the publications referred to no mention is made of the fact that the delay was augmented by the failure of the signalling staff in the *Lion* to transmit, efficiently and without delay, the signal to the *Barham* to alter course to the south-eastward. A signal was made by flags which was not clear to the *Barham*, owing to smoke interference and the distance between the ships, and Beatty's staff knew, or should have known, it was not clear because it was not at once "answered". Responsibility for the reception of the message rested with him and his staff, and with nobody else.

2
THE GUNNERY EFFICIENCY OF THE BRITISH BATTLE-CRUISER FLEET

In referring to the first phase of the engagement between Beatty's and von Hipper's battle-cruisers the Admiralty narrative states: "The damage done to the German battle-cruisers in this phase of the action was considerable, but German information on the point is not conclusive."[40]

The German evidence on this point is very definite and conclusive. Von Hipper himself has referred to the inaccurate shooting of our battle-cruisers, and compared it most unfavourably to that of the Fifth Battle Squadron and other battleships.[41] It is very doubtful if any serious damage was done to the enemy battle-cruisers by the fire of our battle-cruisers, excepting the *Queen Mary*, during this stage of the action.

The *Admiralty Narrative* makes no mention of the mistake whereby the distribution of fire in our battle-cruiser squadron was such that the German battle-cruiser *Derfflinger* was unfired at for some time. This serious blunder is not referred to in any detail in any of the other publications under review, in spite of its far-reaching effect.

This same *Narrative* states: "At 4.33 the fire of the *Lion* and *Princess Royal* forced the *Lutzow* to turn away."[42]

No evidence is forthcoming to support this statement. This "turn away" of the enemy battle-cruisers was made to avoid the torpedoes from our attacking destroyers; actually it was not completely successful as the *Seydlitz* was hit. In fact, there is very strong evidence that the fire of the *Lion* and the *Princess Royal*, which ships were ordered to concentrate on the *Lutzow*, was anything but effective.

The gunnery officer of the *Lutzow*, Commander Paschen, states: "Neither *Lion* nor *Princess Royal* hit us once between 4.2 and 5.23 p.m.; their total hits were three in 95 minutes."[43]

Mr. Winston Churchill states: "As the action proceeded the British battle-cruisers, although reduced to an inferiority in numbers, began to assert an ascendancy over the enemy. Their guns became increasingly effective, and they themselves received no further serious injury."[44]

It has been shown conclusively that the gunnery of our battle-cruisers was not of a high standard, and the evidence is quite clear that, at the time to which Mr. Churchill alludes, it was not the guns of the battle-cruisers which "began to assert an ascendancy" but those of the Fifth Battle Squadron.

Again, he [Churchill] says: "In this phase of the action, which is called 'The Run to the North', firing was continued by the battle-cruisers on both sides."[45]

Here again it is the Fifth Battle Squadron which should be given the credit; that squadron was almost continually in action, whereas very little firing took place from our battle-cruisers during this time, as they lost sight of the enemy shortly after 5 p.m. and did not regain contact for half an hour.

After mentioning the loss of the *Indefatigable* and *Queen Mary* the author [Churchill] continues: "It is difficult to compare sea war with land war. But each battle-cruiser was a unit comparable at least to a complete infantry division. Two divisions out of his (Beatty's) six have been annihilated in the twinkling of an eye. The enemy, whom he could not defeat with six ships to five, are now five to four. Far away all five German battle-cruisers … are still intact."[46]

This quotation appears from the context to be intended as praise for Beatty. Why any commander should be praised, and not blamed, for losing two "divisions" out of six when opposed by only five "divisions" which were left intact is not clear.

Mr. Churchill, however, again ignores the Fifth Battle Squadron – part of Beatty's force. Beatty had ten ships to five, not six to five, and after the loss of his two "divisions" the odds in his favour were still eight to five; and yet, as Mr. Churchill says, he "could not defeat" the enemy. It is well that land war cannot be compared to sea war – the author would find some difficulty in withholding blame from any army commander with ten divisions at his disposal if he failed to defeat, and left intact, an enemy force of only five divisions.

3
INFORMATION GIVEN TO JELLICOE BEFORE MAKING CONTACT WITH THE ENEMY BATTLE FLEET

The Admiralty narrative makes little mention in the text of the lack of reliable information given to Jellicoe. It does, however, state that from 5.0 p.m. to 5.30 p.m. no reports came in.

Commander Bellairs states: "He (Beatty) maintained contact with the enemy, reported his movements …"[47]

Mr. A.H. Pollen states: "It is to be supposed that Sir David Beatty kept Admiral Jellicoe informed from time to time of the position, speed and course of his fleet and of the enemy."[48]

Here we have one mis-statement of fact and one supposition, without foundation. Beatty did not maintain contact with the enemy, he lost touch shortly after his turn to the northward, and sent no reports to Jellicoe during the time when accurate information would have been of inestimable value to him. In his despatch Beatty states: "The visibility was for the most part low and fluctuating and caution forbade me to close the range too much with my inferior force."

It is not clear to what phase of the action this remark applies, but this period was the only one in which he was in inferior force as compared with enemy ships of similar power and speed. Nevertheless, it is a clearly recognized principle that undue caution should not be allowed to interfere with the most important duty of the advanced forces, viz.: to give the Commander-in-Chief regular and precise information of the enemy's movements. Caution did not forbid Commodore Goodenough from closing the enemy, with his very inferior force, for the purpose of obtaining information.

4
THE DEPLOYMENT

So many criticisms have been made on the method of deployment that it is quite impossible to deal with them all. In many cases critics have treated this as a geometric problem; they have pointed out what might, or might not, have occurred if Jellicoe had deployed sooner than he did; they have assumed that Jellicoe knew, or could see, the exact position, strength and disposition of the German battle fleet.

No one will deny that an earlier deployment would have been to our advantage, but the information essential to a Commander-in-Chief before deployment can be made with any confidence was lacking. An early deployment made on accurate information is good, but one made on insufficient knowledge of the position of the enemy is the negation of sound tactics.

Scheer's early deployment has been quoted as an example of what Jellicoe might have done; but Scheer, when he deployed, had an enemy – our battle-cruisers and Fifth Battle Squadron – in sight. Scheer deployed, not against our battle fleet, but against our advanced forces, with whom his battle-cruiser Admiral had kept touch ever since he first sighted them, to the moment of leading them up to his main battle fleet. When he did meet our main fleet he found that his early deployment resulted in his joining action under most unfavourable conditions. Tactically his position could hardly have been worse. It was a striking example of the danger of deploying without adequate information or, having deployed, of being forced into action by an enemy who had secured an initial advantage.

The *Admiralty Narrative* makes no adverse criticism of Jellicoe's deployment – it only hints; thus, on page 47: "The battle fleet after deployment could only occasionally get into action. Its actual firing was confined to two periods of about 20 minutes and a quarter of an hour respectively."

The implication is that the method of deployment was responsible for curtailing the time during which the enemy could be fired at. This was not the case; the avoiding tactics persistently pursued by Scheer was the main cause. Incidentally, the battle fleet was in action from 6.17 to 6.54, and again from 7.10 to 7.25 p.m., or two periods of 37 minutes and a quarter of an hour respectively. Mr. Wilson[49] states: "A deployment to starboard would have brought the British into a line ahead on an opposite course to the Germans, but it would have facilitated an annihilating attack on the old German battleships at the rear of Scheer's line and have forced the German Dreadnoughts to go to their aid."

The author does not explain how Jellicoe could know that the old German battleships were at the rear of Scheer's line at a time when he had not even been given accurate information as to the whereabouts of the enemy battle fleet, much less of its course and composition. This writer continues: "Though, normally, a battle passing on opposite courses will be indecisive, yet here were special conditions favouring a decision. But for such a deployment to give great results it ought to have begun at 6 p.m., or even before. It did not begin, and Beatty had to pass at full speed across the front of the fleet in order to clear the range and obtain a favourable tactical position."

The fact that deployment could not take place earlier than it did, owing to lack of reliable information, is, it will be observed, not even mentioned. Beatty crossed the front of the fleet, at full speed, to take up his assigned station and for no other reason.

Again, to quote Mr. Wilson: "Jellicoe's deployment, if much delayed, and made to port instead of to starboard, none the less placed the British battle fleet in a position of distinct advantage."[50]

The author has already argued that advantage would have been gained by a deployment to starboard; it would, therefore, appear that, in his opinion, a deployment either way was tactically sound. If so, his reason for condemning Jellicoe's deployment is not clear.

Again, he says: "The British were in an extremely favourable position"[51]: but the fact that Jellicoe's deployment enabled this extremely favourable position to be attained is ignored.

Mr. Wilson's criticisms on this point are those of an amateur and might be ignored but for the fact that he perverts the views expressed in the German Official History on the British deployment. He says: "The deployment to port is not strongly condemned by the German Official History."[52]

This is a peculiar interpretation of the actual views expressed in this publication, which are to the effect that the deployment to port was to the British advantage, whereas deployment to starboard would have led our fleet into a position which would have been only too acceptable to the German fleet.[53]

Commander Bellairs never loses an opportunity in his book of using the words "away from the enemy" when mentioning the deployment to port. A deployment on the wing nearest the enemy need not necessarily be a deployment "towards" the enemy, and one on the wing farthest from the enemy need not be "away" from the enemy. He condemns the deployment on the port wing column so frequently that one tires of the repetition.

Commander Bellairs is another critic who is not too particular about the accuracy of his statements. He states: "At 6.50 the *Lion* was well inside towards the enemy, three miles S.S.E. of the *King George V* ..."[54] As a fact, at 6.50, and for some time after this, the *Lion* was farther away from the enemy than the van of our battle fleet.

Again, he states: "7.17 p.m. Battle-cruisers were now on starboard bow of Grand Fleet, from four to five miles ahead of the van ..."[55] This was not the case. The battle-cruisers were at this time on the port bow of the battle fleet and farther from the enemy than any British battleship.

A deployment to starboard, as advocated by the writers referred to above, would have exposed our weakest division of battleships to the concentrated fire of the best German ships, and would also have placed our fleet in a very favourable position for a massed attack by enemy destroyers, and within range of the torpedoes from the German battleships. Furthermore, our fleet would not have been between the enemy and his base.

A deployment on a centre column, in favour of which Mr. Winston Churchill argues with a wealth of geometrical reasoning and no practical knowledge, was possible, but had nothing whatever to commend it tactically. It is a clumsy and complicated manoeuvre at the best of times, and one which, undoubtedly, does not commend itself at such close quarters. The effect of it would have been that our battle fleet would not have straightened itself out and developed its gunfire as soon as it did, nor would Jellicoe have interposed the Grand Fleet between the enemy and the latter's line of retreat with such certainty as he did by his deployment to port.

When we remember that the deployment, as ordered by Jellicoe, enabled our fleet to attain at once a position of immense tactical and strategical advantage there seems little object in exploring alternative methods. No other method could have attained a *more* favourable tactical position for the British fleet.

4
THE "FOLLOW ME" EPISODE

Commander Bellairs' most flagrant misrepresentation of actual facts centres round an incorrect statement of time at which a signal was made by Beatty. This he proceeds to use as a lever to strengthen his criticism of the "turn away" manoeuvre.

To begin with, he states: "From about 7.21 to 7.33, while this turn away was in progress, Beatty steered well to the Westward towards the enemy and engaged them."[56]

This is untrue. During this time Beatty did not steer well to the Westward and his battle-cruisers did not fire a shot.

The author continues: "He made one desperate effort to save the situation by a signal, taken in by the whole fleet, imploring the van of the battle fleet, led by the *King George V*, to follow him, cut off and surround the enemy. But the rigid line could not be broken! The signal from the *Iron Duke* was a thing that must be obeyed, and the Grand Fleet went out of action … it is a matter of common knowledge throughout the Navy that a signal of this nature was made."

Again he says: "No response was made by the Admiral of the Second Battle Squadron to Beatty's imploring signal at 7.20 p.m. to follow him and cut off the enemy. In all probability he signalled for permission to follow Beatty and got no answer, or a refusal."[57]

At the time Commander Bellairs' book was published the signals made during the battle had not been made public. The message referred to was a wireless message, sent in cipher, and should therefore only have been known to those who had access to confidential   documents. As, however, Commander Bellairs seems to have acquired information sufficiently authentic to enable him to refer to the text of a secret message, it is pertinent to suggest that he would also have been aware that the message originated from Beatty, *not* at 7.20 p.m., when the battle fleet was about to turn away to avoid the enemy's torpedoes, but at 7.50 p.m., sometime after the battle fleet had reformed and hauled round to south-west to close the enemy again.

If the correct time of origin of this signal had been stated by the author, he would have been unable to connect it with the turn away of the battle fleet. It is, apparently, equitable, in the author's opinion, to ignore accuracy if such action is necessary to glorify Beatty at the expense of Jellicoe. The matter can best be summed up by quoting an extract from the review of Commander Bellairs' book which appeared in *The Times* of 19th February, 1920:

"Here we come to close quarters with our author and shall not spare him. He makes a statement which, in his judgment, at any rate, is gravely prejudicial to the professional reputation of the Commander-in-Chief of the Grand Fleet, and writes him down to the level of a Calder or even of a Byng. He adduces no evidence for this statement beyond saying that 'it is common knowledge throughout the Navy that such a signal was made and logged', and he makes it clear by implication that he has not himself seen the logs, from which alone, as he acknowledges, the true facts can be ascertained and their true bearing on Lord Jellicoe's conduct of the battle appreciated. Now this, in our judgment, is outrageous and intolerable. It is stabbing a man in the back and then running away."

We feel sure that, to all fair-minded persons, this criticism of the author's methods errs on the side of moderation. The truth of the incident of this "follow me" message, which was as unnecessary as it was meaningless, and only likely to mislead Jellicoe, has been stated in Chapter VI.

The reckless and totally inaccurate statements made by Commander Bellairs in regard to this incident were seized upon by those who wished to find a new "stick" wherewith to beat Admiral Jellicoe, and the dust thrown in the eyes of the public stuck, as dust will stick, until the publication of the Official Despatches and signals in December 1920, and even then the inaccuracy was only contradicted in certain quarters.

The "fact" that this signal, which became known as the "follow me" signal, was made at 7.15 p.m. was stated in the *Daily Mail* of 21st September 1920, 1st November 1920, and 3rd November 1920; in the issue of 12th October 1920 the time was quoted as 7.32 p.m. Among other publications which mentioned this incident was the *Globe* of 21st September 1920, which also quoted 7.15 p.m. as the time the signal was made. It will be seen, therefore, that Commander Bellairs' false and unwarrantable statement had widespread results.

Mr. H.W. Wilson refers in his book[58] to this incident and concludes with the words, "Yet once more a great chance offered". Mr. Wilson does not here connect this signal with the turn away, but he does misquote the times somewhat, thus emphasizing the alleged delay. The time of origin of Beatty's signal was 7.50, not 7.45 as stated by Mr. Wilson; it could not have reached Jellicoe himself until about 8 p.m. Yet the Commander-in-Chief's order to the *King George V* to do what Beatty asked was received by that ship, according to her log, at 8.7. pm. It is not clear what "great chance" the author refers to; turning towards the battle-cruisers would only have delayed the van of our battle fleet, which was already closing the enemy more directly than the former.

Mr. Churchill, alluding to this episode, quotes this signal, giving the time as 7.47 instead of 7.50, and comments: "The British battle-cruisers would soon be engaged. Where was the van of our battle fleet?" If, before asking this question, he had taken the trouble to look at the plans of the action published with the *Official History,* or even the *Admiralty Narrative,* he would have observed that at this time the whole of our battle fleet was heading for the enemy.

6
TURNING AWAY FROM TORPEDOES

Mr. Winston Churchill, when discussing the first retreat of the German Fleet, at 6.35 p.m., states: "Jellicoe, threatened by the torpedo stream, turned away according to his long resolved policy."[59]

This is a complete fabrication on Mr. Churchill's part. He sets out to give his arm-chair version of Jutland and, even at this late date, does not take the trouble to verify essential facts. Jellicoe did *not* turn away from any torpedo attack at 6.35. After the first German retreat, and as soon as he was clear of the perilous wake of the enemy, he, at 6.44 p.m., *closed* the enemy, first 11 degrees and, ten minutes later, by a 45 degree turn, making 56 degrees in all. He thereby brought the battle fleet right across the head of the High Seas Fleet when Scheer blundered back seventeen minutes later.[60]

Much uninstructed criticism has been levelled at Admiral Jellicoe for the one occasion when he countered torpedoes by using the only recognized manoeuvre for frustrating such an attack as that made by the Germans on their second retreat at 7.22. This was a manoeuvre which had been fully discussed, and concurred in beforehand, by all Flag officers; it was used on a number of occasions by a variety of British and German admirals, not only at Jutland but in other engagements. At Jutland this manoeuvre was used by Admirals Sturdee, Evan-Thomas, Burney, Hood, Beatty, and also by von Hipper. In some of these cases the turn away was greater than that used by Jellicoe. No one had evolved an alternative.

Let us suppose for one moment that the battle fleet had not turned away for a few minutes to avoid these torpedoes. What would the result have been? If no alteration had been made in the course it is reasonable to suppose, judging by all peace-time practices, that several ships would have been hit and the battle fleet, as a fighting force, considerably reduced in strength.

Another alternative would have been to turn towards and "comb" the torpedoes; or, in other words, take the risk of being able to see the tracks in time to enable ships to take individual avoiding action. This would have been a risky proceeding in low visibility, in water churned up by the passage of numbers of vessels, making it difficult to see the tracks.

And having done so, what next? Our battle fleet would have been steaming through a smoke-screen in the wake of the retiring enemy fleet, incurring the risk of damage by floating mines, dropped by the Germans for this very purpose, and presenting a most favourable target for renewed torpedo attacks, especially from a screen of submarines, such as Beatty fully believed he had encountered earlier in the action.

It is easy to be wise after the event and to reply that the tracks of the torpedoes could have been seen; that the enemy did not drop mines and that there were no submarines on the spot. If the carefully considered lessons of peace-time practices are to be totally ignored on the day of battle, of what use are these practices?

In 1920, after the publication of Commander Carlyon Bellairs' book, numerous articles appeared in the Press referring to this phase of the battle, and Admiral Jellicoe was accused of breaking off the action when it might have been successfully continued.

The following few extracts will indicate how persistently, and ignorantly, that author criticizes Jellicoe in this respect: "It was to avoid this attack of eleven destroyers that twenty-seven battleships turned away … It is impossible to imagine a more definite break from the whole spirit of naval tradition."[61]

And again: "Decisive victory is impossible in the misty North Sea if a fleet turns away from a destroyer attack, for such a movement involves losing sight of the enemy fleet and throwing away our gunnery supremacy …

turning away in the North Sea must be ruled out as Beatty ruled it out when he succeeded to the Command of the Grand Fleet."[62]

This is incorrect: Beatty himself employed identically the same tactics at the Dogger Bank and twice during the Battle of Jutland, with the difference that on two occasions he wrongly turned away from the reported position of a submarine instead of turning towards it to prevent it firing torpedoes.[63]

Jellicoe, and the other Admirals referred to above, turned away from torpedoes which had actually been fired at them at long range by destroyers, and Jellicoe rightly turned *towards* the position of a submarine (which proved to be a myth) reported, shortly before 7 p.m., as having been sighted by one of the ships ahead during the heat of the action.

Mr. Churchill, when referring to the massed torpedo attacks at about 7.20 p.m., says: "'Once more Jellicoe, obedient to his method, turned away from the torpedo stream, first two points and then two points more. Here at any rate was a moment when it would have been quite easy to divide the British Fleet with the Fifth Battle Squadron leading the starboard division, and so take the enemy between two fires. But the British Commander-in-Chief was absorbed in avoiding the torpedo attack by turning away."[64]

It was not only "his" method which Jellicoe employed to avoid the torpedoes, he used the method proved best by long practice, and agreed with by all his Admirals. The visibility conditions are ignored. It may appear easy, from the study of a diagram prepared with our present knowledge, to divide the fleet in the way suggested. Jellicoe did not have the diagram to guide him!

He had no accurate knowledge of the course of the enemy; the mist and smoke prevented him, and others, from visualizing the situation with any accuracy. It would have been the height of folly, and could only have led to complete chaos, to divide the fleet when the visibility was not sufficiently good to enable the detached squadrons to work in co-operation with one another and to co-ordinate their movements according to the movements of the main fleet.

7
THE ESCAPE OF THE GERMAN FLEET AT NIGHT

The fact that Jellicoe had little or no information of the enemy's movements during the night has either been ignored by most of his critics or the scanty information vouchsafed to him has been given undue weight.

The *Admiralty Narrative* states: "To the Commander-in-Chief the situation may have appeared in a still more favourable light, for he did not know the full extent of the British losses, and was spared any anxiety as to the *Queen Mary* and *Indefatigable*. He knew only that *Invincible* had been sunk. ... For an estimate of the state of, and efficiency of, the German Fleet the Commander-in-Chief could rely on his own observation."[65]

It is correct that Jellicoe did not know the extent of our own losses. Beatty had failed to inform him of the disasters to the battle-cruiser fleet. How, therefore, could he have known, by his own observation, what damage had been done to the enemy?

In the Admiralty narrative is a diagram showing the British and German minefields and the swept channels by which the enemy fleet could enter German protected waters. It is stated that the "general directions" of these channels had been communicated to the Commander-in-Chief. The diagram shows a swept channel running West (true) from Heligoland. Was Jellicoe informed that a channel running in this direction existed, without being told the position of its outer end? Had Jellicoe any reason to suppose that this channel might extend through our own minefields? These are points on which the narrative is silent when it could have been definite.

The *Admiralty Narrative* states: "At about 10.25 p.m. the head of the German line, by this time well on the port quarter of the British fleet, cut through the line formed by the 9th and 10th Flotillas. ... These engagements were seen by the battle fleet."[66]

The implication here is that our whole battle fleet saw firing which indicated the passage of the enemy battle fleet, an altogether unwarrantable assumption. Only some of the battleships saw the firing and only two ships, the *Malaya* and the *Valiant*, identified enemy battleships. The fact that a battleship was identified by the *Malaya* is tucked away in a footnote and no mention is made of the omission to report this to Jellicoe.

Reference is made[67] to an important signal sent from the Admiralty at 10.41 p.m., and also[68] to another important message sent at 1.48 a.m. No mention is, however, made of the time of receipt of these messages in the *Iron Duke*.

Again,[69] it is stated that "the Admiralty's 10.41 signal was not received in the *Lion*". In the absence of any explanation being given, there is some justification for doubting the accuracy of this statement. When the *Lion*'s wireless was put out of action, another ship in the squadron would, normally, be detailed to receive and pass on messages intended for Beatty. We know that signals from the Admiralty were received in the *New Zealand* and passed to the *Lion*[70] and, unless the signal department in the battle-cruiser squadron was yet again at fault, this signal would also have been received by the *New Zealand*, and passed on.

Commander Carlyon Bellairs, when dealing with the information available to Lord Jellicoe during the night, is as inaccurate, and biased, as he is in other details. He states: "A message was sent to the Grand Fleet, at 1.52 by wireless, as follows: 'Enemy battleships steering S.E. approximate bearing S.W. My position 10 miles astern of First Battle Squadron.'"[71]

It will be noticed that Commander Bellairs again purports to give the definite wording of a message which, if made, would have been in cipher and, at the time his book was published, should have been known only to those who had access to confidential documents. He also gives the time at which the signal was made, but omits the name of the ship from which it originated. No message containing the words, as quoted, can be traced in the Official list of signals. A message was, however, sent by the *Faulknor*, at 1.52 a.m., which read: "Enemy's battleships in sight. My position 10 miles astern of 1st B.S."

Commander Bellairs then continues: "Whether the message reporting the course and position of the German fleet at 1.52 was taken in by the Grand Fleet can only be settled by an examination of the signal logs; and in particular the *Iron Duke*'s wireless logs should be produced ... it seems hardly conceivable that the 1.52 message, to which all other signals should have given precedence, from a few miles away was not taken in by a single ship. The difficulty of providing an explanation may possibly be responsible for the allegation that it was logged in the *Iron Duke*'s wireless log."[72]

It is not clear what the author implies by this last sentence. At first sight it would appear that the wording should be "was *not* logged in the *Iron Duke*'s wireless log"; but then, why use the word "allegation"? The impression left on the mind, after reading Commander Bellairs' book, is that he suggests the *Iron Duke*'s log is being deliberately withheld, for the purpose of hiding the fact that this signal was received by Jellicoe, but not acted on by him. Such a suggestion, if intended, is merely a further example of the "mischievous and misleading character"[73] of the book. It is now known that this signal was not received in the *Iron Duke*[74] or in any other ship except a destroyer quite close to the *Faulknor*.

When referring to the firing which took place astern of the battle fleet during the night Commander Bellairs states: "Some of these explosions were seen from the Grand Fleet."[75] No mention is made of the fact that only a few ships saw anything definite enough to report, and that this information was not passed to Jellicoe.

Having weighed all the evidence, most of which is founded on speculation and conjecture, Commander Bellairs sums up the situation thus: "We have now seen that the failure to destroy the enemy was due neither to lack of information nor to any other cause such as low visibility, or mist, but to the deliberate steps taken by Lord Jellicoe, all of which had as their one controlling thought the preservation of his own ships."[76]

Could criticism be more unscrupulous?

Mr. H.W. Wilson states: "Had he (Jellicoe) given his fleet a rendezvous for Horns Reef and vigorously attacked there at dawn, it is morally certain that a great victory would have been achieved. ... But any real doubt as to the whereabouts of Scheer should have been removed by the noise and flash of fighting noted soon after 10 by various battleships."[77]

It is easy to be wise after the event and to make suggestions with the knowledge available some years later. There would have been an outcry, and justifiably so, if Jellicoe had staked his all on the enemy fleet returning by Horns Reef, and had taken no steps to safeguard other approaches. Jellicoe had no reason to know that the Horns Reef Passage had been, or would be, selected by Scheer.

As for the doubts being dispersed by the firing heard, soon after 10 p.m., it was not only Jellicoe who misinterpreted the meaning of this – as has been stated before. Such information as was received by Jellicoe during the night was also available to Beatty. Both Admirals made similar appreciations of the situation. It is sometimes forgotten, too, that there were no less than eleven other Admirals of experience present, and not one of them came to any different conclusion or made any better use of the scanty information available.

When referring to the *Castor's* action, at about 10 p.m., Mr. H.W. Wilson states: "Many opportunities of using the torpedo were lost because the British destroyers were ignorant of the German whereabouts and took the approaching vessels for friends, thus deliberately refraining from discharging torpedoes and losing good opportunities."[78]

The author ignores the fact, clearly stated in the published report from the *Castor*, that the element of doubt in the minds of the Captains of the destroyers, on this occasion, was caused by the enemy ships making our secret challenge. An explanation of the possible cause of this challenge being known to the Germans has been given previously.

To quote one more extract, which is a good example of Commander Bellairs' obvious intention to show that Jellicoe could do no right under any circumstances, he states: "In regard to the big ships, Lord Jellicoe says that the Germans exaggerated our losses by one battleship and one armoured cruiser, but he omits to comment on his own list of German losses."[79]

The author then gives Jellicoe's list of estimated German losses as 3 battleships (certain) and 1 battleship or battle-cruiser and 1 battleship (probable); a total of 5 capital ships, of which 2 were "probable". He continues: "Here was exaggeration indeed, given, of course, in good faith. Still, it is an exaggeration natural to one who builds pictures rather than concentrates all his energies on obtaining decisive results."

If, in Commander Bellairs' opinion, this over-estimation of the German losses is any evidence that Jellicoe is one who "builds pictures rather than concentrates all his energies on obtaining decisive results", what fate would Beatty suffer at the hands of this critic if he was dealt with on the same lines as Jellicoe? In his despatch Beatty (again, of course, in all good faith) estimates the German losses at 6 capital ships sunk, and 2 seriously damaged; as against Jellicoe's, more modest, estimate of 5 capital ships of which 2 were "probable".

Mr. Churchill[80] uses many arguments to show that Jellicoe ought to have realized that the Horns Reef Channel was the most likely one for Scheer to select for his final retreat. There is a good deal in the conclusions he draws, on the evidence he gives, but – and it is a big *but* – he omits to mention that Jellicoe had good reason to suppose there were two channels running towards Heligoland which must be considered.

The author [Churchill] says: "The Horns Reef Channel and the Heligoland Channel … were not far apart."[81] True – the entrance of the channel running in a north-westerly direction from Heligoland was not far from the Horns Reef Channel; but the one running west (true) from Heligoland was some distance to the southward, and Jellicoe could not ignore the possible existence of this channel, or of the route by the Ems.

Again he states: "Scheer was left free to retreat by the Horns Reef."[82] This is inaccurate: our destroyer flotillas stationed astern of the battle fleet acted as a check to this passage, and events proved that Scheer's retreat was by no means "left free". Not only was his fleet continually attacked by the British flotillas, but it was actually sighted by ships of the Fifth Battle Squadron; no report of this was, however, made to Jellicoe, but the author ignores this omission.

Mr. Churchill criticizes Jellicoe for his appreciation of the situation made on the meagre information he received during the early hours of the night; it would be equitable if he had mentioned that a similar appreciation was made by Beatty, who had the same information, and no better one by any Flag Officer present.

In summing up the action Mr. Churchill, after saying, "The British Battle Fleet was never seriously in action"[83], draws attention to the small damage received by our battleships; he omits the considerable material damage done to the enemy *by* the fire of our battleships.

A large volume could be written on the misconceptions and misrepresentations of these, and less important, writers who have presumed to express views on a matter which they have prejudged and only vaguely understand; but it would weary the unprofessional reader. The public, as a whole, wants a clear-cut verdict on Jutland. This they will find in the concluding chapter.

There only remains one aspect of the subject to be dealt with in this chapter. Assertions have been made that if the German battle fleet had been annihilated at Jutland the war would have ended there and then; or, in any case, it would have prevented intensive submarine warfare against our commerce.

In the first place, no British Admiral has ever succeeded in annihilating an enemy fleet; and in the second place, although the material damage inflicted on the enemy at Trafalgar was very considerably greater, proportionately, than at Jutland, this very definite victory did not prevent the French from harassing our trade for the next ten years. What frigates and privateers could accomplish during that period, submarines would have accomplished in our day.

Chapter 11
The Verdict

Was Jutland a British victory? This is a question which is frequently asked, and before a verdict can be given it is essential to be clear as to what is meant by "victory". The material losses were:

	British.	German.
Battleships	0	1
Battle-Cruisers	3	1
Cruisers	3	4
Destroyers	8	5
Total	14	11

The casualties in personnel were:

	British	German[84]
Killed	6,097	2,551
Wounded	510	507

The heaviest British losses occurred during the first phase in the engagement with the German battle-cruisers and just prior to the actual clash of contact between the main fleets, when the *Invincible* and our armoured cruisers found themselves, without warning, under the concentrated fire of the enemy's battle-cruisers and leading battleships.

With regard to the battle-cruiser action, which was in the nature of a distinct and separate encounter, we must admit that the Germans have considerable justification in claiming a victory. What are the facts?

Beatty had under his immediate control a fleet of considerably greater power than that under von Hipper. Taking capital ships alone, the British force consisted of 4 battleships and 6 battle-cruisers as compared with the German one of 5 battle-cruisers, a majority of two to one in our favour.

In this duel we lost 2 battle-cruisers and 2 destroyers as against the enemy's loss of 2 destroyers. Moreover, our surviving battle-cruisers had received more damage than they had inflicted. The enemy had made no attempt to avoid action; von Hipper's tactics were entirely sound and the fighting efficiency of his command proved to be of a high order. We can only acknowledge frankly, that the first "round" went definitely in the enemy's favour.

The final verdict in any match does not, however, depend on the result of the opening rounds. Let us recapitulate the succeeding stages of this great contest.

When the main action was joined and Jellicoe had assumed control, we again had the stronger fleet, but the proportion in capital ships in our favour was not now two to one, but about seven to five. From then on, including the phase already alluded to when contact was being made, the British losses were 1 battle-cruiser, 3 cruisers and 6 destroyers, as compared with the enemy's of 1 battleship, 1 battle-cruiser, 4 cruisers and 3 destroyers.

The German fleet received far more damage than it inflicted, both in actual losses and in hits on surviving ships. Scheer's tactics were chiefly devoted to extricating his command from situations in which he was threatened with annihilation. This, to give him his due, he achieved with considerable ability; but he was like a boxer, knowing himself to be outmatched and outfought, who concentrates his wits on avoiding punishment, while he waits anxiously for the call of "time". The "call" came at length when darkness gave him a much-needed respite.

It was not the real end; his opponent remained, fit and ready to meet him, only anxious for a fight to a finish when daylight should clear the arena again: but Scheer had had enough. He declined and successfully evaded further combat by working his way home under cover of the night, as the pugilist who has lost heart and knows himself defeated "throws up the sponge" and leaves the ring, never again to challenge his victorious adversary.

To Jellicoe, therefore, must go the verdict of that impartial referee – accurate history.

As the misconceptions and misrepresentations which have surrounded the facts about Jutland are gradually, and we hope now finally, cleared away, and the success, which was attained on the day when the whole issue of the Great War hung in the balance, is more generally recognized, credit will be given where credit is due.

Appendix I

ORGANIZATION OF THE BRITISH FLEET ON LEAVING HARBOUR ON 30 MAY 1916

BATTLE FLEET
Iron Duke (Fleet Flagship)

Organization No.2   *Organization No.5*

Second Battle Squadron

	King George V Ajax Centurion Erin	1st Division
1st Division		
	Orion Monarch Conqueror Thunderer	2nd Division

Fourth Battle Squadron

	Iron Duke Royal Oak Superb Canada	3rd Division
2nd Division		
	Benbow Bellerophon Temeraire Vanguard	4th Division

First Battle Squadron

3rd Division
{
  Marlborough
  Revenge
  Hercules
  Agincourt
} 6th Division

  Colossus
  Collingwood
  Neptune
  St. Vincent
} 5th Division

Attached Light Cruisers
Boadicea
Bellona
Blanche
Active

Attached
Oak (Destroyer)
Abdiel (Mine-sweeper)

BATTLE-CRUISERS

Third Battle-Cruiser Squadron
Invincible
Inflexible
Indomitable

CRUISERS

First Cruiser Squadron
Defence
Warrior
Duke of Edinburgh
Black Prince

Second Cruiser Squadron
Minotaur
Hampshire
Cochrane
Shannon

LIGHT CRUISERS

Fourth Light Cruiser Squadron
Calliope
Constance
Caroline
Royalist
Comus
Light Cruiser: Canterbury

DESTROYER FLOTILLAS

Twelfth Flotilla	*Eleventh Flotilla*	*Fourth Flotilla*
Faulknor	Castor	Tipperary
Marksman	Kempenfelt	Broke
Obedient	Ossory	Achates
Maenad	Mystic	Porpoise
Opal	Moon	Spitfire
Mary Rose	Morning Star	Unity
Marvel	Magic	Garland
Menace	Mounsey	Ambuscade
Nessus	Mandate	Ardent
Narwhal	Marne	Fortune
Mindful	Minion	Sparrowhawk
Onslaught	Manners	Contest
Munster	Michael	Shark
Nonsuch	Mons	Acasta
Noble	Martial	Ophelia
Mischief	Milbrook	Christopher
		Owl
		Hardy
		Midge

BATTLE-CRUISER FLEET

BATTLE-CRUISERS
Lion (Fleet Flagship)

First Battle-Cruiser Squadron	*Second Battle-Cruiser Squadron*
Princess Royal	New Zealand
Queen Mary	Indefatigable
Tiger	

Fifth Battle Squadron

Barham
Valiant
Warspite
Malaya

LIGHT CRUISERS

First Light Cruiser Squadron	*Second Light Cruiser Squadron*	*Third Light Cruiser Squadron*
Galatea	Southampton	Falmouth
Phaeton	Birmingham	Yarmouth
Inconstant	Nottingham	Birkenhead
Cordelia	Dublin	Gloucester
		Chester

DESTROYER FLOTILLAS

First Flotilla	*Thirteenth Flotilla*	*Ninth and Tenth Flotillas*
Fearless	Champion	Lydiard
Acheron	Nestor	Liberty
Ariel	Nomad	Landrail
Attack	Narborough	Laurel
Hydra	Obdurate	Moorsom
Badger	Petard	Morris
Goshawk	Pelican	Turbulent
Defender	Nerissa	Termagant
Lizard	Onslow	
Lapwing	Moresby	
	Nicator	

Seaplane Carrier: Engadine

Appendix II

ORGANIZATION OF THE HIGH SEAS FLEET ON 31 MAY 1916

BATTLESHIPS

Third Squadron

König
Grosser Kurfürst
Kronprinz
Markgraf
— 5th Division

Kaiser
Kaiserin
Prinzregent Luitpold
— 6th Division

First Squadron

Friedrich der Grosse
(Fleet Flagship)
Ostfriesland
Thuringen
Helgoland
Oldenburg
— 1st Division

Posen
Rheinland
Nassau
Westfalen
— 2nd Division

Second Squadron

Deutschland
Hessen
Pommern
— 3rd Division

Hanover
Schlesien
Schleswig Holstein
— 4th Division

CRUISERS

First ScoutScouting Group (Battle-Cruisers)	*Second ScoutScouting Group* (Light Cruisers)	*Fourth Scouting Group* (Light Cruisers)
Lutzow	Frankfurt	Stettin
Derfflinger	Wiesbaden	München
Seydlitz	Pillau	Hamburg
Moltke	Elbing	Frauenlob
Von der Tann		Stuttgart

DESTROYER FLOTILLAS

Rostock, Light Cruiser, First Leader of Torpedo Boats	Regensburg, Light Cruiser, Second Leader of Torpedo Boats
First Flotilla (1st half)	Second Flotilla
Third Flotilla	Sixth Flotilla
Fifth Flotilla	Ninth Flotilla
Seventh Flotilla	

PART II

THE JUTLAND SCANDAL

Admiral Sir Reginald Bacon KCB, KCVO, DSO

AUTHOR'S NOTE TO FIRST EDITION

Every detail of the Battle of Jutland is of intense interest to any naval officer who, like myself, has spent his life in the Navy during its gradual development from sailing ships to super-dreadnoughts. While dealing with every phase, problem and doubt during this great change we always looked forward to the great ordeal which awaited our modern Navy with a feeling akin to awe. So much had never been subjected to the stern realities of war, so much had necessarily to depend on forecast and theory, so much doubt was bound to exist as to whether other nations had not forestalled us in invention, adaptation and assumption; that, in spite of all our labours, we felt that the outcome of a naval war in the future might largely lie in the lap of the gods.

That we had done our best was all we could claim, that that best had in no particular been surpassed by others was all we dared to hope. For the remainder, our officers and men might well be trusted to see the country through.

To us, therefore, Jutland had a superlative interest, and we looked forward to the publication of the official Admiralty account of how the battle had been fought and the Germans beaten, with eager expectancy. Delays occurred in its production, sinister rumours were whispered abroad, culminating in a report that the account which had been drawn up by the independent Admiralty experts was undergoing alterations to suit official views.

After delay, Volume III of the *Official History of the War* was issued, and, while waiting for the Admiralty narrative, was at once accepted as the standard history of the battle. Then one year afterwards came the *Admiralty Official Narrative*, an anaemic production, whose claim to be regarded as an authoritative statement weakened and faded more and more as each succeeding sentence was read.

This long delay had affected adversely the prestige of the Admiralty. The *Official Narrative* when issued merely added to its discredit.

When the report was published an article appeared in the *Daily Express* purporting to be a recent interview with Admiral Scheer, who commanded the German High Sea Fleet at Jutland. Also in the *Sunday Express* an article appeared from the pen of Mr. Filson Young which, as a masterpiece of inaccurate imagery, can rarely, if ever, have been surpassed. These two articles most ignorantly condemned Lord Jellicoe's conduct of the British operations. I therefore wrote to both papers pointing out certain facts which should have been apparent to all who had devoted study to the details of the battle. The *Daily Express* courteously excused itself on the grounds that they had closed the discussion. The *Sunday Express* attempted no excuse for refusing to have its misrepresentations confuted.

It is this smoke-screen which has been raised by a section of the Press to prevent the British public from learning the truth about Jutland that constitutes the scandal regarding that battle and furnishes the reason for writing this book.

Not uncommonly, after a war, praise and blame are apportioned most unfairly among those who have held command. Three officers have been blamed unjustly for operations in the North Sea.

The German cruisers escaped in the Dogger Bank Action through a series of errors made by Lord Beatty. For this escape Admiral Sir Gordon Moore has popularly and most unfairly been held to blame.

A want of tactical appreciation on the part of Lord Beatty led to the 5th Battle Squadron not being engaged during the majority of the action in Jutland, Phase I [31 May]. Admiral Sir H. Evan-Thomas has been ungenerously and unjustly blamed for this in the *Admiralty Narrative* of the Battle of Jutland.

Lastly, the failure of Lord Beatty to keep in touch with the High Sea Battle Fleet, on his run north to join the Grand Fleet at the end of Jutland, Phase I, deprived Lord Jellicoe of vital information as to the position of that fleet and caused him to deploy in less rapid a manner than he would have, had the requisite information been available. For this, Lord Jellicoe has been blamed.

It is hoped that this book will help to readjust the incidence of blame in these matters, and that it will be carefully studied by all who value justice.

I have been at pains to verify all statements and details. I must add that Lord Jellicoe has had no hand directly or indirectly in the inception, writing, editing, or publishing of this book.

Admiral Sir Reginald Bacon
January, 1925

AUTHOR'S NOTE TO FIFTH EDITION

When *The Jutland Scandal* was first written an excess of blind hero-worship had apparently led to the belief that the surest way of belauding Lord Beatty lay in belittling Lord Jellicoe. As a result, grossly inaccurate statements regarding the Battle of Jutland appeared from several sources in the Press. I considered that the situation called for drastic action; and, knowing that my statements could not be controverted, I wrote the plain, unvarnished truth in a bald and perhaps aggressive manner. I did not hesitate at personal criticism and defied detractors to prove that my statements were incorrect. The effect was magical and the unworthy campaign came to a hasty conclusion.

Now that all such aggression is ended I have modified my previous remarks so that they are more general than personal and therefore less likely to wound the susceptibilities of others.

Since the issue of the first edition, two publications of importance which deal with the battle have appeared. One is by Vice-Admiral J. Harper, C.B., entitled *The Truth About Jutland*, and the other a chapter on the battle in Volume III of *The World Crisis* by Mr. Winston Churchill.

The first of these commands the respect of all readers, since it comes to us from the pen of the officer who was responsible for writing the first official report of the battle; which, although approved by Admiral of the Fleet Lord Wester Wemyss before he left the Admiralty, was suppressed after Lord Beatty became First Sea Lord. While compiling that report, Admiral Harper had access to every official log-book, report and document; so that his knowledge of the subject became unique. Moreover, he was specially selected as the compiler, since he had not been present at the battle, and his report was therefore bound to be untinged by any bias which might unconsciously have been created by direct personal association with the combined fleets.

In his book, Admiral Harper has dealt faithfully with critics of minor importance, such as Mr. A.H. Pollen and Commander Bellairs, so it is unnecessary here to controvert their extravagant statements. Mr. Churchill's account requires separate examination.

This duty is by no means a pleasant one; in fact, I should have preferred to ignore his account altogether had it not been for the prestige which attaches to the writings of that famous politician, not only by reason of his wide international reputation and a most fascinating, persuasive and forceful style of writing, but also from the fact that for some years he filled with distinction the office of First Lord of the Admiralty.

The several volumes of *The World Crisis* have spread widely over the globe, and while the better informed officers of the Navies of the larger countries, who have studied the accounts of the Battle of Jutland as chronicled in Volume III, must have been filled with a wonderment not devoid of amusement; yet the majority of lay readers must have imbibed totally erroneous ideas regarding that engagement.

In addition, therefore, to correcting the errors into which Mr. Filson Young had fallen, it is also imperative in the present edition to expose the flights of critical imagination of which Mr. Churchill has been guilty.

It is not an easy matter to give a simple and clear description of the various stages of the battle and, at the same time, to deal with the misinterpretations of technical evidence by non-technical writers. I have been forced to the conclusion that the most satisfactory compromise is to leave the greater part of the text of the earlier editions of *The Jutland Scandal* unaltered except in minor details, so that the main features of the engagement may be easily grasped, and to add a fresh chapter dealing with Mr. Churchill's account of the battle. By so doing, the clarity of the general description is preserved, while by secondary repetition the main details of the fight should be more fully impressed on the general reader.

I have retained the account of the Dogger Bank Action in justice to Admiral Sir Gordon Moore, KCB.

Admiral Sir Reginald Bacon
January, 1933

Chapter 1

The First Essential

Of all our public services the Royal Navy is probably the one that for the last hundred years has been most honoured by the confidence reposed in it by the people of this country; but at the same time it has been throughout that period the least understood. Banished from view to the sea, where its life was spent in constant manoeuvres and training, our fleet was only conspicuous on the special occasions of official parades and functions, when the work of a fighting service is paralysed, and the essential life of a navy is hidden under a cloak of artificiality.

Modern ships are marvels of engineering skill and development. Guns, armour, engines, electrical appliances, torpedoes – all tend to challenge the accurate knowledge even of those who daily live in contact with them. To the average person ashore they remain abstract terms. In the old days it was much the same; masts, sails and rigging, the art of sailing a ship in all weathers and tides, navigation and the handling of a fleet were sealed chapters for the man ashore.

The progress from the ship of the early years of the nineteenth century to the *Hood* or *Nelson* of the present day was a matter of slow evolution of detail and of patient following in the footsteps of the growth of science and invention ashore. Even men afloat often failed to grasp the full bearing that this slow progress had on strategy and tactics at sea. Can it be wondered that the British public remained ignorant also?

The deeds of our ships and fleets in the old wars were duly chronicled by historians, largely with an eye to public consumption, victories being emphasized and defeats and failures minimized. Between the era of the old wars and that of the Great War, no active naval operations of any magnitude were undertaken; almost unbroken peace reigned at sea, there was nothing to chronicle that would appeal to the imagination of the public. Hence instruction in modern naval war, its battles and its methods, was denied to the country, and the nation as a whole culled its ideas of sea warfare from the deeds of a Navy of ancient and obsolete construction, and from methods of fighting which had long passed away.

When, therefore, the late war burst on the nation with meteoric suddenness, the minds of the people were imbued with old ideas of naval warfare which created vast expectations of spectacular achievements and victories similar to those of Trafalgar and the Nile. But nothing happened. The end of 1914 passed, 1915 came and left behind nothing much to remember at sea except some cruiser actions.

The facts that the whole of the German Oversea Navy had been destroyed or interned, and that, through sea power, nearly all the German Colonies had been conquered, escaped the close attention of the nation, whose eyes were longingly fixed on the glories of a Fleet action.

People asked: "What is wrong? Where is our Nelson?" The Public only remained partly satisfied that the cause of the apparent inaction was due to the disinclination of the German Fleet to put to sea. Discontentedly and grumblingly they asked: "Why was it not forced from their harbours?", and looked each day to find that the German ships had been forced to come out and had given battle to our fleet. Then they confidently believed our day would at last have come – Trafalgar would be repeated, and ship after ship of the German Navy would be sent to the bottom.

Such were the uneducated hopes of the British nation.

In the early months of 1916 the day came – issue was joined and the battle fought. The news of the result spread dismay – apparently our fleet had been more damaged than that of the enemy. True, the latter had fled to their harbours and never came out again with any intention of fighting, but where was the victory, the crushing defeat so eagerly anticipated? Surely someone had blundered, and surely some gross mistake had been made? Time went on; the war was won; but still there remained a feeling that the chapters in Naval History written by our sailors in the war lacked the glory of those handed down by our ancestors.

Vainly have the more sober of our contemporary historians pointed out the essential differences that exist between the old-time sea conflicts and those of the late war. They have pointed out the strategical results that our Navy obtained, the steady policy and tactics pursued, and the absence of tactical and strategical gambling. Yet the feeling persists that the country was robbed of a glory which should have been equal to that earned in the days of our great-grandfathers, and which should have added lustre and prestige to the nation as a whole.

Explanations after an event always savour of excuse and meet with distrust; but, in the case of the late war, such distrust is not greater than that which would have greeted accurate forecast had it been made before the war. Any attempt to educate the country in modern naval pre-war thought would have ended in failure. Human nature can rarely be brought to believe that which is unpalatable to its preconceptions. Belief is so largely a matter of inclination that actual occurrence is the only evidence that will break down fixed notions and pave the way for new ideas. To have preached in pre-war days that inaction of the sea-going fleet would be the commonplace, and battles the exception, would merely have provoked incredulity.

Yet such has always been the case in war. The long years of blockades in the old wars were barely touched on in popular writings, since accounts of battles were the theme that stirred the populace. Hence the multitude pictured naval war as a succession of sea combats and not merely dull, commonplace sea coercion. But if in our pre-war desire to instruct we had gone still further, if we had asserted that modern conditions favoured, yea even necessitated, our fleets remaining the greater part of each year in harbour, so seemingly pusillanimous a contention would merely have provoked derision.

Now that the late war is becoming ancient history the minds of laymen are better prepared to consider dispassionately the real meaning of sea power and strategy. So much is this the case that they may even be prepared to acknowledge that a war at sea can be won without ever a fleet going to sea or a gun being fired.

To grasp the real significance of war and warlike operations, it is necessary to appreciate that all things living have at all times waged a war of existence. The inexorable law of animal life in the forest, to fight and be fought, to eat and be eaten, governs human nature in principle; although modified in its cruder aspect by civilization. Individuality in persons and nations necessitates rivalry in the struggle for existence; commerce is the modern battlefield for national rivalry. All countries carry on, daily, the war of rival commerce. In the past, wholesale robbery, revenge, the lust of territorial possession, and the pride of rulers were the predominating causes of physical warfare. These are fast fading and may in time cease to exist; but the rivalry of commerce will remain as long as nations preserve their nationality, and until individuality is obliterated and altruism alone reigns in the world.

Commerce is the source of national wealth. Without trade no nation can exist; moreover, the priority of countries in the councils of the world is regulated by the force behind them; this force can *au fond* be traced to wealth, and wealth is the offspring of commerce. The commerce of this country has been built up by adherence to sound principles, good judgment and bold enterprise. Its chief enemy has been and always will be a spirit of gambling. Our vast national resources in coal and iron have helped in the past; our national characteristics have turned these resources into wealth. The process has been slow; in fact so slow, that few, at the time, grasped the full significance of the victories that they were gaining in their commercial war; nor even, owing to the slowness of their maturing, have we perceived that they were as surely victories physical to the country as those that are gained in battles and in war.

Physical war is merely a sporadic outburst of national rivalry in a virulent form. Physical war and commercial war bear the same comparisons to each other as a violent conflagration does to slow decay; force must be met by force, scores of years of wealth accumulated in slow commercial war has to be drawn on and sacrificed to check the conflagration of physical war, and place a limit to its waste. But the same principles should underlie the conduct of violent war as those by which the slow commercial war is successfully carried on.

Hence we should in physical war look for adherence to sound principles, mature judgment and justifiable boldness, but above all the absence of gambling due to the taking of unjustifiable risks. Yet so perverse is human nature, so ingrained are certain sentiments by heredity, that boldness, even up to gambling, is apt to be more applauded than a safe policy. Physical prowess was a god worshipped by our ancestors and is still revered by us. Brain power in war then received, and still receives, scant acknowledgment. Vestiges of this ancient religion remain engraved in our minds and will not die for several generations to come. Deeds of daring, even if unsuccessful, make the pulse tingle and the human frame to glow. The glory of deeds done by a compatriot seems to reflect honour on each individual of a nation, so that each seems, to himself, to have been endowed with a bravery and valour which he values all the more, forsooth, if they happen to be totally absent from his physical equipment.

The emotional tendencies of a nation constitute a great danger in war. The unbalanced judgment of the masses, which sets a greater store on scintillating valiance than on the drab soundness of strategy or tactics, is a great danger in physical war; and is, moreover, one which may be accentuated in the wars of the future.

The first essentials therefore, in approaching the analysis of warlike operation, is to put aside all emotional tendencies, to look on war as a matter of business, most vitally important business, to the nation. The younger and more irresponsible of the fighters can treat war as a game, or as a means of obtaining a reputation for gallantry, and for many reasons these feelings should be encouraged; but for those in high command, on whom the responsibility of this vital business of the nation rests, no such ideas are permissible. War to them must never be anything but a cool, calculating business in which sentiment – except so far as sentiment in others increases morale – can find no place. If, therefore, we are to judge the proceedings of a war we must adopt a like course; each step taken must be judged solely from the standpoint of how it affected the general strategy of the war.

The nation may revel in luxuries such as the charge of Balaclava and similar feats of heroism; and to a certain extent such sporadic outbreaks

100

may at times be useful in keeping up the morale of a nation and inspiring the fighting forces; but they must be looked on as relaxations and extravagances, and not as part of the business of war. However much we may hanker after our pride being stimulated by accounts of heroism and gallantry in battle, we must, as critics, assess such pleasurable indulgences at their basic worth, and coldly inquire whether they did or did not assist us to win the war.

Chapter 2

Nelson and His Times

The latter portion of 1805 was one of suspense to the people of Britain. The great war with Napoleon had lasted with but brief intermission since 1793. On land the French arms had been victorious. Europe lay under the domination of the newly-crowned French Emperor. The war at sea, at first largely confined to a struggle to capture or retain colonies, had gradually assumed a more threatening aspect so far as invasion of England was concerned. Events had brought home to Napoleon that his real enemy was Great Britain. He had imposed his rule and peace, at will, on all the European nations except those of these islands, and it was they who, with money and their fleet, energetically continued to oppose his autocratic assumption of ruling the destinies of Europe.

The two weapons at his disposal to reduce this country to obedience were actual invasion and commercial starvation. The former was the one which appeared to be the more feasible, and it was this threat that lay most heavily over our nation. Our one hope for immunity from the consummation of Napoleon's designs lay in the Navy. Our Navy was but slightly numerically stronger than that of the French Navy combined with those of the varying Allies of France. It was, therefore, fortunate for us that our Navy was at that time vastly superior to the French and every other European nation in sea experience. For a moment let us trace the causes that led to this superiority.

The great war which began in 1793, and which convulsed Europe for over twenty years, was the direct outcome of the French Revolution. The Revolution had shaken the structure of French social organization with violence, destroying both bad and good alike, and disorganizing all the public services; none of which suffered more than the French Navy.

In 1790 the French Navy was a service to be proud of: in 1794 it was a disorganized rabble. In Lord Howe's victory at the battle of the 1st of June, 1794, the three admirals and twenty-six captains of the French Fleet had three years before held the following positions: The Commander-in-Chief had been a lieutenant; one of the two other admirals had been a lieutenant and the other a sub-lieutenant. Of the captains, three had been lieutenants, eleven sub-lieutenants, nine had been merchant ship officers, one a seaman in the navy, one a boatswain, and one unknown.[1] The French Navy, therefore, was at that time as regards its officers in a thoroughly disorganized condition. As regards the men it was little better.

Moreover, energetic action on the part of our naval authorities had instituted blockades off all the French naval ports. This was with a view to preventing the various units of their fleet leaving and combining without being brought to action; but it had a secondary and far-reaching effect, in that it imposed idleness on the crews of the French vessels, and denied them that constant practice and experience in handling and working sailing ships, as well as in gunnery, which was absolutely necessary for reasonable efficiency in action.

With us the blockade had the exact contrary effect: our ships were constantly at sea, sometimes for two years or more, always sailing, always practised in manoeuvring and working the ships; reefing, trimming, shortening and making sail, until sea-lore was a commonplace.

When the French fleet put to sea it was more or less a rabble. Unused to the motion, the men suffered from sea-sickness; but, beyond all, that feeling of accustomedness to sea work, and the confidence begotten by it, were absent. In their place a feeling of diffidence and uncertainty supervened, increased almost to despair by the early evidences of the inexperience of officers and crews as their vessels passed the heads of their ports and met the ocean swell and the shifting winds. It is useless to make a cavalry charge with raw recruits, or to fight a naval action in sailing ships with unpractised crews.

Confidence is an asset of incalculable value to a fighting force, and this was even more so in the old sailing days, when the whole crew were implicated in the sailing and handling of the ships, and often were called on to take a part in hand-to-hand fighting. In present years the handling of the ships is largely independent of the crew, who merely tend the oil fuel and keep an eye on the lubrication of the turbines or load the guns. The movements of the ship are controlled by one or at the most two officers, and the fire of the guns is, again, in the hands of half a dozen officers; the men merely load and lay the guns mechanically in obedience to the movements of certain pointers.

Such then was the condition of the French Navy in Nelson's time. It is well to keep these facts in mind when we look back on the old-time victories. We may well be filled with admiration of the deeds of our old sea heroes, but at the same time we must give due weight to the conditions prevailing in those times which aided our seamen in gaining the sweeping victories that history has recorded, and which we are apt to ascribe solely to a superiority of courage or genius in our race.

It is not infrequently the practice of modern writers to compare some existing popular naval officer with Nelson, and to judge the actions of others by what they call the "Nelsonic standard". Nelson was, and always will be, a unique personality; but much of the picturesqueness of his complex character was due to the conditions of the times in which he lived. Had Nelson lived in the twentieth century he would appear to those writers to be totally different to the Nelson of whom they write, and who lived in the early nineteenth century.

The day of complete freedom of action at sea has gone, wireless telegraphy and telegrams have destroyed the conditions which developed much of the independence of his character. Hand-to-hand combats have passed; little chance remains of exhibiting exceptional gallantry in an action. The fiery longing to exhibit personal prowess and the love of close combat can now be satisfied only on the rarest occasions, and then only in vessels of small value like destroyers. Those impulses would develop into a positive danger to the nation if indulged in by those in command of our more valuable vessels.

The kernel of Nelson's character would still remain if he were alive today; his devotion to duty and prompt decision, the result of earnest thought, would persist; but the conditions that govern the use of these qualities in a modern navy are so different that they would appear to be totally different attributes. The one predominant quality that Nelson exhibited, and which stamps him as a great sea commander, was a swift and unerring judgment and quick determination in a crisis in battle. He had many other high qualities as an officer: restless activity, a high sense of duty, a natural love of fighting, which, of course, endowed him with a personal gallantry conspicuous even in his own day of gallant fighters.

Many others have possessed these qualities to as great an extent as Nelson, although perhaps they have not given expression in words, or writing, so fully to their feelings regarding duty and love of fighting as Nelson through his peculiar singleness of character was wont to do. It is this constant repetition in correspondence and conversation, of "doing his duty" of "getting at the enemy" that reveal the constant thought and rumination over the problems that confronted him, and undoubtedly it was the constant thought over possibilities, and visualizing probable and possible conditions, that sharpened his natural rapidity of thought and caused him to recognize and to act instantly in a critical phase of an action.

Independence of action bred of profound belief in himself and his judgment (a most necessary quality in every officer) led him immediately to take the action he considered to be right. It is utterly improbable that Nelson, like many other officers, considered personal gallantry as anything but a matter of course. Thousands of officers would not hesitate to place themselves in positions of risk and danger when they considered such action necessary. Nelson never threw himself into a position of danger

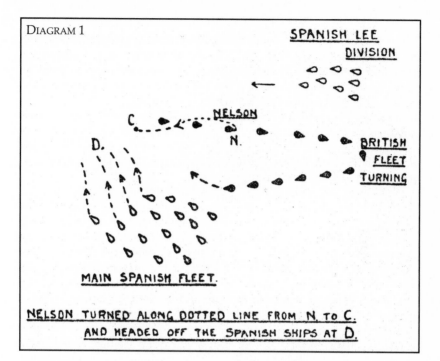

DIAGRAM 1

SPANISH LEE DIVISION

NELSON

C.

D.

N.

BRITISH FLEET TURNING

MAIN SPANISH FLEET.

NELSON TURNED ALONG DOTTED LINE FROM N. TO C. AND HEADED OFF THE SPANISH SHIPS AT D.

merely to exhibit his gallantry. He was to himself merely one of the ship's company; to share with them the hazards that duty demanded – this is the correct spirit of an officer.

In every action at sea in which Nelson was engaged he showed unerring judgment at some crisis. In the battle of Cape St. Vincent, his first fleet action, he commanded the *Captain*, which according to seniority was stationed as the thirteenth ship in the line. Sir John Jervis, afterwards Lord St. Vincent, led the British line of battle down between two portions of the Spanish Fleet which had become separated from each other – one group of ships lay to *windward* of him, and the other group to *leeward*. Now, in sailing days, it took a long time for ships to *leeward* to beat up and join those to *windward*, since the wind was blowing dead against them, and they had to make long zigzags to reach the desired point. In fact, for a line-of-battle ship to reach a point three miles to windward, it had to sail approximately sixteen miles through the water. On the other hand, ships to windward had only to steer a straight course with the wind behind them to join their consorts to leeward of them.

When the Spaniards detected Jervis's design, the captains of the ships to windward altered course to join their detached unit to leeward, in order to reunite their fleet in one compact body and so defeat the British tactics. Nelson saw their intention and at once appreciated the full measure of their manoeuvre; without hesitation, he left the line of battle and threw his ship in the road of the ships bearing down, bringing his broadside to bear and raking the leading ship. His resolute action miraculously stopped the remainder of the Spanish ships following the example of their leaders. The ship next astern of Nelson followed suit and supported him; thus the success of Jervis's manoeuvre was assured.

Now the details of this operation give much food for thought. Nelson exhibited a rapid appreciation of the crisis and prompt action in carrying out his decision. The captain next astern was equally gallant, but Nelson was solely responsible for the quickness of brain and independence of action that led to the brilliant manoeuvre.

In discussing this action we must give due weight to the traditions of the times. To break out of the line might well have been considered by some admirals a deadly sin, and had the action been lost Nelson might have been made a scapegoat. It was his decision to do, against precedent, what he considered was right that showed a moral courage far more rare than mere gallantry. A man who had merely lived in the present, without daily analysing the past or visualizing the future, would have let the opportunity slip. Moral courage, prepared thought and accurate judgment were the attributes Nelson showed at the battle of St. Vincent.

Let us now pass over two years and turn to Nelson's next sea fight, that of Aboukir Bay, probably the most dramatic of all sea battles, fought at night, with all the weirdness of night fighting, where the grappling hand-to-hand struggle in the darkness was illumined by the flash of guns and explosions. The young Rear-Admiral, selected specially to command the fleet detached to watch the French in Toulon, had, through no fault of his own, allowed their vessels to escape from that port in a gale. He had fruitlessly chased to the east to find them.

Mortified in spirit, he was perfectly conscious that it was luck merely that had favoured their escape; but he also knew the ignorance of the British public and their avidity for blaming all but successful officers; painfully he felt that his chances of serving his country, as he knew that with the right opportunity he could serve her, were slipping by. When almost in despair the French Fleet was sighted at anchor in Aboukir Bay. He decided to attack at once, although darkness would close down before the battle could be decided. Let it not be forgotten that the deterrents to modern night fighting were all absent – no torpedoes or torpedo-craft existed; the enemy was at anchor, and there was no chance, therefore, of mistaking friend for foe.

Captain Foley led the line, and when approaching the French Fleet had one of those flashes of thought which experience only can originate. The ships at anchor conjured up to his mind their swinging round their anchors at the full scope of their cables, and therefore he recognized intuitively that there was enough water inshore of them to float his ship. The unpreparedness of guns on the disengaged side, because of the lumber

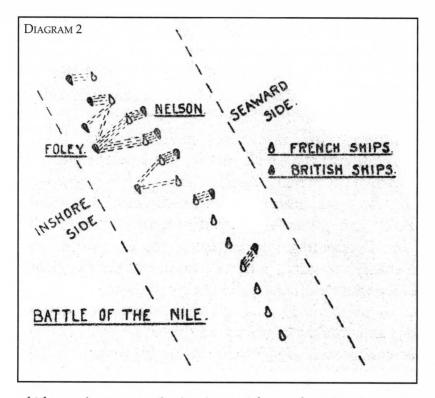

DIAGRAM 2

NELSON

SEAWARD SIDE.

FOLEY.

♦ FRENCH SHIPS.
♠ BRITISH SHIPS.

INSHORE SIDE

BATTLE OF THE NILE.

which was often temporarily placed around them in the sudden emergency of a surprise fight, flashed into his mind. So without hesitation he led the line *inshore* of the enemy and engaged them on their unprepared side. The next six ships followed him and passed inside, till Nelson, in the *Vanguard*, reached the head of the French line. Without hesitation he led the remainder *outside* and placed them to seaward of the enemy, thereby having, roughly speaking, one English ship on each side of each ship in the northern half of the French Fleet; while the southern half of that fleet was left with their broadsides pointing harmlessly to the east and west altogether out of the action, and totally unable to assist the head of the line, which was being sorely engaged, and rapidly crushed by the overwhelming force of a one to two fight.

Disputes have centred round the point as to whether Nelson or Foley doubled the line. Some, who have been unable to give credit to anyone but Nelson, have suggested that the situation had been previously discussed, and that Nelson had indicated the action to be followed. This is most unlikely, since there is no reason to suppose that Nelson ever anticipated fighting the French Fleet at anchor – an utterly improbable situation. Let us give Foley the credit of leading the ships round to the disengaged side

– a flash of genius bred of experience – but let us take the common-sense view that Foley never intended by his action to "double the line", that is, to place one ship each side of each of the French vessels. That was due to Nelson's genius. As a sea officer, Nelson must have appreciated that Foley had given him the enormous advantage, the great initial advantage, of engaging the unprepared side of the enemy's vessels; but, as a master of tactics, he saw that every minute given to the enemy allowed the French vessels to prepare the guns on their shoreward side for action; and that the doubling of two of our ships to one of the enemy was fifty times more valuable than the temporary advantage that Foley's action had given to the leading vessels.

Let us note most carefully that Nelson's tactics were not what modern critics would call "Nelsonic"; personal bravery was subordinated to the end to be achieved. He did not disdain to place his ship, coming fresh and without a shot having been fired at her, alongside a half-beaten ship to complete her destruction. He did not dash in a fiery manner to engage a new and unattacked enemy; he did merely what his unerring judgment told him was the right course, one dictated by the brain and not the lust of the fighter.

Years elapsed and Nelson was in the North Sea, second-in-command to Sir Hyde Parker. He had reconnoitred the offing of Copenhagen and decided in his mind that he could attack and reduce the batteries.

No previous attack of this nature had been tried on a grand scale; there was no previous experience to guide him and to enable him to appreciate the advantages that well-prepared shore positions possess against the attack of ships. He persuaded the Commander-in-Chief to allow him to make the attack with a portion of the fleet. Nothing was left to chance that could be done previous to the engagement. The passage was surveyed and all made ready.

The fight began and its progress showed that the outcome was, to say the least, doubtful. Nelson's judgment suppressed his fighting ardour: he arranged an armistice and saved his squadron. Brain and clear thought in the middle of a fierce fight saved the ships. Nelson showed himself in a new light; no similar deed had ever been done by a naval commander, but his unfaltering judgment in action suppressed his love of fighting. The course he followed can hardly again be called "Nelsonic" in the popular sense, but in no action has Nelson, as an admiral in command, shown greater brain power or judgment than at the Battle of Copenhagen.

One word in passing. The famous episode of Nelson disregarding Hyde Parker's signal to discontinue the action has its lessons. The Commander-in-Chief had given his consent to the undertaking – the attack was launched, and he had no right to cancel his permission unless some new information had reached him to cause him to reconsider the position; or, unless conditions had arisen whereby his portion of the fleet was compromised by the absence of Nelson's ships.

Neither of these had occurred, and therefore he had no right to get "cold feet" and cancel the operation. Or, perhaps, since "cold feet" are constitutional, and it is out of the power of the individual to avoid them, he might bitterly regret having given his sanction – but it was his duty to maintain sufficient self-control not to hamper a subordinate to whom he had assigned a definite detached operation. Nelson's conduct in disregarding the signal was dictated by common sense. He knew his Commander-in-Chief, and we may let it rest at that: or, to put the matter in a nutshell, if St. Vincent had recalled him, Nelson would have put his telescope to his good eye, for he would have known there was a reason for the signal; but his blind eye came into use with Hyde Parker because Nelson knew Hyde Parker.

The Battle of Trafalgar saw Nelson at his prime as a naval Commander-in-Chief. The years between the Battle of Copenhagen and 1805 had been full of experience and incident. He had had unique opportunities for making an accurate estimate of the French Navy and also the Spanish Navy as fighting forces, and on those estimates he was able to base the tactics of his fleet. The quiet of Merton had given him the opportunity of reviewing the past and of thoroughly analysing the busy years of the war. Whilst at Merton he evolved the future tactics of any fleet he might command. It is not difficult to trace the lasting impression made on him by the Battle of the Nile in his development of the "Nelson touch", as he loved to call his tactical scheme for a fleet action.

Briefly the scheme was to divide his fleet into two squadrons; to throw one half on to a lesser number of the enemy while he, with the other, took up a position to threaten the unengaged portion of the enemy's ships should they attempt to go to the succour of their engaged vessels.

Here, again, we have the true Nelson spirit shown. Not the "Nelsonic spirit". He did not propose to engage; he did not propose to rush helter-skelter into the action; but to remain clear of the fighting, because by so doing he was free to bring his mature judgment to bear, and to seize the critical moment when the disengaged section of the enemy might attempt to turn to assist their heavily beset comrades. His time for fighting would come later when the first stage of the battle was decided; then he would hurl himself on the disengaged half of a fleet whose other half had been beaten.

Let us then, above all, correct any mistaken ideas we may have imbibed from sensational writings about Nelson as a sea officer. He was not in any way merely "a bull at the gate" fighter; there were, at that time, dozens of such men in the British Navy who never rose above mere passing distinction. He was essentially a thinker and an organizer and a great leader of men.

Loyalty and single-mindedness were such marked features in his character that never would he have permitted anyone to let their adulation overstep the limits of propriety and seek to magnify Nelson at the expense of any of his Commanders-in-Chief.

His action at St. Vincent was that of a man who had a profound grasp of the essentials of fleet tactics, and the eye to size up the situation and to seize the opportunity. His doubling his ships on those of the enemy at the Nile and not disdaining to engage a ship already being engaged instead of choosing one that was not being fought, again stamps him as a tactician who could keep his thirst for glory under control.

At Copenhagen his adroitness in getting his fleet out of what might have been a disastrous dilemma again shows an appreciation of when to fight and when to retire. He mastered every detail of supply, health and gunnery of his fleet; the men consequently were healthy and his ships could be relied on to shoot with considerable accuracy.

Lastly, his tactic known as the "Nelson touch" was designed to keep half of the fleet under his immediate command, in reserve ready to help the other half and ward off any concentration on the part of the enemy. If, therefore, Nelson the great sea officer had been in command of the Grand Fleet at Jutland, we may be perfectly certain of one thing; that he would have done nothing foolish, he would never have allowed any gallery display to lead him to risk the Grand Fleet, he would never have applied Trafalgar tactics to twentieth-century fighting. It is grossly libellous to imagine he would have done so. We may be quite sure that the sound tactic was the one that would have been followed by him instantly as the occasion for it might arise.

Chapter 3

Ships – Guns – Torpedoes
Armour – Projectiles
Submarines and Mines

All of us have some conception, more or less, of the size of a modern battleship, but it is interesting to compare the *Victory*, Nelson's flagship at Trafalgar, with the *Iron Duke*, Lord Jellicoe's flagship at Jutland.

The *Victory* cost one hundred thousand pounds, the *Iron Duke* two million and eighty thousand pounds, or twenty *Victories* could have been built for the cost of the *Iron Duke*. The tonnage of the *Victory* was 2,500 tons, that of the *Iron Duke* 25,000, or ten times as much. The length of the *Victory* was 200 feet, and that of the *Iron Duke* 600 feet.

Now a few words about the different kinds of ships used in battlefleet actions. We will for clearness omit the subsidiary uses of such vessels.

The battleship is the strongest vessel afloat; that is, it has more guns and heavier armour than any other class of ship. It therefore has to be slower in speed than the more lightly armed and protected vessels, since it is impossible in a limited size of ship to have all the great qualities.

The battleship, therefore, is a hard nut to crack, and a fleet of such ships forms a solid rampart of sea power. Enemy's vessels that are not equal in strength to the battlefleet cannot count on remaining at any place without being chased away or fought by the battlefleet; and the battlefleet provides protection to which its own more lightly-armed vessels can run.

It is this concentrated power that invests a battlefleet with the ability to control oversea operations; as, for instance, the invasion of a country. Invasion can only be successful if subsequent sea-communication can be maintained between the mother country and the troops landed. The transports may, in the first place, have evaded hostile sea forces; but should the enemy's battlefleet be strong enough to dominate the line of sea-communication, no reinforcements, ammunition or other supplies can be sent to the force landed.

The value of our battlefleet in the late war was well shown by the fact that, since the German battlefleet was thoroughly dominated by Admiral

Jellicoe, our merchant vessels could use all the waters of the world with practically complete freedom from ship attack.

The battle cruiser is less heavily armed and less heavily armoured than the battleship, but it is faster. Its chief function is to scout and get in touch with the enemy and convey any   information gained to the Commander-in-Chief of the battlefleet, and, of course, incidentally, to chase and fight enemy fast cruisers. The origin and original intention of the battle cruiser was to provide a fast ship able to push home a reconnaissance through and past the enemy's cruisers.

Battle cruisers cannot usefully fight in the line of battle against battleships on account of their weaker gun fire and poor armour protection; but they can dominate the situation outside the line by controlling the activities of the enemy's cruisers and destroyers. Also during an action, by keeping in close touch with the enemy they can inform the Commander-in-Chief of his every movement.

Battle cruisers can only take a direct part in a battlefleet action if, by virtue of their speed, they have attained a position where they are at considerable tactical advantage; but such occasions are rare, since, usually, attempts of this nature can be frustrated by a watchful enemy.

The lighter cruisers are mainly of use for scouting purposes, backing up destroyers and assisting to ward off enemy destroyer attacks.

The destroyer is a fast vessel that carries its torpedoes to a place where they can be discharged at the enemy's fleet with advantage. It engages and fights enemy destroyers attempting similar attacks on its own fleet or ships. It is the deadly enemy of the submarine. Destroyers are the main defence of a fleet against submarine boat attack. A submarine hates a destroyer more than a cat hates a terrier. Not only can the destroyer ram, but it carries explosive charges to drop on the back of the submarine – a most unpleasant form of attack.

Although a battleship is the strongest unit offensively, it is weak defensively against torpedo attack. A fleet, therefore, is accompanied by destroyers to make up for this inherent weakness.

The above are the only classes of vessels that we need mention in connection with the Battle of Jutland.

Now about guns. It would take fifty of the guns carried by the *Victory* to supply sufficient iron to make the steel for one of the large guns of the *Iron Duke*; and forty-six of the round shot of Trafalgar days would be required to make one modern heavy projectile. But the advance of weight in guns from 2¾ tons to 103 tons, and from a projectile of 30lbs to one weighing close on 1,400lbs had small effect on naval tactics compared with the increase in range of the guns that took place between Trafalgar and Jutland. The heaviest gun fired at Trafalgar had a maximum range of 3,000 yards, and was extraordinarily inaccurate at such a range; at Jutland 20,000 yards could have been obtained. About 500 was considered to be a fighting range at the time Trafalgar was fought; now no action would be fought under 12,000 yards, and 15,000 yards would be the usual distance.

The difficulty of hitting a ship at long ranges is due to the impossibility of seeing exactly in what position, as regards the enemy fired at, the projectile that was last fired fell. It is obviously useless to fire away round after round if all of them are falling to the right or left, or short of, or over the ship fired at.

We can all appreciate that it is easy to see if the splash made by a projectile on striking the water is *in line* with the ship fired at; and should it happen to be in line, whether the splash was between us and the ship or beyond the ship. We can also appreciate that at seven miles distance it would be impossible to say whether a splash that was between us and the ship was 1,000 or 50 yards short of her; or, in the case of a splash on the other side of the ship, if it was 50 or 1,000 yards over her.

Now when a broadside, say, of five shell, is fired (all the guns being aimed at the same object), all the shell fortunately do not drop into the same hole in the water; there is a certain *spread*, some are beyond the others, some to the right or left of the others. It is this *spread* that enables *ranging* to be carried out. If all the splashes are seen to be *short* of the ship, the next time a broadside (or *salvo*, as it is called) is fired, then the range is put up, say, 500 yards. If still all are short, another 500 yards is added to the range. If the next *salvo* puts them all *over* then the range is dropped until some of the splashes are seen to be *over* and others to be *short*. Then the spotting officer says, "Hurrah", for he has got the enemy's ship right into the middle of his salvo and thus has found his correct range.

Many other calculations in order to allow for the change of the position of the enemy between salvos and during the time the projectile is going through the air are necessary to get good shooting, but into these we need not enter.

Now the aim and object of every good gunnery officer is to get his guns adjusted so that they make as *close a pattern* as possible. This and constant practice on the part of the control and spotting officers is necessary for a ship to hit another frequently at long range.

Well, believe me, from the point of view of winning an engagement, practice, brainwork and gunnery training are worth all the effervescent gallantry in the world. A battlefleet action in these days is no affair of mere gallantry: it is a pure case of recognizing chances and profiting by the training, practice and experience that those in command have bestowed on the fleet. You may have the most gallant admiral ever born in command of a fleet in these days, but his gallantry is worth nothing in comparison with a cool brain to calculate chances, and the gunnery excellence that he has instilled into his command by constant training. The blame for failure of ships to shoot well must fall on the admiral; others may be and, of course, are also responsible, but the success or failure of an admiral in command of a fleet in these days must, *inter alia*, be judged by the hitting power of his fleet. It is his business to see that his ships are able to shoot accurately, and he cannot be held free of blame if they fail.

And now for the torpedo.

Although fifteen years before Trafalgar was fought a steamboat was carrying passengers above water, it was not for sixty-five years after that battle that the below-water Whitehead locomotive torpedo was invented.

It is impossible here to deal with the fascinating story of the improvements in that weapon from a baby going seven miles an hour for a range of 350 yards and carrying a charge of 40lbs of black powder, to the monsters of Jutland going 25 knots for a range of 10,000 to 15,000 yards and carrying a charge of 300lbs of high explosive.

In the early days, although a torpedo, after once it had settled down on its run, would keep an even depth of 10 or 15 feet below the surface of the water without any considerable variation, its accuracy of running in a given direction left a good deal to be desired. It was, in fact, very inaccurate in direction until a gyroscope was adapted for use in its inside, which corrected any tendency to curve or deflect from the direction in which it was originally discharged. The result of this and many other improvements was that at Jutland the torpedo was a weapon that could run with reasonable accuracy for about 15,000 yards and explode a charge of 300lbs of high explosive below the water-line of a ship.

The speed of a torpedo through the water is very slow compared with the velocity of the modern projectile through the air, namely, about 50 feet per second for the torpedo, while the average velocity of a modern projectile is somewhere about 2,000 feet per second.

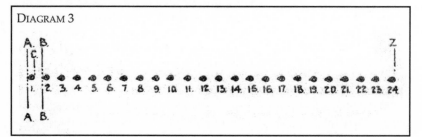

DIAGRAM 3

It is difficult enough to judge the change in position of a ship during the time a projectile is flying through the air when firing at long ranges, but it is infinitely more difficult to do so in the case of a torpedo travelling through the water. In fact it takes a torpedo ten minutes to traverse a range of 10,000 yards, and it is quite impossible to forecast where a ship would be after an interval of ten minutes in a naval action.

Moreover, although the gyroscope straightens the running of a torpedo, it cannot be expected to keep it straight enough to hit a single ship only 200 yards long at a distance of 10,000 yards. The torpedo may be written down as useless in a single-ship action at modern fighting ranges. When, however, a fleet comes to be the target the conditions are totally changed, since no longer is the object a single ship, but the target becomes a line of many ships. Let us see how this works out.

Take the example of the Grand Fleet, say with 24 battleships each about 600 feet or 200 yards long. The space from the bow of one ship to the bow of the next, A, B, was about 500 yards; the length of each ship, A, C, was 200 yards, so that the length of the space C, B was 300 yards.

Now it is easy to see that the whole line of ships from A to Z form one long target with 24 ships each 200 yards long, or 4,800 yards of ships and 23 blanks of 300 yards each.

The total length of the target was, therefore, 11,700 yards, of which 4,800 were vulnerable ships and 6,900 yards was blank space.

The chances of hitting 4,800 yards of ship compared with 6,900 yards of blank is as 48 is to 69, or nearly as two is to three, so that out of every five torpedoes fired at such a line of ships, two should hit ships and three should pass through the blanks. Moreover, the line is so long, nearly 12,000 yards, that if a torpedo were fired at the centre of the line from a distance of 10,000 yards it would have to be deflected 30 degrees to the right or left in order to miss the line.

If we have thoroughly grasped that the chances were that two torpedoes out of every five that were fired from 10,000 yards distance would hit ships of the Grand Fleet in single-line-follow-my-leader formation, we must agree that here was a very real and live danger and one which required all the wits of the Navy to minimize.

Well, of course, the problem had been discussed between naval officers for several years prior to Jutland, and Admiral Jellicoe decided, with the concurrence of all the other admirals, that the best means of defeating such an attack was to turn the ships *away* from an attack if the torpedo were fired from any position between abeam and half-way to right-ahead. This method of defeating torpedo attacks was used by:

Admiral Jellicoe in the Battle of Jutland, Phase III.

Admiral Beatty at the Dogger Bank Action.

Again by him on the way out to Jutland.

Admiral Sturdee during Phase III at Jutland.

Vice-Admiral Evan-Thomas, Phase I, Jutland.

Admiral Burney at Jutland, Phase III.

Rear-Admiral Horace Hood, Jutland, Phase II.

Admiral Hipper, Jutland, Phase I.

This matter will be referred to later; enough has been said here to show that the practice was a general and, we may add, a successful one.

Now let us consider another point, namely, the use of the torpedo when one fleet chases another. The torpedo has a speed of thirty knots. A fleet chasing another, or being chased by another, has a speed of about 20 knots.

A torpedo fired in a right-ahead direction by the chasing fleet towards a fleet they were chasing would, of course, still run its 15,000 yards through the water, but the fleet chased would be running at 20 knots speed away from the torpedo. The torpedo would run for 15 minutes, during which time the ships would have gone 10,000 yards, so that the torpedo would only have gained the difference between its 15,000 and ships 10,000 yards, or 5,000 yards, before its fuel would be exhausted and it would stop.

So it would be no good during such a chase for the chasing ships to fire at ships which are more than 5,000 yards ahead of them; and as no ship would ever be as close as this without being sunk by gun fire, the torpedo may be looked on as a useless weapon to a fleet that is chasing another.

The opposite is true for the fleet chased; for the ships that are chasing are steaming up towards the torpedo fired from the fleet that is being chased; so the distance the torpedo could run would be its own 15,000 yards *plus* the 10,000 yards of the ships steaming towards it, or 25,000 yards. It is, therefore, conceivable that a torpedo might be fired at 25,000 yards distance and still hit a pursuing ship. Of course this is an extreme case and not likely to happen in practice, but it is well to remember that the torpedoes of a fleet chasing have a maximum range of 5,000 yards, but those of the fleet chased have a possible range of 25,000 yards. The same principle applies when one ship is somewhat in front of, but not right-ahead of, another.

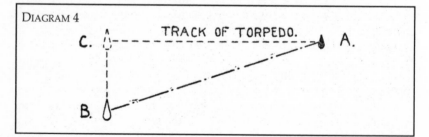

DIAGRAM 4

TRACK OF TORPEDO.

C. A.

B.

If a ship A (Diagram 4) fires a torpedo in order to hit B, she does not aim at B, but at a point C, where B will be when the torpedo reaches her. Naturally the distance A C is less than A B, which is the distance B was from A when the torpedo was fired. In fact B is steaming somewhat to meet the torpedo.

But if (Diagram 5) B fires a torpedo at A, she will have to aim well ahead of A, so that the torpedo will have to cover the distance B C while A steams A C, a very much greater distance than A was from B when the torpedo was fired.

One last point in connection with torpedoes that we must firmly fix in our minds is that the destroyer *plus* its torpedo is particularly deadly to the

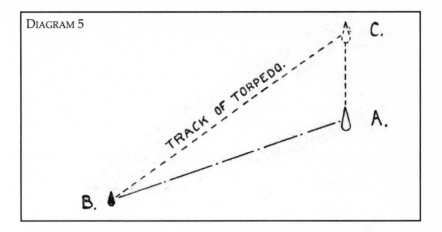

DIAGRAM 5

fleet that is chasing another. Imagine a torpedo attack on a chasing fleet of many ships with destroyers sent back from a chased fleet.

First we have the smoke of the chased fleet which hides the commencement of the attack. In the case of Jutland we would have had mist to help this.

Next the destroyers would steam at thirty knots speed towards the fleet, which would be coming up at twenty knots, or their rate of approaching one another would be fifty knots.

If the fleets were 14,000 yards apart the destroyers would arrive in among the chasing fleet in eight and a half minutes; but they could fire their torpedoes long before this. They could fire with terrible accuracy when they were 6,000 yards off, or about three and a half minutes after they had left

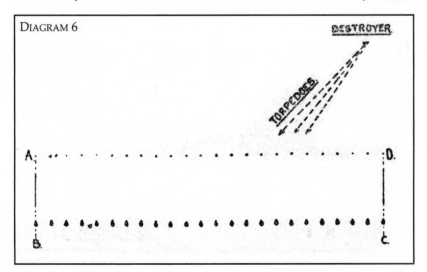

DIAGRAM 6

their own fleet. Not much time would be available for the chasing fleet to avoid the attack, especially in misty weather with volumes of smoke hiding the attack.

Diagram 6 gives an idea of such an attack.

Now if the ships kept on their chasing course they would advance from B C to A D, and the torpedo would find a good target if fired at the angle as shown. If they turned at right angles to the attack (Diagram 7) they would give the good old follow-the-leader target two in five chance of hitting.

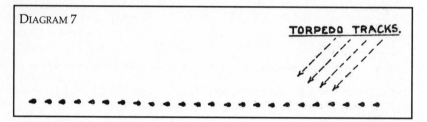

DIAGRAM 7

TORPEDO TRACKS.

If the ships, appreciating in time that the attack was being made, turned away from the attack they would lose ten minutes at the very least; and, before they could get back again on to their chasing course, the fleet chased would have increased their distance by at least 10,000 yards (Diagram 8).

So, please remember, all the advantage of torpedo fire both from the ships and also from destroyers is with the fleet chased, and such attack is a very great menace to the chasing fleet. This point will be referred to again later. To recapitulate:

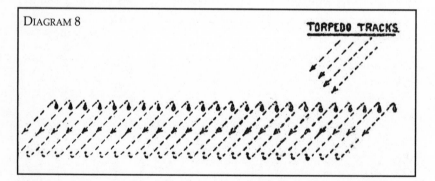

DIAGRAM 8

TORPEDO TRACKS.

(1) The chances are that two torpedoes out of every five, if fired at about 10,000 yards, will hit ships in a fleet in single-line-follow-my-leader formation. This constitutes a very great danger to a fleet.

(2) This was so serious a menace that the manoeuvre generally adopted by the admirals of the Grand Fleet and battle cruisers was to turn the large

ships away from such an attack if the attack came from any direction except right-ahead or within thirty degrees of right-ahead.

(3) The torpedo is useless to a fleet chasing, but a very deadly and valuable weapon to a fleet being chased.

Now a few words about armour and projectiles.

In "Trafalgar days" the sides of a battleship were made thicker than those of a frigate; so that an elementary idea of armour existed even then. The advent of iron afforded a material of greater protective efficiency than wood. Then steel followed on iron. But through the successive stages of development of armour the gun and projectile kept pace. Chilled shell pierced steel armour, and the greater velocity given to the projectile by improved guns, in turn, enabled them to pierce and defeat increase in thickness of the armour plates.

At last a climax in the duel was reached with Krupp cemented armour plates and cunningly hardened projectiles. This armour had a very hard chilled surface which tended to break up the projectile, but the back of the plate was made very tough so as to drag and stop it while it was forcing its way through.

In turn, shells were given soft steel caps fitted to their hardened points to afford lateral support to the delicate point while it pierced through the hardened steel face of the armour. And so this beggar-my-neighbour went on.

Now a great difficulty always faced the constructor and ordnance officer when they came to test armour or shell. The only practical method of testing a plate was to fire at it; this destroyed the plate. And the only practical method of testing the projectile was to fire it at an armour plate, and this irretrievably damaged the shell. So a compromise had to be arranged. One out of a batch of plates destined for a ship was taken by hazard and fired at; if this test proved to be satisfactory, then all were passed as probably correct. But even such a test was subject to doubt as to whether the shell fired was of standard quality. So doubt crept in in spite of every precaution.

A similar procedure was carried out with the shell. One or more of each "cast" of steel was selected and fired at a plate at a prearranged velocity. If these went through, all were passed; if they failed another sample was tried, and if that failed all the cast were condemned. Again doubt was introduced, as it was always possible that the plate might be rather weak or else a specially good one. Still, no better system could be devised. Of course there were border-line failures; that is, a projectile might just fail to get entirely through, or a plate just, and only just, fail to keep a projectile out. These failures received special consideration. The whole system left doubt, but no better methods of test have as yet been devised.

Speaking personally, and I dare say many other officers shared the same feelings, I had a haunting fear that an enemy might in peacetime develop some invention or improvement and keep it up his sleeve ready to be produced when we went to war. Guns, armour, shell, propellants, torpedoes, all presented chances of some secret.

I think we may claim that in gunnery efficiency our battleships had a decided superiority. The only matter in which the Germans had the advantage of us was in the penetrating power of their armour-piercing projectiles when striking armour at an oblique angle. This superiority was obtained by thickening the walls of the shell and therefore it entailed sacrificing the amount of bursting charge contained in the inside cavity.

The constructive reason for the tragic loss of the *Indefatigable, Queen Mary* and *Invincible,* when each of these ships blew up with a terrible explosion, requires a word of explanation.

In modern ships the heavy guns are mounted in turrets; there are generally two guns in each turret. Immediately below the turret is a circular chamber called the working chamber; and as a continuation of this a central tube some twelve feet in diameter goes right down to the bottom of the ship. All these three units – the turret, the working chamber, and the central hoist-tube – move together as the turret is swung round by the trainers to keep the guns pointing on the enemy.

In the process of loading, a cordite charge is taken from the magazine, which is close at hand, and placed in the tray of a hoist in the central tube. A shell is placed into another tray in the same hoist, and up they go to the working chamber. Here they are transferred to *waiting* trays, where they lie ready to be placed in another hoist which takes them up immediately behind the gun. The hoists in the working chamber have "flash doors" fitted to them to prevent flames finding their way down the central tube to the magazine.

There is no doubt that, when one or two charges were ignited by a shell bursting in the turrets of these doomed ships, the flash forced its way past the flash doors in the working chamber and penetrated down the central hoist, probably igniting a charge there, and so on down to the magazine. Or perhaps a direct explosion of a German projectile in close vicinity to the magazine itself may have occasioned the disaster.

A similar fate nearly overtook one of the German battle cruisers in the Dogger Bank Action. So, before the Battle of Jutland, alterations in the German magazine approaches were made which did away with the danger. Unfortunately the Dogger Bank Action did not reveal to us our weakness in this respect, so that no warning was given as to the doom that threatened the existence of our large ships in action.

A word about submarines. Submarine attack differs from destroyer attack in that it is essentially a short-range attack; moreover, is made by isolated vessels and not in mass as with destroyers. If submarines attempted to work in flotillas they would be continually bumping into each other; in fact it would be a game of blind-man's buff.

The essence of defeating submarine-boat attack is to turn *towards* the boat whenever possible, and by the threat of ramming, to put it off its stroke. The principle of the disposition of escort destroyers is to place them in such positions that the submarine is in danger of being rammed, should it take up the most favourable position for attack. Any officer of experience would turn towards a submarine attack if the boat was between right-ahead and 30 degrees before his beam and away from it if 30 degrees abaft his beam. Between 30 degrees before and 30 degrees abaft it does not matter much which way he turns.

By turning *towards* an attack made by a submarine before the beam the quickest means are being taken of reducing the size of the target your ship presents to the torpedo; and by turning *away* from a submarine attack abaft the beam the same result is obtained.

Mines. It will be found that mines are referred to in connection with destroyers. The Germans were known to have practised laying mines from their destroyers, and also from certain of their large ships, with the idea of dropping them in the path of an advancing fleet in order to blow up the leading ships. It was, therefore, well, as far as possible, to avoid steering up water through which the enemy's ships had recently passed.

Chapter 4

A Few Simple Manoeuvres

In order to understand the Battle of Jutland, it is necessary to master a few of the elementary movements of a fleet. These are very simple, in fact only matters of common sense.

Suppose you were in command of 24 large battleships, how would you arrange them? Well, the simplest way would be in a single "follow-my-leader" line. This is the simplest formation, since the leading ship steers any course it may wish and the others follow on behind, each keeping the proper distance from the ship in front of it.

What is the proper distance for the ships to be apart? Naturally the least distance at which it is safe to manoeuvre; because the nearer the ships are together the shorter and less unwieldy the line. Experience has fixed this distance at a little more than double the length of a single ship, or 500 yards.

Now the first thing that strikes us about our single line of ships is that a line of 24 ships will be very long, nearly 24 times 500 yards.[2] That is 12,000

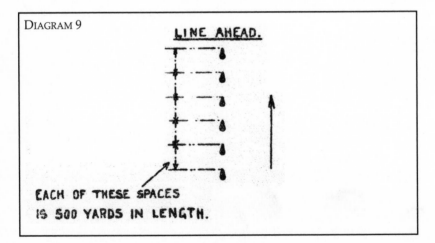

DIAGRAM 9

LINE AHEAD.

EACH OF THESE SPACES
IS 500 YARDS IN LENGTH.

yards or six sea miles. Rather a long serpent to trail about the sea! Moreover, as we have seen, a long line of ships is open to very deadly torpedo attack: two hits out of every five torpedoes fired; so, naturally, when cruising about in wartime, when submarines may be met with at any moment, some more compact arrangement is desirable.

You may say, "Why not arrange them in a line so that all the ships are abreast of each other like soldiers marching in line across a barrack square?" (Diagram 10). Well, the answer is that it is very difficult to keep accurate station when steaming like this, and experience has led to this method of progression being rarely adopted. Some half-way house is better.

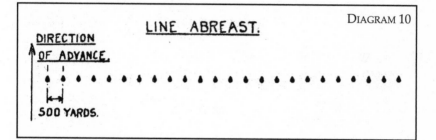

Now two lines of ships would still leave the fleet three miles long; and to cut the matter, like the fleet, short, six lines of four ships each is the formation adopted for 24 ships, as shown in Diagram 11. In this formation it is not difficult for the six leaders (each shown by a flag) to keep good station on each other; each lot of four ships finds the follow-my-leader station-keeping simplicity itself, and the length of the side of the fleet, that part open to torpedo attack, is reduced to one mile in length.

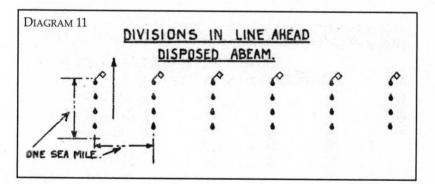

So that, had you been in an aeroplane and seen the battleships of the Grand Fleet cruising, you would have seen them arranged like the six teeth of a comb without a back to it, each tooth being made up of four ships.

Now what would you say the right distance should be for each of these six leaders to be apart? Naturally it might be necessary at any moment to bring the three ships up from behind each leader to form a single line, so the distance between each leader should be the distance taken up by three ships, or the same as a line of four ships, or nearly one mile. So our fleet now is, for cruising purposes, formed into an oblong measuring five miles along its least vulnerable side, and one mile on the side vulnerable to torpedo attack.

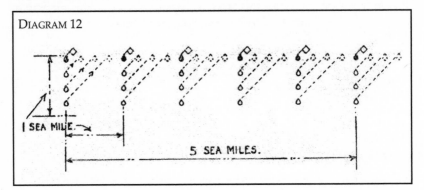

DIAGRAM 12

I SEA MILE.

5 SEA MILES.

Now, although for cruising purposes such a formation is excellent, it is a hopeless one for fighting. Stick a pin to represent an enemy in any direction you like, say a foot away from Diagram 11, and you will see that many of the ships could not fire at the pin without firing over their friends, who in turn would be obscuring clear vision with their hulls or smoke. No, to get clear gun fire for each ship we must go back to a "single line follow-my-leader" formation.

Now stick a pin away on the side of Diagram 9 and you will see that every ship can get all her guns pointing on an enemy away out on either side of the line of ships, with nothing in between to interfere with clear vision.

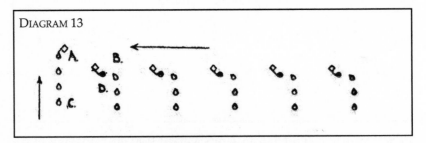

DIAGRAM 13

A

B.

D.

C.

Now how can we get from our six-teeth-of-a-comb formation into single line by a follow-my-leader method? (For follow-my-leader is the simplest

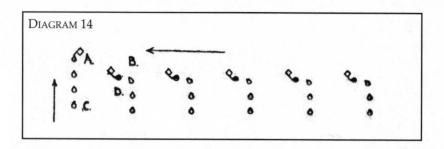

DIAGRAM 14

method of keeping accurate station.) Well, it is quite simple. Suppose we tell the leader of the left-hand tooth, shown as A in Diagram 13 to go straight on as if nothing was happening, and all the other leaders to turn to the left at right angles to the course on which they had been steaming. The distance between A and B we have seen was one mile, or a little more than the length of the line A C. Therefore C will be clear by the time D gets to the line A C, and D can turn up behind C.

Now if each ship in each of the five teeth follows its leader exactly, the whole come, first into a line D E, then each ship again turns as it comes behind the line AC. So in the end a single line is formed behind the leader A, who is still steering on the same course the fleet was on when in its cruising formation.

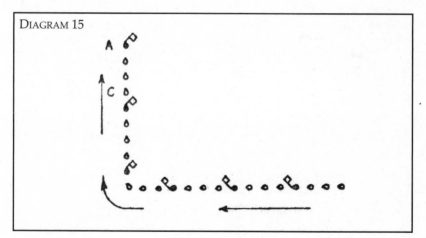

DIAGRAM 15

Now the double wriggle from the teeth-of-the-comb to single line is called *deployment*. It is absolutely necessary to grasp the manoeuvre thoroughly to understand a much disputed point in the Battle of Jutland.

It would have been equally easy to have done the manoeuvre by telling the leader of the right-hand tooth to go straight on, and the other leaders to turn *right* instead of *left*. All the other ships would then have ended behind

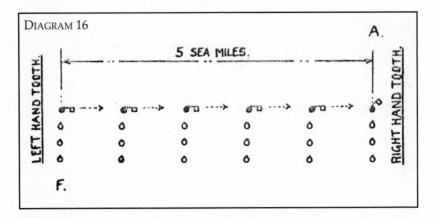

the right-hand tooth instead of the left-hand tooth; and in the end the only difference between the positions of the fleet in the two cases would have been that, after forming on the right tooth, it would be five miles more to the right than when it formed on the left-hand tooth.

One more small matter; namely, what is the time taken by the manoeuvre? Well, suppose the ships to steam 20 miles per hour, the last ship F would have to traverse a distance equal to the length of the whole line of 24 ships, or six miles. Now 20 miles per hour is the same as one mile in every three minutes, so the manoeuvre would take 18 minutes to complete; quite a long time if by any chance you were in a hurry to fight the enemy.

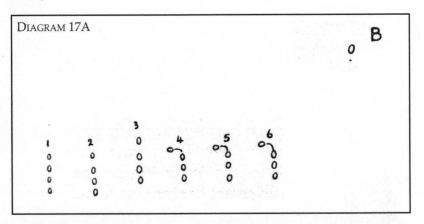

There is one point to note: any division could be ordered to steam straight on, as say, No.3 (Diagram 17A); and Nos. 4, 5 and 6 could be ordered to form as I have previously described. But Nos. 1 and 2 would be left at a loose end. They would have to steam on until column 6 was in

Above left: The 1st Earl Beatty (17 January 1871 – 11 March 1936) whilst a Vice Admiral.
(Historic Military Press)

Above right: Admiral John Jellicoe (5 December 1859 – 20 November 1935), pictured
wearing the uniform of Admiral of the Fleet, the rank he attained in 1919. (US Library of
Congress)

Below: The British Grand Fleet on its way to meet the warships of Imperial German
Navy's High Seas Fleet in the North Sea on 31 May 1916. (NARA)

Above: The bow and stern of HMS *Invincible* sticking out of the water as the battlecruiser sinks. The destroyer HMS *Badger* is desperately searching for survivors. *Invincible*'s remains were first located in 1919 and she was found to have been blown in half by the explosion. Pieces of the wreckage rest on a sandy bottom near each other, the stern right-side up and the bow upside-down. The roof of the aft 12-inch turret is missing, the guns still loaded. (Historic Military Press)

Below: Damage caused to a British light cruiser at Jutland. Unfortunately, it is not known which of the light cruisers damaged this is. Two, HMS *Black Prince* and HMS *Tipperary*, were sunk, whilst HMS *Southampton* was the light cruiser hit the most times – with eighteen shells striking her. (Historic Military Press)

Taken from the deck of HMS *Inflexible*, the next ship astern, this picture shows the massive plume of smoke caused when HMS *Invincible* exploded during the Battle of Jutland after she was hit five times by shells from the German battlecruisers *Derfflinger* and *Lützow*. The last hit blew the roof off 'Q' Turret and set fire to the cordite propellant. The flash soon spread to the magazine and *Invincible* was ripped in two by the explosion. She sank with the loss of all but six of her crew of 1,021 (though the number of survivors varies from account to account). One of the survivors, Gunnery Officer Hubert Dannreuther, was the godson of the composer Richard Wagner. Admiral Hood was among the dead. (Historic Military Press)

HMS *Royal Oak*, HMS *Acasta*, HMS *Benbow*, HMS *Superb* and HMS *Canada* in action during the battle. The latter had originally been built for the Chilean Navy, but was purchased by the British on the outbreak of war in 1914. During the Battle of Jutland, HMS *Canada* fired forty-two rounds from her 14-inch guns and 109 6-inch shells. She suffered no hits or casualties. Amongst the targets engaged was the cruiser *Wiesbaden*. (Historic Military Press)

Left: The Royal Navy's battlecruiser HMS *Indomitable* pictured in port. She damaged the German battlecruisers *Seydlitz* and *Derfflinger* during the Battle of Jutland. (US Library of Congress)

Below: Damage to SMS *Derfflinger* pictured after the Battle of Jutland. During the course of the engagement, *Derfflinger* was hit seventeen times by heavy calibre shells and nine times by secondary guns. She was in dock for repairs until 15 October 1916. *Derfflinger* fired 385 shells from her main battery, another 235 rounds from her secondary guns, and one torpedo. (Bundesarchiv, Bild 134-B2100/CC-BY-SA)

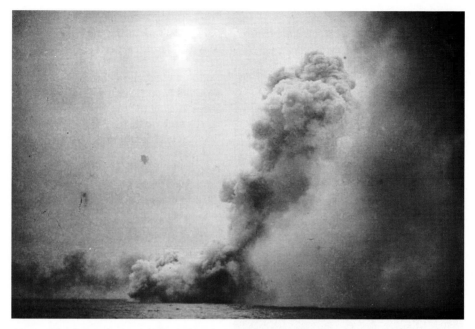

Above: The funeral pyre of HMS *Queen Mary* during the Battle of Jutland. After a German salvo had hit this battlecruiser amidships, her bows plunged down and her stern rose high in the air. A few minutes later there was nothing to be seen but this pillar of smoke rising hundreds of feet into the air. All but nine of her 1,266 crew were lost – two of the survivors were picked up by German ships. (Historic Military Press)

Above: HMS *Lion* leading the battlecruisers during the Battle of Jutland. At one point in the battle, a heavy shell struck HMS *Lion*'s Q-turret, entered the gun-house, burst over the left gun, and killed nearly the whole of the guns' crews. It was only the actions of Major F.J.W. Harvey, RMLI that saved the flagship from sudden destruction; in spite of both his legs being shot off he was able to pass the word down to close the magazine doors and flood the magazines. Harvey thus prevented the fire which had started from reaching the ammunition, an action for which he was posthumously awarded the Victoria Cross. (Historic Military Press)

Top Left: The German battlecruiser SMS *Seydlitz* on fire during the fighting on 31 May 1916. (NARA)

Middle Left: A chunk of armour knocked from HMS *New Zealand*'s 'X' Turret during the Battle of Jutland. It can be seen on display at the Torpedo Bay Navy Museum in Auckland.

Below: The German battleship SMS *Schleswig-Holstein* fires a salvo during the Battle of Jutland. (NARA)

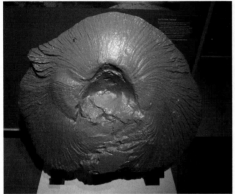

Above: The Revenge-class battleship HMS *Royal Oak*. Completed in 1916, *Royal Oak* first saw action at the Battle of Jutland. (US Library of Congress)

Below: British and German sailors buried side by side in Frederikshavn Cemetery. Pictured here during the 1920s, the British memorial is on the left; the German one nearest the camera. Frederikshavn is a port in northern Jutland, about twenty-five miles from the northernmost point of Denmark. Buried there are four First World War casualties, all naval ratings killed in the Battle of Jutland. (Historic Military Press)

Above and Below: A surprising relic from Jutland – the last surviving warship that participated in the battle which is still afloat. HMS *Caroline*, a C-class light cruiser, was built by Cammell Laird at Birkenhead, and launched in December 1914. Along with her sister ships of the Fourth Light Cruiser Squadron, HMS *Caroline* formed part of the anti-submarine screen for the Royal Navy battleships as they rushed south towards the German battlecruisers. During the main battle she took part in the destroyer clash between the main fleets; towards the end of this main action, her squadron caught sight of a group of German capital ships, believed to be their battlecruisers and pre-dreadnaught battleships, and fired two torpedoes at them. (Courtesy of NI Science Park)

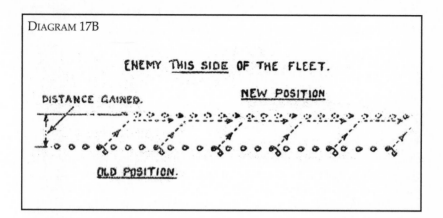

station and then turn up, or they would have to reduce speed and edge in behind. In any case the mobility of the fleet would be reduced and the columns 1, 2 and 3 would form a bunched target to an enemy firing guns or torpedoes from a direction B.

We have now brought all the ships into single line ready to fight the enemy (Diagram 17B); and we have the ships that were the leaders of each tooth of the comb (the ones with the flag) spread along the line, each with its three ships behind it, so if we want to "sidle" the whole fleet towards, or away, from the enemy we can tell all the leaders to turn a small amount towards or away, to the right or left, and their own ships to follow them; and when the desired amount *to* or *from* the enemy has been gained, we tell the leaders again to turn together back to the old direction and their ships to follow them round. Our single line will then again be formed, but the fleet has been sidled to the right or left.

When a line of ships is steaming in single line follow-the-leader formation and the admiral desires to turn the line round to steam in exactly the opposite direction, he can do it in two ways – (Diagram 17C) either he can turn the leader and let each ship follow round the same point (this is called altering course in *succession* – ships are altering in *succession* round the point A) or he can tell each ship to turn at the same moment (Diagram 17D).

All ships then put over their helms at the same instant and each ship turns on the spot it happens to be. It will be seen that the great advantage

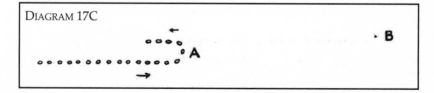

of the latter turn, the turn *together*, is that, supposing it is necessary to avoid an enemy at B, the whole fleet can be made to steam away from him in the shortest time possible; whereas by the turn in *succession* the whole of the ships are dragged in turn round the point A under fire of his guns. Eighteen minutes would elapse before a fleet of 24 ships could be completely turned in succession, whereas the turn *together* would only take a little under three minutes to complete.

One word about gunnery as allied to tactics. Battleship tactics are mainly the handmaiden of gunnery: they exist to help to bring the greatest volume of *hitting* on to the enemy. As the volume of hitting not only depends on volume of fire, but also on the accuracy of that fire, the less ships are swung about at the time they are firing at the enemy the better. Hence violent alterations of course while the ships are actually engaged are bad.

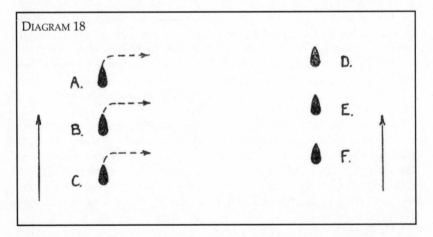

It may seem natural to the layman to say perhaps if, as in Diagram 18, A B C suddenly sight D E F out of the mist, why not turn on them at once and try to squeeze closer quickly in that way?

The reason for not doing so is that by so doing you would give the enemy two great points of advantage. *First*, your own hitting would be entirely upset while your ships were swinging round; and all this time the enemy's hitting would be helped by your slow advance from the point at which you were turning. *Secondly*, you would only have your four right-ahead guns bearing on the enemy instead of the ten you could use on the broadside; and all the time you would be slated by the ten guns of each of the enemy's ships.

So, although at first sight such a proposal might appear seductive, second thoughts, and abstention, are by far the best.

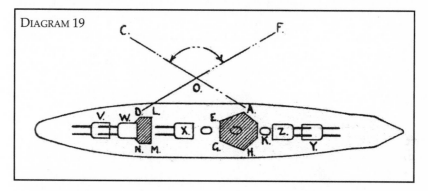

Let us now look at how the guns in a ship are placed. Take a deck plan of the *Iron Duke* as she would look viewed from an aeroplane.

Now it is necessary to have the funnels and masts and other obstructions on the upper deck of ships; these are reduced to a minimum, but they still exist; they are shown by the shaded parts at A E G H K, D L M N. The guns cannot fire through these, so that the arc of gun fire is limited. Hence in firing ahead W turret is checked by D L M, and X turret is checked by A E G H K. The same obstruction checks Z turret in firing astern.

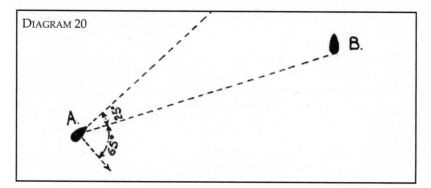

Speaking roughly, the whole of the gun fire of a ship can only be obtained through the arc of C O F, which is approximately from 60 degrees before to 60 degrees abaft the beam.

Any ship visible in a direction between D F and right-ahead cannot be shot at by W turret, V turret or X turret. This has a very important bearing on tactics, for obviously if, A sights an enemy B (Diagram 20), the enemy B can shoot at A with all his guns; whereas A can shoot at him with only the four guns that point ahead. A will therefore turn at once till all his guns will bear (Diagram 21). B will probably turn up parallel to A also and still keep all his guns bearing on A, and A cannot get closer to B unless he can steam faster than B. But B, being ahead of A, is in a better position to fire torpedoes at A.

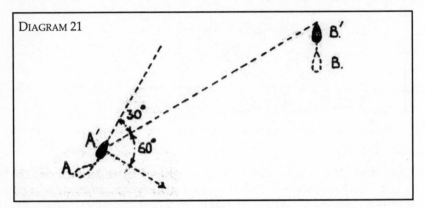

DIAGRAM 21

So remember, a ship is not able to close on an enemy merely because he is sighted ahead, unless the ship foolishly likes to allow ten guns to fire at her while she can only reply with four. She must therefore turn till she gets all her guns bearing on him. He can then turn parallel to her course and keep his distance. Also she is in a bad position from considerations of torpedo attack.

The same principle applies when two fleets meet. This is then called crossing the T.

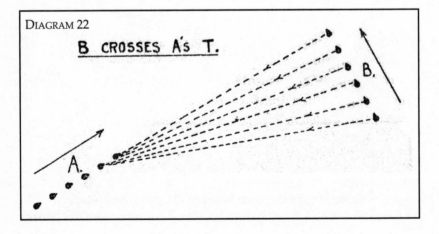

DIAGRAM 22

B CROSSES A's T.

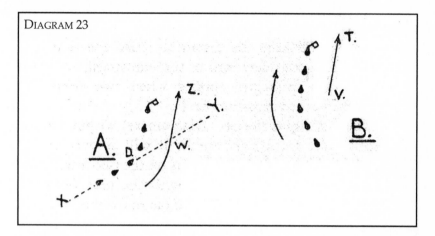

DIAGRAM 23

If fleet A sights fleet B (Diagram 22) within a bearing of 30 degrees from right-ahead, B will at once open fire with all its ships and all their guns on the two leading ships of fleet A. A can only reply with the four right-ahead guns of its leading ships, and the range for the other ships gets longer and longer the nearer they are to the tail of the line. So A must at once alter course to W Z (Diagram 23) to get all the guns of each ship to bear as it turns at the point D. But the unequal action will continue until all A's ships have passed D.

If B does not want to let A close him, he alters course to a direction V T, parallel to W Z, and still slates A with all the guns of all the ships.

The fact that sighting a fleet ahead does not mean that you can necessarily close it is a point generally overlooked by the casual critic. This will be referred to later, so let us get it well into our minds.

There is one term that requires a little explanation, and that is *chasing* a fleet or a ship. To "chase" does not necessarily mean to run behind, such as a ship A (Diagram 24) running after a ship B. Of course, in such a case A is chasing B, but the two ships can only bring their right-ahead and right-astern fire respectively to bear on each other.

Chase far more often assumes the condition (Diagram 25) where A and B can both bring all their guns to bear on each other. A is still chasing B in that she is behind her, and as soon as B is disabled can gobble her up, but the ships are not *directly* one behind the other.

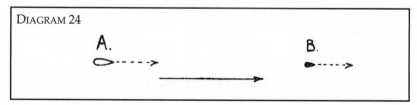

DIAGRAM 24

A.

B.

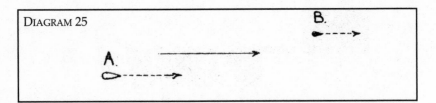

DIAGRAM 25

A.

B.

There is one manoeuvre that I have kept till the end. It was not used at Jutland, but in all probability it would have been had our battle cruisers on joining the battlefleet been able to give Admiral Jellicoe exact information regarding the whereabouts of the German battlefleet.

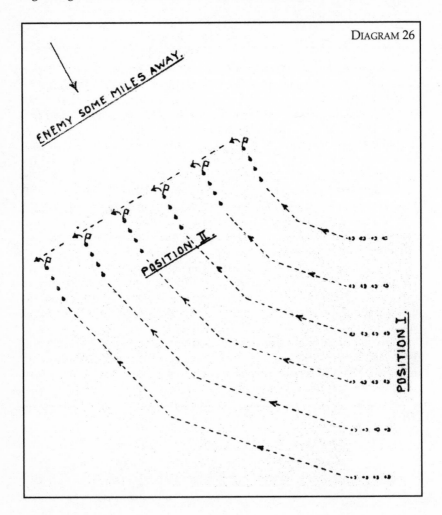

DIAGRAM 26

ENEMY SOME MILES AWAY.

POSITION II.

POSITION I.

If a fleet is cruising in the tooth-of-a-comb formation and the enemy is reported some miles off, steering as shown by the arrow, (Diagram 26) the fleet can be wheeled as shown into position II. It can then go on steaming in this direction, and when the enemy is sighted a simple turn on the part of each leader together, and then the three ships behind them following round, brings the whole fleet into line across the enemy's path.

This is called *Direct Deployment*.

The time taken depends of course on the angle of the wheel; but, as this is done before the enemy is sighted, the time taken is not of importance.

The time taken to form single line from position II is only three minutes, instead of the eighteen minutes required for the deployment on the right or left hand tooth – a matter of great advantage.

Chapter 5

General Description of
The Battle of Jutland

We will now give a brief outline of the Battle of Jutland, and then deal with each phase in greater detail.

PHASE I

(1) The Battle Cruiser Fleet, composed of six of our battle cruisers, together with the 5th Battle Squadron, which consisted of four of our fastest battleships, as well as 14 light cruisers and 27 destroyers, all under Admiral Beatty, met five of the German battle cruisers, five light cruisers and 22 destroyers. Our six cruisers engaged the German five cruisers for three quarters of an hour and inflicted no serious damage on them, but two of our cruisers were sunk by German gun fire. The 5th Battle Squadron was in action for a quarter of an hour only.

(2) Our battle cruisers sighted the German High Sea Battlefleet and immediately turned and steamed back to the Grand Fleet, engaging the German battle cruisers at intervals on the way. The 5th Battle Squadron engaged the leading ships of the German High Sea Fleet and, at intervals, the German battle cruisers.

(3) Our battle cruisers on the run north lost touch with the German High Sea Battlefleet, so that when Admiral Beatty in the *Lion* sighted the *Iron Duke* (Admiral Jellicoe's flagship) he was unable to report the position of the High Sea Fleet, which information was absolutely vital to the Commander-in-Chief to enable him to determine on which tooth of the comb to deploy, or whether to wheel the fleet ready for a direct deployment.

PHASE II

The cruisers ahead of the Grand Fleet while engaging some of the German light cruisers came under the fire of the leading ships of the German battle cruisers and battle-fleet as they emerged from the mist, and the *Invincible* and *Defence* were sunk.

PHASE III

The reckoning of the Grand Fleet was in error four miles to the east, that of the *Lion* seven miles to the west. Admiral Jellicoe therefore put the position of the *Lion*, and consequently the approximate position of the German Fleet, eleven miles different from what it really was. This error could only have been corrected by the reception of exact information from the *Lion* as to the position of the German Battlefleet when she sighted the *Iron Duke*.

Admiral Jellicoe, in vague doubt as to the exact position of his enemy, deployed on his left hand tooth. The advantages of deploying on this tooth and not on the right-hand tooth were:

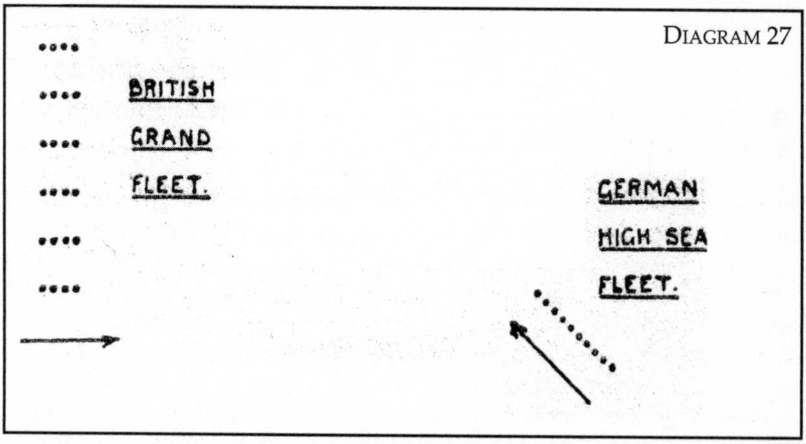

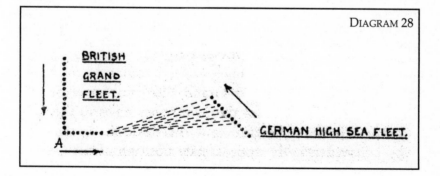

DIAGRAM 27

(1) He estimated the German Fleet to be somewhat as shown in Diagram 27. If he deployed on his right-hand tooth he expected the German Fleet would have crossed his T. This was quite enough to determine his deployment on the left hand, for then (Diagram 29) he crossed the German Fleet's T. This is what actually happened, and our battleships gave the leading German battleships a very warm time.

DIAGRAM 28

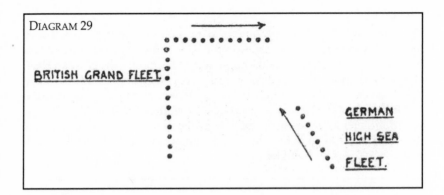

(2) Another reason for deploying on the left-hand tooth was to interpose our fleet between the German High Sea Fleet and their harbour. This is broadly shown in Diagram 30.

Owing to Admiral Jellicoe's masterly deployment the leading ships of the German High Sea Battlefleet sighted our battlefleet right-ahead, and those ships, as we have said, received a good hammering.

Admiral Scheer therefore turned and ran, using what he called "a short turn" movement, which in plain English was that every ship in his fleet turned and ran away from ours as fast as their engines would carry them. Almost immediately they were lost in the mist and the extent of the turn could not be seen by Admiral Jellicoe.

Admiral Jellicoe had now to think quickly. There were two possibilities. Either (a) the enemy's ships had run out of sight under cover of the mist to turn into a line parallel to that of our fleet; or (b) they had run away.

If (a), then the Grand Fleet would come across them again if he closed the enemy gradually by altering course towards the place where they had last been seen; this would also bring him between them and their harbour.

If (b), he could never catch them up because his speed was insufficient, and he had only two and a half hours before nightfall in which to attempt to do so.

If he had chased he would have left the road to their harbour open for them, and therefore such an action would have been grossly idiotic as well as also extremely hazardous. But by closing and feeling for them he managed to get the Grand Fleet in between them and their port. So he closed by successive alterations in course towards the enemy.

When Admiral Scheer pulled himself together he found that instead of running *towards* his harbour he was running to the westward right *away* from it; so he formed his fleet again into line and steered so as to pass astern of our fleet to make for the passage at the Horn Reef which led him back to his harbour. But, to his intense disgust, for the second time he ran into our

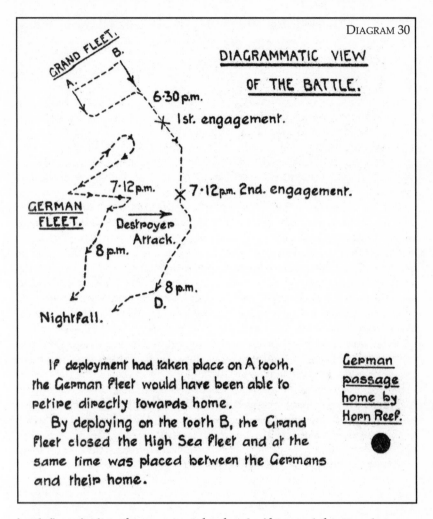

DIAGRAM 30

DIAGRAMMATIC VIEW OF THE BATTLE.

GRAND FLEET.
A.
B.
6·30 p.m.
1st. engagement.
7·12 p.m.
7·12 p.m. 2nd. engagement.
GERMAN FLEET.
Destroyer Attack.
8 p.m.
8 p.m.
D.
Nightfall.

If deployment had taken place on A tooth, the German Fleet would have been able to retire directly towards home.

By deploying on the tooth B, the Grand Fleet closed the High Sea Fleet and at the same time was placed between the Germans and their home.

German passage home by Horn Reef.

battlefleet, finding them again right ahead of him and this time between him and his harbour. Again he got a hammering.

So bad was this pounding that he made a flamboyant signal to his battle cruisers and destroyers to charge the Grand Fleet and save the High Sea Fleet; which they did most gallantly, and of course, in so doing, got badly mauled, while he, with the battlefleet, for the second time was forced to run away from his harbour.

Darkness now fell on the two fleets, with Admiral Jellicoe between Admiral Scheer and his harbour.

There were three principal passages through the German minefield: one on a bearing of about S.S.E. and 85 miles distant, another bearing about

137

south and 160 miles distant. The third lay between the other two. Which was he going to make for? The only way to cover all three was to keep the fleet steaming south and extend the length of the battle-fleet by spreading the destroyer divisions out behind to attack the enemy if he tried to force his way through.

It was the duty of all ships to give warning to the Commander-in-Chief if any of the enemy's large ships were sighted. Much depended upon the look-out kept by the Grand Fleet, which had been specially lengthened for look-out purposes.

Here Admiral Jellicoe was badly served. Two battleships, the *Malaya* and *Valiant*, one light cruiser, the *Champion*, and five destroyers all sighted the enemy's large ships.

All except *Faulknor* failed to report that the enemy's battlefleet were passing through the destroyers in the rear of our fleet; and the *Faulknor*'s signal, probably jammed by the Germans, never got through. Hence the High Sea Fleet passed behind the Grand Fleet and entered their swept passage through the minefields in the early morning.

Had Admiral Jellicoe received a report from any of the vessels that the large German ships were breaking through astern, the battlefleet could have again been placed in front of the Germans, and would have engaged them at daylight.

Such was Jutland. It proved what everyone already knew, that you cannot make an enemy fight if he does not want to fight, unless you have greater speed and sufficient daylight in which to overtake him; or unless you can get between him and his harbour and keep there till he does fight. Admiral Jellicoe had neither speed nor sufficient daylight to force a decisive action; so he adopted the latter course; and had it not been for the failure of ships to report sighting the large ships of the enemy, *which it was their very first duty instantly to do*, the Germans would have been headed off their harbour and brought to action at daylight.

Chapter 6

Phase I:
The Battle Cruiser Action

The German plan of operations that led directly up to the Battle of Jutland was a simple one. Admiral Scheer's plan was to bombard Sunderland with his battle cruisers. This port was not far from Rosyth, where our battle cruisers were lying. Twenty-two submarines were to be stationed off our coasts to attack the various portions of our fleet as they put to sea. If any of the battle cruisers got through this screen of submarines, Admiral Hipper, with the German battle cruisers, was to entice them down to be crushed by the German battlefleet. The whole operation was to be helped by airship scouting. Thick weather which persisted for nearly a fortnight prevented airship scouting, by which time the submarines had approached the limit of their endurance. The plan had therefore to be put into operation without the assistance of the airships. Had these been with him, ample warning that our battlefleet had put to sea would have been conveyed to Admiral Scheer and Jutland would never have been fought.

Our Admiralty soon discovered that there was something special afoot, and warned Admiral Jellicoe that the German Fleet might go to sea.[3]

On May 30 an operation signal, undecipherable at Whitehall, was made to the German Fleet. Orders were therefore sent to Admiral Jellicoe and Admiral Beatty to concentrate as usual at a rendezvous in the North Sea. Whether the German operation would be aimed at the East Coast of England or the English Channel no one knew. The whole of the Grand Fleet was at sea by 10.30 p.m. on May 30.

Admiral Beatty left Rosyth, having with him a force consisting of 6 battle cruisers, 4 fast battleships, 14 light cruisers and 27 destroyers. The four battleships had been specially placed under his command by the Commander-in-Chief to take the place of the 3rd Battle Cruiser Squadron which was carrying out gunnery exercises at Scapa.

Shortly after two o'clock in the afternoon of May 31 a chance steamer brought the two cruiser fleets into contact. The German cruiser admiral detached a destroyer to look at the steamer, and at the same time Captain Alexander-Sinclair in the *Galatea* took a look at her also. The destroyer sighted the *Galatea*'s smoke. The German light cruisers altered course to investigate, and the *Galatea* sighted and reported them. Both battle cruiser squadrons moved to support their smaller vessels, and at 3.20 the two battle cruiser fleets sighted each other.

Let us follow very carefully the movements of the battle cruiser fleet.

Admiral Beatty had been cruising with the 5th Battle Squadron five miles distant from the battle cruisers. There no justifiable reason for these two units being so far apart on a N.N.W. bearing. The Admiral should have chosen a cruising formation which would have allowed line of battle to be formed in the shortest possible time, or one which would have stationed the slower ships nearest to the German base. This dispersion was a tactical error.

The only reason that has been advanced for this formation is that Admiral Beatty expected shortly to sight our Grand Fleet. The battle cruisers and the 5th Battle Squadron would, when in this formation, have been in their relatively correct positions, one to form ahead and the other astern of the battleships. This in no way excuses the adoption of such a formation when cruising in wartime. There would have been ample time to assume this purely evolutionary formation after the Battle Fleet had been sighted.

At 2.20 *Galatea* reported: "Urgent. Two cruisers probably hostile in sight bearing E.S.E."[4] Clearly the first thing for the Admiral to do was to close up his capital ships. This he did not do. In twelve minutes he could have repaired the original error of dispersion; moreover, this time was available, as it was not till 2.32 p.m. that he signalled to the whole fleet to alter course to S.S.E.

Then, without making certain that the 5th Battle Squadron had received the signal to alter course,[5] he, full of ardour, raced away at high speed. His signal staff failed to repeat so important a signal by searchlight. The result was that owing to delay in receiving the alter-course signal the distance of the 5th Battle Squadron from the battle cruisers was increased to *ten miles*.

This was the action of an impulsive fighter but not that of an experienced Admiral. Now what was the result?

Admiral Hipper, commanding the German cruisers, came on until he sighted our cruisers, and, owing to this helter-skelter way of bringing our battle cruiser fleet into action, instead of our battleships being in the line of battle with the battle cruisers, when the action began they were several miles away. Had our battle cruiser fleet been closed up, the ensuing action, instead of being practically a defeat for our ships, might well have been a brilliant success. Annihilation should always be the result aimed at. Annihilation can only be achieved by numbers.

The *Admiralty Narrative* excuses Admiral Beatty and places the blame for not closing up on Admiral Evan-Thomas, by saying that "an admiral commanding a squadron sighting, or in touch with, the enemy would anticipate that his supporting squadron would close without further orders".[6] No such assumption can absolve the senior officer from not having ordered the squadron to close. Nor is the statement fair to Admiral Evan-Thomas.

At 1.30 p.m. Admiral Beatty had definitely stationed the 5th Battle Squadron N.N.W. five miles from his flagship, and the senior officer of the squadron had no right to depart from that station without orders. The 5th Battle Squadron had, by the stationing signal, become a definite part of the cruiser fleet and was no longer an independent squadron.

No general instructions as to the conduct of the 5th Battle Squadron when in action with the battle cruisers seem to have been issued by Admiral Beatty before sailing. It was the business of the Admiral in command to concentrate his fleet and to help the concentration as much as possible himself. In this he failed when an experienced admiral would have succeeded, and his battle cruisers paid dearly for the omission, and the nation missed what should have been an annihilating victory.

Meanwhile Admiral Jellicoe was steering to his rendezvous, and, having been definitely informed by the Admiralty that the German Battlefleet were not at sea, he was saving the fuel of his destroyers and steaming only at 15 knots.

The reason for this misapprehension was a simple one. The German Battlefleet flagship had exchanged its wireless call-up sign with a shore station, so that as the call sign remained in harbour, apparently the flag ship was still there also, although in reality she had put to sea.[7]

Immediately on receiving a wireless report that the German battle cruisers had been sighted, Admiral Jellicoe stopped zigzagging, worked up to full speed, and sent the three battle cruisers attached to his fleet to reinforce Admiral Beatty.

About 3.20 the two battle cruiser fleets sighted each other; the German Admiral fulfilled the role which had been given him and fell back towards his battlefleet, drawing, of course, our ships with him.

At 3.45 the German and English battle cruiser squadrons opened fire at about 16,000 yards; the 5th Battle Squadron was not able to open fire *until thirty minutes later*.[8] Had the 5th Battle Squadron been closed up, Admiral Hipper would have caught a veritable Tartar, and would, without doubt, have lost two or more of his cruisers.

The visibility of the enemy from our ships was not good. The enemy here had an advantage.

As there were only five German cruisers to our six, the *Lion* ordered, by signal, both our two leading ships to fire on the ship leading the German line, and for each of the other ships to fire at her opposite number, counting from the *rear* of the German line. The third and fourth ships in our line missed the signal and therefore counted from the *bow*, hence the second ship in the German line was left unfired at. A very fatal blunder reflecting gravely on the signal organization of the battle cruisers.[9]

The distribution of fire, owing to this error, was thus:

Lutzow at *Lion* and *Princess Royal;*
Derfflinger and *Seydlitz* at *Queen Mary;*
Moltke at *Tiger* and *New Zealand;*
Von der Tann at *Indefatigable.*

The fire was rapid, but on our side not good; the visibility was against us, and a destroyer division helped to obscure the enemy with its smoke; but, even so, our gunnery was poor. Our ships were hit several times, but we inflicted little damage on the enemy. Shortly after four o'clock the *Indefatigable* received a shell in her magazine, blew up and disappeared in a pall of smoke.

It was not till 4.5 p.m. that Admiral Evan-Thomas and the 5th Battle Squadron sighted the German battle cruisers. Our battle cruisers had then for a short time withdrawn out of range of the German battle cruisers, and the absence of their smoke revealed the German ships to our battleships.[10]

At 4.15 *Barham,* the flagship of the 5th Battle Squadron, opened fire at about 18,000 yards range. Her firing was reported by the Germans to have been magnificent, and this in spite of the fact that owing to the great range, and the smoke when the Germans again opened fire, the 5th Battle Squadron officers could see little to aim at through the haze and smoke.[11]

What a tragedy that they, good gunnery ships, had not commenced the action at the same time as the battle cruisers!

At 4.26, while the *Queen Mary* was being engaged by the *Seydlitz* and *Derfflinger,* a salvo struck her upper deck, penetrated below, and, with one loud explosion, she immediately sank. Her magazine had been fired by the plunging salvo.

The German destroyers now advanced to deliver an attack. The leader of the German flotilla saw the plight in which his battle cruisers were now that the 5th Battle Squadron had joined in the engagement and had found their range. He therefore determined to attack the 5th Battle Squadron in order to relieve his friends from the scouring they were undergoing.

Shortly before this move on the part of the German destroyers, Commander Hon. E. Bingham in the *Nestor,* leading our 13th Destroyer Flotilla, had also seen an opportunity to bring off an attack, and had already commenced to race across the water separating the two fleets. As soon as he saw the German destroyers advancing, he turned straight towards them and broke up their attack, forcing them to fire their torpedoes at so long a range that none reached our 5th Battle Squadron.[12]

At the conclusion of the mêlée the only destroyer left with the *Nestor* was the *Nicator*, Lieutenant-Commander Beattie. Yet these two solitary vessels went on to carry out their attack, and arrived undamaged within 5,000 yards of the *Lutzow*, where they let fly two torpedoes.

The German battle cruisers turned away and foiled the attack, but on went Commander Bingham again until he got within 3,500 yards. Again the enemy dodged, and *Nestor* and *Nicator* came back in a veritable hail of shell. The *Official History* gives the following inimitable description of the end of this fight.

By this time Lieutenant-Commander Thompson, in the *Petard*, having become separated from his division, was endeavouring to attack with the *Turbulent*, followed by the *Nerissa* and *Termagant*, as well as the *Morris* and *Moorsom* of the 9th Flotilla, who had attached themselves to the party.

In the first onset he had fired a torpedo at the leading German destroyer, *V 27*, which seems to have taken deadly effect, for she was soon seen to be lying stopped with her decks awash, but all the boats were too much engaged in the mêlée with the enemy's destroyers to be able to get at the squadron. It was a wild scene of groups of long, low forms vomiting heavy trails of smoke, and dashing hither and thither at thirty knots or more through the smother and splashes and all in a rain of shell from the secondary armament of the German battle cruisers as well as from the *Regensburg* and the destroyers, with the heavy shell of the contending squadrons screaming overhead.

Gradually a pall of gun and funnel smoke almost hid the shell-tormented sea, and beyond the fact that the German torpedo attack was crushed, little could be told of what was happening, when at 4.43 the *Lion* ran up the destroyers' recall. As they all turned to obey it was seen that midway between the lines the *Nestor*'s first antagonist, *V 27*, and another destroyer, *V 29*, were sinking.

Near to them was the *Nomad* in a like condition, and as the *Petard* ran back she came across the *Nestor* hardly able to crawl. Commander Bingham, in dodging back from his second gallant attack, had had two boilers put out of action by the *Regensburg*. The *Petard* offered him a tow, but he refused to expose another destroyer to what looked like certain destruction.

At 4.33 the *Southampton*, light cruiser, Commodore Goodenough, sighted the German battlefleet. At 4.40 Admiral Beatty promptly and quite properly altered course right round and made for the Grand Fleet. Again the signal to alter course never reached the 5th Battle Squadron,[13] which carried on until eight minutes later, when they actually passed the battle cruisers, who were well on their return journey; they then turned also, but owing to the delay they were, after turning, only about 17,000 to 18,000 yards from the leading ships of the German Battlefleet.

The *Nomad* and *Nicator* had perforce to be left to their fate. Their crews were taken off by the Germans and the boats sunk.

A desultory action was carried on between the British and German battle cruisers on the run north. By 5 o'clock Admiral Beatty had lost sight of the German Battlefleet.

The following table gives the distances the *Lion* was from the German Battlefleet on the run back to the Grand Fleet.[14]

Time	Distance from German battlefleet (yards)	Remarks
4.40	24,000	The German Battlefleet was in sight.
5.0	22,000	Lost sight of German Battlefleet through gathering mist. Battle cruisers had turned to N.W.
5.20	24,000	German Battlefleet out of sight.
5.40	21,000	German Battlefleet out of sight.
5.56	19,000	Joined Grand Fleet. German Battlefleet out of sight.
6.14	14,000	Sighted German Battlefleet again.

At 5 p.m. the German battle cruisers were dimly visible when 17,000 yards away. The German Battlefleet at 22,000 yards must have been well out of sight. The 5th Battle Squadron came north, fighting the leading ships of the German Battlefleet, and also at times the German battle cruisers, until at 5.30 the fight was gradually broken off, to be renewed again on joining up with the Grand Fleet battleships at 6.10.

A torpedo attack was made by the *Onslow* and the *Moresby* destroyers, and torpedoes were fired, but the attack was unsuccessful though gallantly attempted.

Thus ended Phase I of Jutland, when a British force was worsted by a squadron of one half its strength, our losses being two battle cruisers and the *Lion* badly damaged, while the enemy suffered little. And why? Because our Admiral in command was inexperienced and showed no tactical ability. Apparently he forgot the existence of the four battleships that had been specially put under his command and also the light cruisers that were attached to his fleet. At all events he failed to co-ordinate their movements to those of the battle cruisers.

Except for a signal to the battleships at 3.35 p.m. to alter course to east (three minutes after the same signal had been made to the battle cruisers), not a single signal was made specially to the battleships until after the turn north had been carried out by the battle cruisers;[15] nor was a single signal made specially to the light cruisers between 3 p.m. and 5.47 p.m.; their existence was practically ignored.[16]

What a chance existed in the action, both on the run south and on the run north! But the run south was merely a helter-skelter mêlée, when only half the force available was engaged for the majority of the time. During the run north the battleships were left to fight the High Sea battleships without the combined aid of the battle cruisers or even that of the light cruisers; the latter were never ordered to attack with torpedoes until 5.47 p.m., one hour and a quarter after the run north had commenced.

Then again on the run north Admiral Beatty completely lost touch with the High Sea Battlefleet, so that when he joined the Grand Fleet Battlefleet he was unable to supply the Commander-in-Chief with the information which was vital to him to determine the method of his deployment.

Chapter 7

Phase II

There were many units, consisting of vessels of various classes, attached to our battlefleet as semi-independent commands. All these were steaming, many were attacking, repelling attacks, or scouting, at the same time as the battle-fleets were grimly approaching each other. It is impossible to give an account of all their various activities and at the same time to weave a consecutive story.

Much, therefore, that is worthy of comment and record has been omitted in the interest of clearness of narrative. For a detailed account of this subsidiary work the *Official History of the War* should be consulted. One name, however, among the Senior Officers of the Light Cruiser Squadrons stands out pre-eminently, namely Commodore Goodenough of the *Southampton*, Senior Officer of the Second Light Cruiser Squadron. He was always to the fore in scouting and in conveying accurate and reliable information, a model that may well be studied by Scouting Admirals in the future.

The part of the action we have styled Phase II took place ahead of the battlefleet between the time that the battle cruisers arrived in sight of the *Iron Duke* and the complete deployment of the fleet. As these engagements were subsidiary to the main battlefleet operations they have been treated as a separate phase of the main action.

About 5.40, half an hour before the deployment of the battlefleet, conflict was brewing out to the eastward of the fleet.

The *Invincible*, flying the flag of Rear-Admiral the Hon. Horace Hood, with two other ships of the Third Battle Cruiser Squadron, had been sent by Admiral Jellicoe, the moment he had heard of the enemy battle cruisers being sighted, to reinforce Admiral Beatty.[17] At 5.27, when about twenty-five miles ahead of the battlefleet, the *Chester*, one of Admiral Hood's light cruisers, sighted an enemy ship. Then out of the mist suddenly appeared the German Second Scouting Group, comprising the *Frankfurt*, *Wiesbaden*, *Pillau* and *Elbing*.[18]

Within five minutes the *Chester*, under this concentrated fire, had three guns disabled and the majority of her guns' crews killed. With only one gun in action, she turned and made off at full speed, dodging the shell salvoes, twisting and turning like a snipe.

Admiral Hood was close at hand. Steering at once to the sound of the guns, his three ships suddenly burst through the mist on to the German light cruisers, who turned to escape; but they were too late, for before the mist hid them the *Wiesbaden* was a wreck and the *Pillau* and *Frankfurt* were badly damaged. To save his ships from the torpedoes launched from these vessels, Admiral Hood had to turn the Third Battle Cruiser Squadron sharply again to the east. Our destroyers, under Commander Loftus Jones, engaged the destroyers that had come to the assistance of the German vessels. A fierce fight ensued.

The following is an account of the end of the *Shark* as described by Lord Jellicoe in his book, *The Grand Fleet*.[19]

> The attack of the British destroyers was carried out with great gallantry and determination, and, having frustrated the enemy's torpedo attack on the Third Battle Cruiser Squadron, Commander Loftus Jones turned his division to regain his billet on our battle cruisers. At this moment three German vessels came into sight out of the mist and opened a heavy fire, further disabling the *Shark* and causing many casualties on board; Commander Loftus Jones was one of those wounded.
>
> Lieutenant-Commander J.O. Barren, commanding the *Acastar*, came to the assistance of the *Shark*, but Commander Loftus Jones refused to imperil a second destroyer and directed the *Acastar* to leave him. Commander Loftus Jones, who was assisting to keep the only undamaged gun in action, ordered the last torpedo to be placed in the tube and fired; but whilst this was being done, the torpedo was hit by a shell and exploded, causing many casualties.
>
> Those gallant officers and men in the *Shark* who still survived continued to fire the only gun left in action, the greatest heroism being exhibited. The Captain was now wounded again, his right leg being taken off by a shell; but he still continued to direct the fire, until the condition of the *Shark* and the approach of the German destroyers made it probable that the ship would fall into the hands of the enemy, when he gave orders for her to be sunk, countermanding this order shortly afterwards on realizing that her remaining gun could still be fought. A little later the ship was hit by two torpedoes and sank with her colours flying. Only six survivors were picked up next morning by a Danish steamer.

Another brilliant attack was carried out by the *Onslow*.

Lieutenant-Commander Tovey, who had fired the torpedo which hit the *Wiesbaden*, found that, as a result of the action, the engines of the *Onslow* were only able to drive the vessel slowly. Suddenly, five miles off, he saw the German battleships steering towards him. In spite of his slow speed and the faint hope of surviving unless he at once retreated, he turned and attacked them, firing his torpedoes at 8,000 yards. Then he slowly limped away, fortunately escaping what seemed almost certain destruction. He presently joined the *Defender*, a fellow cripple, and the two towed each other to Aberdeen, where they arrived forty-eight hours after.

Two tragedies were shortly to occur near the *Wiesbaden*. Rear-Admiral Sir Robert Arbuthnot in the *Defence*, seeing the flashes of the guns of the *Chester* action, immediately steered towards them and, shortly after, sighted and opened fire on the *Wiesbaden*. The *Defence* at once drew on herself the fire of the leading German battle cruisers, and within four minutes of engaging the *Wiesbaden* was struck by two salvoes. A shell exploded her after magazine and she immediately disappeared in the roar of a terrific explosion. The *Warrior*, her consort, nearly shared a similar fate.

The *Warspite*, the rear ship of the 5th Battle Squadron, whose steering gear had broken down, now came in for the attention of the German Battlefleet, and escaped, only after having had a particularly warm shelling from the leading ships. Diagram 31, shows the following features of the general situation:

The battlefleet deploying across the enemy's T.

The First and Second Battle Cruiser Squadron taking station ahead of the line.

The Third Battle Cruiser Squadron leading ahead.

The place where the *Defence* sank.

The disabled *Wiesbaden* and damaged *Warspite*.

The second tragedy was now maturing.

It will be seen that the Third Battle Cruiser Squadron, and the German battle cruisers and battlefleet, were steering on courses which quickly shortened the distance between them. Soon the *Invincible* came under the fire of four of the German battle cruisers and perhaps one of the leading battleships. Well as the *Invincible* was shooting – and she was shooting magnificently – the conflict was too unequal. Several salvoes struck her, and like her sisters, the *Indefatigable* and *Queen Mary*, she disappeared in a sheet of flame and a dense pall of smoke.

After this the German battleships became conscious of the presence of our battlefleet, and had their attention fully occupied in returning the heavy fire that was being concentrated on them.

The action of the *Invincible* with the Second German Scouting Group gave Admiral Scheer later on the impression that the *Invincible* and her consorts were the leading ships of the British line of battle. Working back from this, he fixed the tail of our fleet as being five or six miles further ahead than it really was. Hence, as we shall see later, when he tried to dash astern of our fleet at seven o'clock he struck the tail of our battle fleet instead of

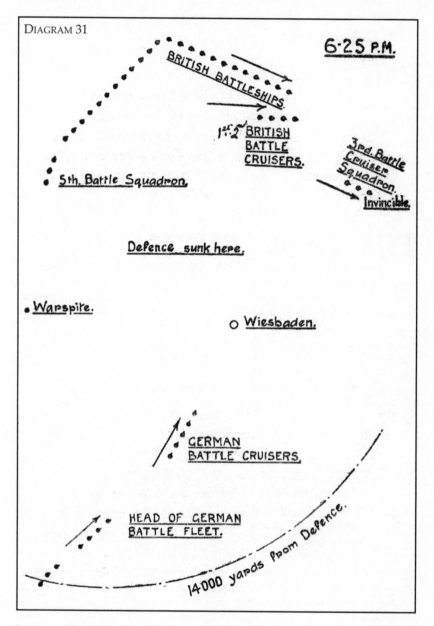

DIAGRAM 31

6·25 P.M.

BRITISH BATTLESHIPS.

1ᵗ 2ᵗ BRITISH BATTLE CRUISERS.

3rd. Battle Cruiser Squadron.

Invincible.

5th. Battle Squadron.

Defence sunk here.

Warspite.

o Wiesbaden.

GERMAN BATTLE CRUISERS.

HEAD OF GERMAN BATTLE FLEET.

14·000 yards from Defence.

being well astern of it. This led, temporarily, to a complete upset of the German Admiral's plans.

So ended Phase II, the first blast of the storm that was shortly to break on the two battlefleets.

Chapter 8
Phase III:
The Battlefleet Action

We now come to what we may call Phase III of the Battle of Jutland, when the two battlefleets came into action.

As we can well imagine, the time from 6 p.m. to 6.30 p.m. was one of expectation and suppressed excitement in the battlefleet. Everyone knew that at any moment the German High Sea Fleet might appear in sight and the long-looked-for action be engaged in. To Admiral Jellicoe the time was one of tense expectancy. As soon as he was informed of the exact direction of his enemy he would have to deploy, that is, to change from his teeth-of-the-comb cruising formation to single line follow-my-leader. How exactly the enemy did bear from him was the all-important question.

It was of great importance for Admiral Jellicoe:

(1) Not to deploy until he knew the position of the German Battlefleet; because after deployment it was highly desirable that his line should be steaming at right angles to the direction in which the German Fleet would be sighted. Had he deployed at random he might have had to alter the direction of his six-mile-long fleet, an operation requiring eighteen minutes to complete.

(2) If time permitted to "wheel" his fleet so that the method of *direct deployment* could be used; the subsequent deployment would occupy three minutes instead of eighteen minutes.

(3) To have his deployment completed by the time the German Fleet was sighted, so that all his ships could at once open fire.

Now let us say a word or two about scouting. If a ship is out of sight and you want to find out what her bearing and distance are from you, you must ask her where she is. She can only answer your question by giving you the latitude and longitude she thinks that she is in. We must say "think", because at sea the exact position of a ship that has been for some time out of sight of land, or without observation of the sun or stars, is always a matter of doubt.

You also know the latitude and longitude you think your ship is in.

So you see there are two "thinks" involved; either one or both may be wrong. If either is wrong, then any estimate you make of the bearing and distance the ship is from you will be wrong also. Hence, to fix the exact bearing and distance that a ship is from you it is necessary to *sight* the ship.

Take now the case of a cruiser scouting. When the cruiser sights the enemy she can measure the bearing and distance he is from her. If at the same time you sight the cruiser, you can measure her distance from you. You can then from these two pieces of information with great accuracy find the distance and bearing that your ship is from the enemy, although the enemy may not actually be in sight from your ship. But, until you actually sight your friend the cruiser, you must remain in doubt of her exact bearing and distance from you and therefore the exact bearing and distance of your ship from the enemy she has sighted.

Now, as a matter of fact, at 6 p.m., owing to zigzagging, the estimated position of the Grand Fleet was four miles more to the east than it should have been;[20] and, owing to the battle cruisers having been engaged in an action and other causes, the position the battle cruisers estimated they were in was seven miles west of their true position, so that there was a difference of eleven miles between the estimated and the true position of the battleships relative to the battle cruisers.

Admiral Jellicoe had every reason to count on the fact that when Admiral Beatty came in sight he would give him the accurate bearing and distance of the German Fleet from the *Lion*. Time would therefore still be available to Admiral Jellicoe to deploy on the proper course for fighting. But in this he was badly disappointed, for when the *Lion* hove in sight she had lost touch with the German Fleet, and Admiral Beatty was unable to supply Admiral Jellicoe with the information that was vital to him to determine his deployment.

At 6.1 Admiral Jellicoe signalled to the *Lion*: "Where is the enemy's battlefleet?" The only reply was at 6.6, "Enemy's battle cruisers bearing S.E."[21] This was a "thank you for nothing" reply. So that at the very moment when the exact position of the enemy's fleet should have been known to Admiral Jellicoe events conspired to create the greatest ambiguity as to its position:

    (1) First of all Admiral Beatty had lost touch with the enemy. The main reason why the battle cruisers were originated was to provide a Commander-in-Chief with a cruiser force which could push home a reconnaissance and supply him with accurate information, but Admiral Beatty failed to keep touch with the enemy and was therefore unable to report to his Commander-in-Chief.

    (2) Then the eleven miles difference in reckoning had caused the *Lion* to be sighted by the *Iron Duke* in a totally different direction from that which previous reports of latitude and longitude had led him to expect.

Hardly crediting this scouting failure on the part of the battle cruisers, Admiral Jellicoe signalled again: "Where is the enemy's fleet?"[22] but Admiral Beatty had none of their fleet in sight and therefore made no reply. At 6.14, however, the German Battlefleet steamed into sight and he signalled back: "Have sighted the enemy's battlefleet S.S.W."[23]

The *Southampton*, Commodore Goodenough, did excellent work in signalling the movements of the German Battlefleet to the Commander-in-Chief of the Grand Fleet. Unfortunately a wrong estimate of the bearing of the enemy's battlefleet from his battle cruisers, viz. S.W., was made to the *Iron Duke*, and received at 5.54. The information was most confusing to the Commander-in-Chief.

It is best to quote the exact words of the *Official History of the War*, which deals with the position in which Sir John Jellicoe found himself:

> Many had been the critical situations which British admirals in the past had been called upon suddenly to solve, but never had there been one which demanded higher qualities of leadership, right judgment and quick decision than that which confronted Admiral Jellicoe in this supreme moment of a Naval War. There was not an instant to lose if the deployment were to be made in time.
>
> The enemy, instead of being met ahead, were on his starboard side. He could only guess their course. Beyond a few miles everything was shrouded in mist; the little that could be seen was no more than a blurred picture, and with every tick of the clock the situation was developing with a rapidity of which his predecessors had never dreamt. At a speed higher than anything in their experience the two hostile fleets were rushing upon each other; battle cruisers, cruisers and destroyers were hurrying to their battle stations, and the vessels steaming across his front were shutting out all beyond in an impenetrable pall of funnel smoke. Above all was the roar of battle both ahead and to starboard, and in this blind distraction Admiral Jellicoe had to make the decision on which the fortune of his country hung.
>
> His first and natural impulse was, he says, to deploy on the starboard flank, which was nearest to the enemy. But for this the decisive intelligence had come too late, and he was too near. Heavy shells were already falling between the lines of his divisions, and if he deployed as his natural impulse was, it would mean that Admiral Burney, whose squadron was the oldest and least powerful in the fleet, would receive the concentrated fire of the enemy's best ships, and almost certainly a heavy destroyer attack while in the act of deployment.
>
> To increase the disadvantage, he would be compelled as he deployed to turn to port in order to avoid having his T crossed; this would mean that the fleet would be turning at least twelve points in the thick of the enemy's fire, and, what is still more important, the action would be

opened well within torpedo range of the enemy's battleships, a hazard which in Admiral Jellicoe's system it was vital to avoid. It is scarcely to be doubted that his reasoning was correct.

We now know that such an opening with the visibility as low as it was would have given his enemy exactly the opening he prayed for. The tactics on which Admiral Scheer's whole conception of offensive action with an inferior fleet was undoubtedly based were a rapid and overwhelming concentration with gun and torpedo on part of his opponent's line, followed by a withdrawal under cover of a smoke-screen before a counter concentration could be brought to bear – a bold manoeuvre which the High Sea Fleet had persistently practised.

Let us put the matter in the form of a simple diagram. Had the right tooth of the comb been the one selected for deployment, the position five minutes after the signal had been made would have been much as in Diagram 32.

The whole brunt of the action so far as the Grand Fleet was concerned would have fallen, to begin with, on four of our slowest and oldest ships, within torpedo range of the enemy, and all the other 22 ships would have been powerless to fire a shot and only able to come one by one into action as they followed for twenty minutes round at the point A. Admiral Jellicoe deployed, however, on the left-hand tooth. His brain had previously, time after time, ruminated over the possibilities that varying emergencies might suddenly spring upon him, and therefore he was ready and prepared to make a vital decision instantly and correctly.

Some have suggested that his deployment should have been made on the centre tooth. This would have brought our fleet no nearer the enemy. It would only have saved some eight or nine minutes before contact with the enemy was made. It had the great disadvantage that it was a manoeuvre that could not be carried out with rapidity by a simple follow-my-leader method: some of the ships would have had to reduce speed to dead slow, and the flagship would have been brought at one end or the other of the line. So no advantage would have been gained, but several disadvantages would have been incurred.

Now turn to Diagram 33, which shows what actually happened. The whole of the Grand Fleet ships that lay inside the circle shown and marked as the 14,000-yards circle (except some of the leading battleships whose fire was masked by the smoke of the battle cruisers) could, and did, open fire on the enemy.[24]

Attempts have been made by critics to blame Admiral Beatty for obscuring vision with the smoke of the battle cruisers. But it was in no way his fault. He had a definite position to take up, and he most rightly took it up in the shortest time possible. It was quite out of his power to prevent his smoke trailing behind him.

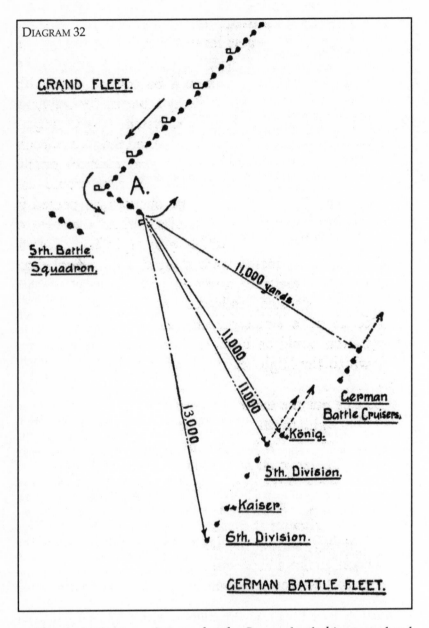

DIAGRAM 32

GRAND FLEET.

A.

5th. Battle. Squadron.

11,000 yards.

11,000

11,000

13,000

König.

German Battle Cruisers.

5th. Division.

Kaiser.

6th. Division.

GERMAN BATTLE FLEET.

The result of our gun fire was that the German battleships turned and ran dead away from the Grand Fleet on a S.W. course, in spite of the fact that the Horn Reef passage lay about S.E. The German Fleet, therefore, in their precipitate retreat to get at all hazards out of the devastating fire of our

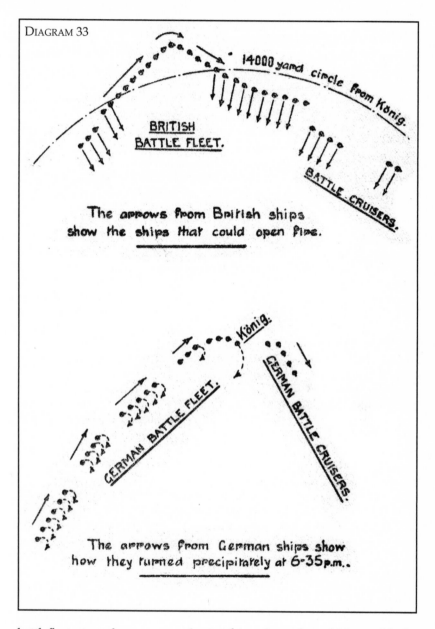

DIAGRAM 33

14000 yard circle from König.

BRITISH BATTLE FLEET.

BATTLE CRUISERS.

The arrows from British ships show the ships that could open fire.

König.

GERMAN BATTLE FLEET.

GERMAN BATTLE CRUISERS.

The arrows from German ships show how they turned precipitately at 6·35 p.m..

battlefleet, steered a course nearly at right angles to that which would take them back to the Jade.

The exact amount that they had turned "away" could not be estimated by Admiral Jellicoe or his Staff. The German battleships had disappeared.

155

But in what direction had they gone? The chances were that they had merely run under cover of the mist to complete forming their line parallel to our fleet, and that they would then come again into sight and continue the action.

Admiral Jellicoe therefore altered course with his fleet 45 degrees towards where the German Fleet were hidden in the mist, so as to close them and also to get the Grand Fleet between them and the Horn Reef.[25]

If he had chased the German Fleet by turning straight towards the spot where they had been last seen, as some lunatics have suggested that he should have done, not only would he have seriously endangered the Grand Fleet, without any prospect of damaging the enemy, but he would actually have been further from the German fleet at dark than he eventually was!

Let us see why.

The German dreadnoughts, except their two oldest classes, the *Heligoland* and the *Nassau* classes, were equal to or greater in speed than the average battleships of the Grand Fleet.[26] Again, the Germans knew the date they proposed to come out to fight and could clean their ships' bottoms in anticipation. They therefore could have all their ships in a condition to steam at their highest speed, whereas our ships could only go singly in rotation to be docked, so that some of them were sure to have dirty bottoms and therefore could only steam at less than their best speed.

Taking this into account, the speed of the slowest German dreadnoughts, those of the *Heligoland* and *Nassau* classes, was probably about as good as the oldest of our dreadnoughts.

It is only when we consider the old German pre-dreadnought ship that we find any marked superiority in favour of the Grand Fleet. Compared with these our Grand Fleet had the advantage of a knot and a half greater speed.

But let us look at the distance that the various units of the German Fleet were from our ships when Admiral Scheer turned away. Owing to the speed of the chase north, the German tail streamed away from our fleet at the distances shown in Diagram 34.

Between 6.30 and 9 p.m. two hours and a half of daylight only remained. Now if Admiral Jellicoe had chased these ships, which (although at the time he did not know it) had already turned round and were running as hard as they could away from our fleet, after a two-hours-and-a-half chase, when darkness had fallen on the fleet, the distances would have been as on Diagram 35.

The nearest German ship would still have been 16,000 yards away and out of sight.

So let this for ever dispel the fiction that had Admiral Jellicoe chased the German Fleet he could have forced a close action. As a matter of fact, he would never again have sighted them. They would never have been seen again; they would have steered straight back to their harbours laughing at his efforts to overtake them.

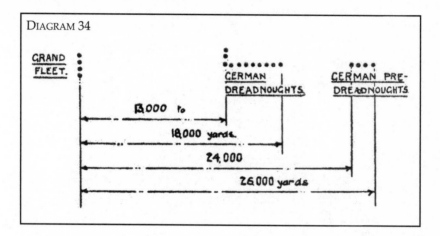

DIAGRAM 34

GRAND FLEET.

GERMAN DREADNOUGHTS

GERMAN PRE-DREADNOUGHTS

13,000 to

18,000 yards.

24,000

26,000 yards

Now to hark back. We have seen that at 6.35 Admiral Scheer turned and ran. At five minutes to seven o'clock he pulled himself together and tried to break across the place where he imagined the rear of our Grand Fleet to be; but he was horribly sold to find that Admiral Jellicoe was between him and his harbour, and that at 7.12 p.m. he ran into a heavy fire from our battlefleet. He found himself in the position shown in Diagram 36 and received smack number two.

His leading battleship was only 12,000 yards from our nearest ship, his leading cruiser was barely 10,000 yards from the *Colossus*, and before he could turn again and get out of range he was badly mauled. In order, therefore, to extricate his fleet, Admiral Scheer made a signal to his battle cruisers to "charge the enemy, ram, ships are to attack without regard to consequences".[27]

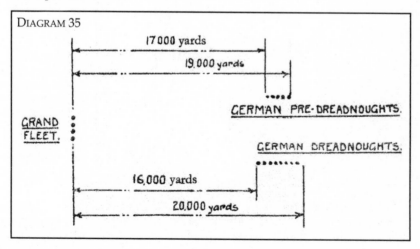

DIAGRAM 35

17000 yards

19,000 yards

GERMAN PRE-DREADNOUGHTS.

GRAND FLEET.

GERMAN DREADNOUGHTS.

16,000 yards

20,000 yards

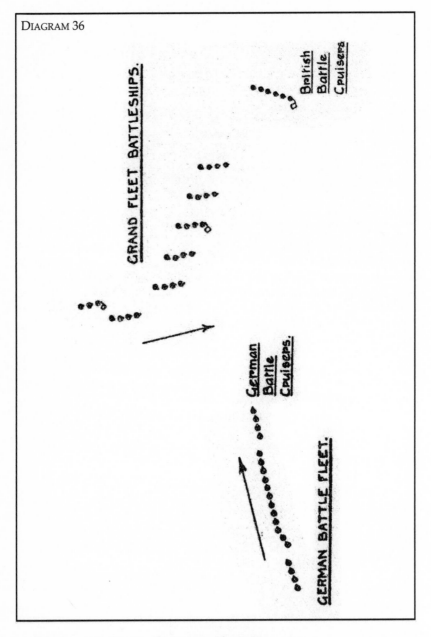

DIAGRAM 36

It was a veritable "death ride" for the battle cruisers.

The battle cruisers by this attack succeeded in attracting the greater volume of fire on themselves. In a couple of minutes the *Derfflinger*, the leading ship, had two turrets blown to pieces, her decks were a shambles, and she was ablaze fore and aft, and all her fire control gear was out of action. She was blinded with the smoke from the fire of the *Lutzow*, one of her sister ships, which was burning close to her, and the other battle cruisers suffered severely in casualties and structural damage.

At 7.20 Admiral Scheer, having turned his battlefleet round, recalled his cruisers and destroyers. *The Official History* records the end thus:

> Fitfully the firing died away; like a Homeric mist the smother of haze and smoke thickened impenetrably between the combatants, and Admiral Scheer, for the time at least, had saved his fleet; but no more. His surprise tactics had not had the effect he expected; they had not upset his enemy's plans for the rest of the day, nor had his attack "fallen heavily enough", as he says he hoped, to facilitate his "breaking loose at night".

Von Hase, the gunnery officer of the *Derfflinger*, describes the attack as follows: "Battleship encounter. A fierce and unequal engagement now developed. Several heavy projectiles struck us with tremendous force and burst inside the ship with terrific noise."

He also describes the position the German Fleet had been caught in as, "in absoluten Wurstkessel", a literal translation of which is, "in the frying-pan". He says:

> A perfect hail of projectiles beat on us; a fifteen-inch burst in the turret called *Caesar*. The flames penetrated to the working chamber, where two other cartridges caught fire; flames leapt out of the turret as high as a house, but they did not explode, as the enemy's cartridge had done. The effect was appalling, 73 out of 78 men of the turret crew were killed outright.
>
> A fifteen-inch shell hit the roof of *Dora* turret; again charges were set fire to, roaring up into the sky from both after turrets like funeral pyres. The enemy had our range to an inch.
>
> The *Seydlitz* was heavily down by the bow. The *Lutzow* was hidden, burning in dense smoke. The *Moltke* and *Von der Tann* had been severely handled. Each of our battle cruisers had suffered a great number of casualties; hundreds had perished in the dauntless attack.

When Admiral Scheer made his "death ride" signal to his cruisers he also launched his destroyers to attack; these rushed forward with determination. The German Battlefleet was lost to view behind the smoke and haze. The attack promised to be a formidable one, and Admiral Jellicoe instantly turned his fleet away, using what had been decided on as the only manoeuvre that would satisfactorily frustrate such an attack.

He turned his ships first of all 22 degrees away; but the officer who was working the instrument for calculating the amount of turn that was

159

necessary according to varying conditions of attack informed him that 22 degrees was insufficient.

Admiral Jellicoe therefore turned yet another 22 degrees, making 44 in all.[28] Three distinct attacks were made by the German destroyers. Twenty-two torpedoes were fired, but thanks to Admiral Jellicoe's manoeuvre all these were avoided by the ships; but it was close work. Had he not turned, we might have had to lament the loss of several battleships with no advantage gained. The total distance in range sacrificed by these turns was only 3,000 yards.[29] Immediately the attacks had been frustrated Admiral Jellicoe turned the fleet again up towards the Germans.

We now come to an episode which has been entirely misunderstood by the general public and also totally misrepresented in passing from mouth to mouth.[30]

At 7.50 Admiral Beatty sent a message: "Submit van of battleships follow battle cruisers; we can then cut off whole of enemy's battlefleet." This was received in *Iron Duke* and given to Admiral Jellicoe about 8.4.[31]

At 8.7, or shortly after, Admiral Jerram received Admiral Jellicoe's order to follow Admiral Beatty.

As a matter of fact there was nothing from which the battle cruisers could cut the German Battlefleet off! They had already been cut off from their harbours. This is, however, dealt with more fully later on.

Darkness was now rapidly coming on; so there is little more left to record. The battle cruisers carried out some fitful firing at the German old pre-dreadnought battleships at long-range; only two projectiles hit the German ships.

Admiral Jellicoe formed his fleet for night cruising, breaking up into divisions to avoid the long line of battle so open to torpedo attack. He also prolonged his line astern by stationing his destroyer flotillas in that direction. In this position they were able better to discriminate between enemy and friendly battleships, and so "regrettable accidents" were minimized, and at the same time they provided a most thorny screen should the Germans attempt to pass behind the Grand Fleet.

Chapter 9
PHASE IV:
THE NIGHT ACTION

There is one class of fighting at sea which has no counterpart in land warfare, namely, a night action. Ashore in a night attack, one army is fixed in position and the exact locality for the attack is known; at sea, both forces are mobile. At the Battle of the Nile the French Fleet were at anchor, and our ships anchored as they arrived opposite the French vessels: there was none of the doubt that accompanies two opposing fleets silently moving through the impenetrable darkness of the night.

The problem presented to Admiral Jellicoe at 9 p.m. on the 31st May was one of surpassing complexity. We will try and explain the various issues.

The Grand Fleet, while closing the German High Sea Fleet, had been skilfully manoeuvred between that fleet and its harbours, but the advantage thus obtained vanished considerably as darkness came on. Darkness cramps and renders the finest ships largely powerless. It degrades the offensive strength of the various vessels down to a common level. The battleship, proud in an armament of ten guns able to fire at ranges up to ten miles, finds her range limited to one thousand yards. The torpedo rises in value, as near approach to a battleship is permitted by the shielding darkness, and the battleship supreme in daytime is at a disadvantage to the destroyer owing to the obscurity of the night.

At night all fleet actions must develop into single ship combats. Mutual support is an impossibility, gunnery skill is effaced. The whole combat becomes one of chance; but a certain advantage attaches to the fleet with the initiative. Let us see what this means.

Take the conditions prevailing on the night of Jutland. Our Grand Fleet was between Admiral Scheer and his harbour. He would have been quite justified in saying: "If I stay out till morning my fleet will be gobbled up in daylight by the Grand Fleet. My game is to charge right through the Grand Fleet in the dark; I may lose some ships, but I shall not lose all."

The fleet breaking through always has the initiative, the ships know to the tick of a second when they will act and exactly what they are going to do.

Let us suppose in carrying out the attempt Admiral Scheer had struck the centre of our battlefleet. The scene of chaos that would have ensued beggars all imagination. With his fleet going about 18 knots he would have charged clean into the middle of our ships. His one and only preoccupation being to go straight on for his harbour. Not necessarily to fight. Collisions? Yes; but he would drive through and would expect an equal number of our ships as of his own to be sunk. Gun fire! After one minute the fog of the cordite smoke would have rendered searchlights useless – what a hellish cauldron those few acres of the North Sea would have been for some quarter of an hour. Friend indistinguishable from foe. The fleet a rabble of single ships. The restraint of doubt at times saving enemies from attack; mistaken identity sacrificing friends. All the peace training thrown to the winds, luck and happy chance the sole arbiters of the conflict. What an action to have been in and lived through!

Admiral Jellicoe, on the other hand, could not take the initiative. He had no reason to charge through the German Fleet – quite the contrary. Had he tried to do so he would probably have missed them altogether. It was best for him to remain if possible between them and their harbours till daylight. There was no offensive action he could take with his large ships which would not be a ghastly gamble, even supposing he could have hit off the exact position of the enemy in the dark. The initiative therefore lay with Admiral Scheer, not with Admiral Jellicoe.

And what about the destroyers?

First of all, a destroyer finds considerable difficulty in distinguishing friend from foe at night unless the ship is lighted up by a searchlight; and, vice versa, the difficulty of a battleship to recognize the nationality of a destroyer is equally great.

The fundamental principle adopted for night work is that it is better to sink a friendly destroyer than to risk the loss of a large ship through withholding gun fire.

A destroyer therefore cannot be certain, merely because she is being fired on, that the ship firing must needs be an enemy. It may well be a friend taking precautions against risks. Everyone's hand therefore is against the destroyer, and she must act warily, for she will get no thanks if she makes a mistake and sinks one of her own ships. Actual attacks using gun fire cannot be carried out in peace-time, so that in night attack in peace-time destroyer education lacks reality.

Now the Jutland night action did not culminate in a clash of battleships. Admiral Jellicoe, knowing that his battlefleet only interposed a short screen between the enemy and their coast, lengthened his line by spreading his destroyers and light cruisers astern; his screen by this means was increased to sixteen miles. His argument was that if the High Sea Fleet tried to break through this screen and missed the battleships, they would be badly mauled by the destroyers, in which case the German Fleet might not care to try to force on through the screen, but would not improbably sheer off again to the eastward. In any case he would have their presence reported. This is what actually did happen.

Admiral Scheer, however, had quite rightly made up his mind to push through at all hazards. Moreover, Admiral Jellicoe's W/T signal stationing the destroyers astern of the fleet had been intercepted and decoded by the German shore station and repeated to Admiral Scheer,[32] so that he knew when he struck our destroyers that he was astern of our battleships, and that if his light cruisers could break down the attack of these vessels the road to his harbour was clear.

We must bear in mind that there were three main passages through the minefields by which the Germans could return to their base, one by the Horn Reef bearing approximately S.E., another further off bearing about south from the Grand Fleet, and a third leading to Heligoland between the two. Which one would the Germans use? There was no hint or clue to go on; at all events there was none before 11 p.m.

Admiral Jellicoe fully expected the fleet to be attacked by enemy destroyers, and therefore anticipated that occasional scraps would be carried on throughout the night in the rear part of the fleet, and perhaps in the main fleet itself.

Nightfall was marked by a gross piece of carelessness on the part of the *Lion*. At 9 p.m. she made to the *Princess Royal* by flashing-lamp: "Please give me challenge and reply now in force as they have been lost." The challenge and reply were passed as requested.

The signal from the *Lion* was seen by the *Castor*.

The reply was taken in by the *Manners*. The *Castor* was seven miles away from the *Lion*, and if the signal was taken in by *Manners* it might well have been taken in by the enemy, as their second squadron was only four miles away and their other battle squadron only six to seven miles distant. The secret signals of challenge and reply were the sole means of destroyers being able to distinguish friend from foe. Not only would the possession of the secret signal enable the enemy ships to escape attack, but it would, under certain conditions, enable them to disarm suspicion on the part of our destroyers and lead them to close sufficiently to be destroyed by gun fire.

It should be noted that this occurred at 9 p.m., so that the making of the signal might well have compromised the safety of our destroyers and the efficiency of their attacks.[33]

Events worked out as had been anticipated on board the *Iron Duke*, several bursts of firing were heard astern. About 11 p.m. Admiral Jellicoe asked Commander Hawkesley, of the light cruiser *Castor*, if he was engaging enemy's destroyers. Crossing the question came the message that he had engaged enemy cruisers. As the light cruisers were certain to support a destroyer attack the reply merely confirmed the inference that the expected attack had taken place. Commodore Goodenough reported that he had engaged the enemy's cruisers bearing W.S.W., and at 11.30 Captain Duff, of the *Birmingham*, reported the enemy's battle cruisers in sight, steering South. This was a course practically parallel to the course of the Grand Fleet.[34]

At 11.5 a message deciphered and delivered to the Commander-in-Chief about 11.30 was received from the Admiralty, summarizing the intercepted German wireless messages that had been received at 9.5 and 9.16 stating that the German Battlefleet had been ordered home, and that its course was S.S.E. ¾ E., speed 16 knots, the battle cruisers being in rear.[35]

Another Admiralty message received at 10.30 and read at 11.0., gave a latitude and longitude of the German Fleet that was obviously incorrect.

The original message intercepted by the Admiralty had asked for an airship to reconnoitre in the early morning off the Horn Reef. This fact was not passed on, as unfortunately the Admiralty thought that the course of the German Fleet as given in their message was a sufficient indication of the probable movements of that fleet. But to those at sea, who had reports as to the position and course of the enemy ships from the light cruisers at times subsequent to those mentioned in the German messages, the position was by no means clear. If the German Fleet had altered course at 9.16, how was it that the German Fleet was well to the westward of Commodore Goodenough at 10.15? Again, how was it that Captain Duff could report at 11.30 that he had seen their battle cruisers steering South, when, if they were making for the Horn Reef, they should have been steering S.E.?

The explanation of the latter is now simple. Owing to an attack by the fourth flotilla the German van, which had been steering to the south-eastward, swung back to south-west, and had pulled up again to south just at the time Captain Duff sighted them. The course on which they had been observed was therefore a temporary and not a permanent one. No further reports after 11.30 came in to the Commander-in-Chief.

Now it seemed inconceivable to Admiral Jellicoe that the German Fleet could pass through the destroyers and light cruisers massed astern without being sighted. He therefore fully expected that that fleet would remain to the westward unless he received news of an attempt made by them to pass astern.

He was partly right. Right to the extent that the German battleships must be sighted, but wrong in assuming that such vital information was bound to be reported.

As a matter of fact, the ships of the main German Fleet were sighted at 11.35 p.m. by the *Malaya* battleship, Captain the Hon. A.D. Boyle, and the *Valiant* battleship, Captain M. Woollcombe.[36]

The *Champion* light cruiser, Captain Farie, and the *Faulknor*, Captain Stirling, and four other destroyers, also sighted the enemy's large ships. The only vessel of these which made a report was the *Faulknor*, who reported both before and after the attack, but his signals never got through. They were probably jammed by the German wireless.

In defence of the destroyers much can be said. They all made gallant attacks, and it is difficult to say whether or not their signal appliances survived and were fit for use nor was it their duty to report other than to their immediate senior officer, who presumably had seen as much as they had.

But the *Malaya* and *Valiant* are in a totally different category. Here were two battleships with every signalling appliance and with experienced officers of rank in command, but who never informed the Commander-in-Chief, nor even their own Admiral, that the enemy was breaking through astern of them.

The escape of the German Fleet must be attributed largely to the failure of the officers commanding these two ships to pass such vital information to the Admiral commanding their Division, or to the Commander-in-Chief.[37] The *Champion*, Captain Farie, must share the blame. The Admiralty also are further to blame for not keeping the Commander-in-Chief fully acquainted of all intercepted signals received at headquarters.

About 2.15 a.m. may be taken as the very latest time that an alteration in course by the Grand Fleet could have brought the German Fleet to a successful action. The last report received by Admiral Jellicoe was that of the *Birmingham* at 11.30, which reported the enemy steering south; that is, parallel to the Grand Fleet. Had the *Malaya* and *Valiant* reported at 11.30, the Grand Fleet could have headed off the Germans, and engaged them at daybreak.

As it was, there was nothing to indicate that the German Battlefleet was not still to the westward.

Admiral Jellicoe has stated that when steering south his original idea was to close the Horn Reef at daylight, but that the difficulties experienced in collecting the fleet, particularly the destroyers, rendered this undesirable.[38] It was, he states, obviously necessary to concentrate the battlefleet and destroyers before renewing action.

This, of course, was a perfectly sound procedure provided that the enemy's fleet were not close enough to the Horn Reef to escape engagement before slipping in. This seemed improbable since no reports of large ships being sighted had been received from the ships astern, and it was almost inconceivable that they could have broken through the sixteen-mile screen without being sighted. It was therefore wise not to go prematurely, without destroyers, into waters that it was certain would be infested by submarines. Had the *Malaya* and *Valiant* reported the enemy as passing astern, there is no doubt that on such definite information our fleet would have been interposed between the enemy and their harbour and a considerable toll of them taken in the morning.

The *Faulknor*, Captain Stirling, with the 1st division of the 12th Flotilla, at 1.45 a.m. made a gallant attack and sank the *Pommern* in the half-light of

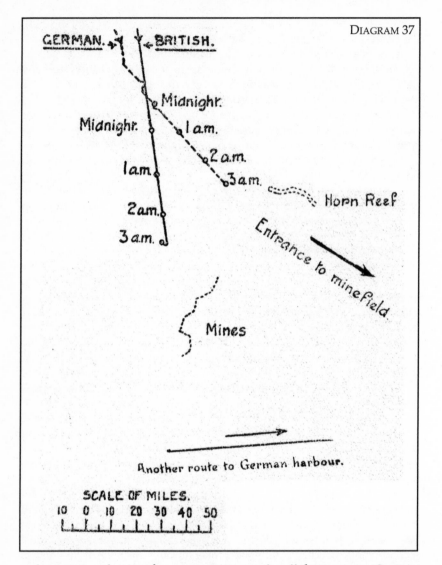

DIAGRAM 37

GERMAN. ← → BRITISH.

Midnight.

Midnight.

1 a.m.

1 a.m.

2 a.m.

2 a.m.

3 a.m.

3 a.m.

Horn Reef

Entrance to minefield

Mines

Another route to German harbour.

SCALE OF MILES.
10   0   10   20   30   40   50

early morning, forcing the enemy temporarily off their course. Captain Stirling reported the presence of the battlefleet by wireless telegraphy, but, as before stated, the signal was jammed and never got through to any flagship of the fleet. Even had it been received it would have been too late to enable the Grand Fleet to reap a sweeping victory.

This was the last attack. When this passed off, the German Fleet was only sixteen miles from the Horn Reef, and at 4 a.m. they entered the passage which they kept swept through our minefields.

166

At 4.15 Admiral Jellicoe received a message[39] from the Admiralty to say that the German Fleet at 2.30 were only 16 miles from the Horn Reef steering south-east at 16 knots. This meant the fleet had escaped.

There was nothing then to do except to pick up any lame ducks the enemy might have left behind in the night attack.

The Grand Fleet remained in the vicinity of the Horn Reef till noon, and then made its way north again at cruising speed.

Of course the general disappointment from Commander-in-Chief to seaman at the chance of a great victory on June 1st having been lost was great. But the 31st May settled for ever the desire of the German High Command for their battleships again to try conclusions with so efficient a fleet, and one, moreover, commanded by so sound a tactician as our Commander-in-Chief.

Although this short account of Jutland is intended only to explain in a popular way the phases of the main battle, it is impossible to end without saying a few words about the gallant actions of our destroyers.

While sombre, unromantic principles and direct calculations of final gain or loss to the country must govern the tactics of the battlefleet, in destroyer attacks officers and men have a vast scope for the display of initiative and gallantry.

To any of us who have borne the burden and heat of the peace development of the torpedo craft, and who have oft-times served in the early manoeuvres of such vessels, and who have, perforce, over and over again attempted to visualize what night destroyer actions and attack in war would be like, the epic of our destroyers and the names of Bingham and the *Nomad*, Thomson and the *Petard*, Loftus Jones and the *Shark*, Wintour and the *Tipperary*, Trelawny and the *Spitfire*, Marsden and the *Ardent*, Tovey and the *Onslow*, Stirling and the *Faulknor*, Terry and the *Fortune*, will long remain in our memories.

Let us take some of the scraps as examples of the class of work done by our destroyers by day and during the night. We have already given an account of Commander Loftus Jones and the *Shark*, one that should ever be remembered, an echo of Grenville in the *Revenge* in his centuries-old but never forgotten fight.

CAPTAIN WINTOUR AND THE TIPPERARY[40]

Again, during the night of the 31st of May, Captain C.J. Wintour, of the *Tipperary*, and the leading boats of his solitary flotilla saw dimly the forms of enemy ships to starboard. They crept up to within 1,000 yards, when the enemy suddenly opened fire.

Salvoes, accurate and rapid, at point-blank range instantly broke on them. The *Tipperary* immediately burst into flames, but discharged both her torpedoes. All the boats attacked, several hits were claimed.

The *Elbing* light cruiser received her death-blow and was rammed by the *Posen*; others also were probably damaged. Captain Wintour had done all that was possible and had made a gallant attack. The first salvo had swept away the *Tipperary's* bridge, and with it her gallant captain, and she was left a mere mass of burning wreckage.

LIEUTENANT-COMMANDER TRELAWNY AND THE SPITFIRE[41]

Lieutenant-Commander C. Trelawny, in the *Spitfire*, was next astern of the *Tipperary*. His torpedo reloading gear had been disabled; unable to fire torpedoes, he deliberately with his guns smashed the enemy's searchlight and then turned back to the assistance of the *Tipperary*.

Suddenly he saw two German cruisers bearing down on him. He wrote afterwards: "The nearer one altered course to ram me apparently. I therefore put my helm hard a-port, and the two ships (i.e. the *Spitfire* and a German cruiser[42]) rammed each other port bow to port bow ... I consider I must have considerably damaged the cruiser, as twenty feet of her side plating was left on my forecastle."

Cannot the scene well be imagined? The dark, the grim forms of the ships silhouetted, the high speed, the sudden heel over of the boat under helm; then the smash, the grinding tear, the flash of the gun, and then blindness from the gunflash; stupefaction, and once more nothing but night and darkness.

BROKE, SPARROWHAWK, AND GARLAND[43]

Again another scene but a few minutes later with the same flotilla. The *Broke*, Commander Allen, had taken the *Tipperary's* place as leader of the flotilla, and saw a large ship heading to cross his course; again a blaze of searchlights and gun fire.

The *Broke* swung to port to bring her torpedo tubes to bear. The *Sparrowhawk* did the same, but the *Broke* was out of control by the damage done from the gun fire; with her steering gear jammed she could not steady her helm, so swung right round and crashed into the *Sparrowhawk* just before her bridge.

The next boat, the *Garland*, missed the two thus locked together by a foot, but before the next in the line, the *Contest*, had time to avoid them she cut five feet *off* the *Broke's* stern!

LIEUTENANT-COMMANDER THOMSON AND THE PETARD[44]

Let us end with the *Petard*, Lieutenant-Commander Thomson, who had a cheerful day and night. With the battle cruisers in Phase I, at the time when the *Nestor* and *Nomad* were disabled, he torpedoed the leading German destroyer, *V 27*. Coming across the *Nestor* practically disabled, he offered to tow her; but as the German Battlefleet were coming fast up astern, Commander Bingham refused to let the *Petard* run the almost certain risk of destruction, so he followed the battle cruisers up to the Grand Fleet.

Again at 4.50 the *Petard* and *Nicator* attacked the German cruisers, and the *Petard* torpedoed the *Seydlitz*.[45]

Lastly, at 12.25 a.m., the *Petard* again came across the German Fleet; being one of the four last boats of the 13th Flotilla, her captain sighted a dark mass only 600 yards away bearing close down on him.[46] It was a German battleship, but bitter was the luck of the *Petard*, for in her previous actions she had fired all her torpedoes; as she turned sullenly away, she only just escaped being rammed by the battleship. The destroyer that had so often attacked was impotent to do anything but retreat. The *Petard* was fortunate enough to escape with but small damage, but close by she saw her companion, the *Turbulent*, crashed into and sunk by the leading German battleship.

Such was the work and excitement of the destroyers. Attacks and hair-breadth escapes followed each other in quick succession whenever our vessels had the good fortune to fight the Germans in the darkness of the night.

Criticisms have been directed against the Admiralty for ordering back Commodore Tyrwhitt's destroyers to Harwich at 5.15 p.m. on the 31st May, after he had started to join the Grand Fleet. Commodore Tyrwhitt, who, beyond all officers, earned the greatest reputation for gallantry and leadership during the war, and, moreover, earned it in spite of absolute self-effacement and hatred of advertisement, was the Commodore in command of the destroyers at Harwich.

It had always been understood that in case of a fleet action being imminent he was at once to join the Commander-in-Chief. At 4.50 Admiral Jellicoe signalled to the Admiralty, "Fleet action is imminent".[47] This was enough for Commodore Tyrwhitt. Anxious to be off at once, he asked for instructions.

At 5.15 none had come, so he informed the Admiralty that he was off to join the Grand Fleet. His message to the Admiralty crossed one to him telling him to "Complete with fuel; you may have to relieve light cruisers and destroyers in Battle Cruiser Fleet later". This was a bad dash to his ardour which he did not accept. He kept on steering north while awaiting an answer to his signal. Twenty minutes later he got the order, "Return at once and await orders".

Now this seems at first sight deliberately to have deprived the Grand Fleet of a magnificent force on the eve of battle. But let us look into the matter more closely.

The Admiralty had no clear indication at the time that the enemy's forces in the north were not intended as a cover to a raid on the Strait of

Dover; such a raid might have done immense damage to our shipping. The Harwich force and the 3rd Battle Squadron of old battleships lying in the entrance to the Thames were the only force worth mentioning in the south. It was from the Admiralty point of view imperative to keep the Harwich force in the southern part of the North Sea until the situation became clear. Moreover, the Grand Fleet was well supplied with destroyers and light cruisers at the time. As a matter of fact, if Commodore Tyrwhitt had left at 5 p.m. on May 31st, he could not have been in touch with the Grand Fleet till 4 a.m. the next morning without exhausting all his fuel.

His arrival, therefore, would have been at too late an hour for him to have participated in any part of the action. So the Admiralty decision was not only a wise one, but in no way militated against success in the battle. When all chance of a raid south was over, that is at 3 a.m., the Commodore was ordered north and arrived in time to relieve and supplement the divisions badly mauled in the night action.

In conclusion, there is one matter of great importance which has been mentioned but to which fuller reference must now be made. It is common knowledge, and in fact assertions have appeared in print without contradiction on the part of the Admiralty, that messages from Admiral Scheer to the High Sea Fleet were intercepted almost hourly by the English stations, decyphered and reported to the Admiralty. These were not passed to Admiral Jellicoe. He only received one that was sent at 9.58 p.m. and one received at 11.5, which latter was an incomplete summary of those which had been received prior to that time. No others were subsequently received by him.

The reason for this omission has never been explained. There is little doubt, however, that had, even some, of these messages been sent to the *Iron Duke* the whole course of the night's programme would have been altered, and our fleet would have been in a position to intercept the High Sea Fleet at daylight.

Chapter 10

"THE ADMIRALTY NARRATIVE"

The publication of the Admiralty official account of the Battle of Jutland was looked forward to with both interest and apprehension – interest, in the hope that it might contain new facts, especially from foreign sources, and apprehension because of the sinister rumours that have shrouded its conception and birth. Our hopes were doomed to disappointment and our apprehensions have been confirmed.

Some months after the Armistice, Admiral Sir Rosslyn Wemyss, then the First Sea Lord, appointed a committee to prepare a report on the Battle of Jutland. Captain J. Harper was appointed president of the committee, since at that time he was Director of Navigation, and therefore officially the proper person to supervise the charting. Moreover, not having been present at the battle, he was free from all bias of association. Sir Rosslyn Wemyss approved of the report, but before it could be issued he had left the Admiralty and the succeeding Board suppressed it.

Not infrequently when cold, hard facts are charted the result does not agree with the impressions that moments of excitement may have implanted in the memory. So something approaching to incredulity and consternation reigned when the report showed that the battle cruisers took but a small part in the battlefleet action, and were practically out of the fight that took place at 7.10 p.m., owing to being to the eastward of the battlefleet. On the other hand, the plotting of the positions of the German Fleet showed that Admiral Jellicoe's manoeuvres were the best possible under the varying conditions of the action.

Then rumour after rumour floated out from the Admiralty and passed from mouth to mouth of the sea-gossips in London: "Harper had been ordered to alter his report"; "Had refused"; "Had been threatened with My Lords' displeasure"; "Had stuck to his refusal"; etc. Then, lastly, "As Harper had refused to alter his report My Lords were going to alter it for him".

These reports went forth in ever-widening circles throughout the Navy and the country. What exactly followed is a bureaucratic mystery. The

Admiralty apparently stood by their suppression of the Harper report, but promised to issue a Staff appreciation of the battle later. Meanwhile, the Government published a collection of original documents known popularly as the *Jutland Papers*. It seems also that some undertaking was given by the Admiralty to Lord Jellicoe to the effect that the new report that was being prepared as a substitute for Captain Harper's would not be published until he had seen the draft.

Lord Jellicoe left for New Zealand in the latter part of 1920. The *Admiralty Narrative* was sent out to him. This he examined, and took objection to a considerable portion. He must have been placed in a most difficult position being in the Antipodes, and having to deal with a document in which innuendo was present, and in which facts were glossed over and suppressed. He replied to the document and asked that his corrections should be included in the *Narrative*; or, at all events, that his remarks should be printed, otherwise he would have to issue a separate publication.

In view of the possibility of the latter alternative, Lord Jellicoe asked me to undertake such publication if necessary, and I consented. I felt, however, that it was only right that I should inform the First Lord of the Admiralty that I had done so. I therefore called on Mr. Amery in 1923 by appointment, and told him of my consent. At the same time I took advantage of my rank and experience of the Navy to appeal to him to appoint an independent committee – I suggested the three Hydrographers of the Navy last retired – to inquire into the Harper and the Admiralty chartings, and to say which one was correct – or, as was possible, if both were correct. I also pointed out that the Navy looked to him as First Lord to see that the balance was truly held and that no biased report was issued. He promised to look closely into the matter, but I heard no more from him.

As I left the Admiralty I told a naval officer of high rank, holding a prominent appointment in that office, what my business with the First Lord had been. His remark, "Thank God! I hope he will do it," showed that the opinion of some officers in the Admiralty regarding the report was much the same as that of the Navy generally.

In August 1924 the *Narrative* was issued, and as it contained Lord Jellicoe's remarks, I refrained from publishing the papers confided to me, in which procedure Lord Jellicoe concurred, and has since asked me not to make use of the papers for any purpose whatever.

The *Narrative* confirmed the apprehensions originated by the rumours referred to. To the technical reader, versed in naval operations and terms, as well as in the sentiment of the Navy, a nasty flavour pervades the whole narrative. Let us take some examples.

We have already discussed the failure of the Admiral commanding the Battle Cruiser Fleet to keep in touch with the German Battlefleet on the run north back to the Grand Fleet. The result was that at the time of sighting

Admiral Jellicoe's flagship he was unable to give the latter accurate information of the position of the enemy's battleships. Since this failure delayed the deployment of our fleet, and in all probability altered the nature of the deployment, the matter is of surpassing interest to the technical reader.

The *Official History of the War* states: "As soon as he (Admiral Jellicoe) made out our battle cruisers heading across his bows and engaged with an unseen enemy, he flashed to Admiral Beatty the query, 'Where is the enemy's?' (6.1 p.m.) ... Just then (6.6 p.m.) Admiral Beatty ... flashed back his reply to the Commander-in-Chief's query, but it only said, 'Enemy's battle cruisers bearing S.E'. This did no more than deepen the obscurity. ... The Commander-in-Chief repeated to Admiral Beatty, 'Where is the enemy's battlefleet?' ... at 6.14 ... Admiral Beatty signalled, 'Have sighted the enemy's battlefleet bearing S.S.W.'."

What we find in the *Admiralty Narrative* is this[48]: "Hardly had the columns turned south than the sound of heavy firing indicated the close proximity of the enemy's heavy ships, and the *Lion* signalled (6.6) that the enemy's battle cruisers bore S.E. ... About 6.14 p.m., and almost simultaneously, a signal came in from *Lion* reporting them (enemy's battleships) in sight S.S.W."

That is all. Nothing more. The whole episode glossed over and the important facts never mentioned.

Two other examples will be sufficient. On page 62 we find: "Admiral Beatty turned at once to the sound of the guns." But on page 64 we read: "At 8.15, when the two fleets were again coming into contact, the British Fleet was in divisions steering west. ... A few minutes later the guns of the *Calliope* and the 4th Light Cruiser Squadron could be heard to the westward. Touch had evidently been regained, and at 8.21 the Commander-in-Chief altered course to W.S.W. *two points away from the enemy*."

The italics are mine. The impression conveyed is that as soon as the Commander-in-Chief, Admiral Jellicoe, heard the guns he altered course away from the enemy – else why add these words gratuitously after W.S.W.?[49]

The truth so skilfully hidden by the *Admiralty Narrative* was: First, the enemy was out of sight and his exact whereabouts unknown; secondly, that Admiral Jellicoe altered course towards the sound of guns which bore from him W.S.W., or even a little more still southward of that bearing. That the firing was to the *westward* was true, for the *westward* was W.S.W., the course altered to by Admiral Jellicoe.

Again, dealing with the escape of the German Fleet at night, we read, on pages 75 and 76: "Admiral Beatty was still in ignorance of the enemy's course to the south-eastward, and imagined him to be to the westward. The battle cruisers had been too far ahead to observe the route of the High Sea Fleet *as indicated by the destroyer actions*."

Now the portion I have italicized can only mean:

(1) That the route of the High Sea Fleet *was* indicated by the destroyer actions.

(2) That had the battle cruisers been less far ahead their Admiral would have interpreted the course of the German Battleneet from the fighting that went on during the night between the destroyers and light cruisers belonging to the two fleets.

Let us see what inferences were drawn from the destroyer actions by the two Admirals nearest to that attack.

Admiral Evan-Thomas, commanding the battleship division near this fighting, in no way interpreted it as indicating the presence of the enemy's battlefleet, since in his dispatch after the battle he reports:[50]

> At 10.15 observed heavy firing a little abaft the starboard beam which I surmised to be attacks by enemy destroyers and light craft on our light cruisers and destroyers. ... At 10.34 heavy firing was observed on our starboard quarter, and destroyers appeared to be attacking the cruisers. At 11.35 a further attack was seen further off right astern. No further incident occurred until the Second Battle Squadron was observed ahead three to five miles at early dawn.

Admiral Sir Cecil Burney, who was also near the fighting, reported after the battle:[51]

> Four night attacks were observed during the night. The first on the starboard beam, others taking place in succession towards the stern; several explosions were heard, and two very large ones with flame shooting into the sky were seen. Star shells were seen. ... About midnight smoke was observed ahead of *Marlborough*, which crossed from starboard to port, and back again to starboard, and then came down the starboard (western) side. It appeared to be a large ship and was challenged by *Revenge*, who was answered by two letters, though they were not the correct ones. She then disappeared.

There was no suggestion that the torpedo attack indicated that the High Sea Fleet were passing astern. The *Marlborough* was six miles off the leading German battleship when it passed astern, while the *Iron Duke* was ten miles off.

It is therefore grossly unfair to hint that Admiral Jellicoe should have drawn an inference which was not apparent to two Admirals four miles nearer to the fighting.

The point raised by Lord Jellicoe regarding the alleged injustice to Rear-Admiral Evan-Thomas would have been more courteously answered by the Admiralty had they quoted portions of Admiral Beatty's dispatch after the action : "Led by Rear-Admiral Evan-Thomas, M.V.O., in *Barham,* the Squadron (5th Battle) supported us brilliantly and effectively."[52]

Again: "I have already made mention of the brilliant support afforded by Rear-Admiral Evan-Thomas, M.V.O., and the 5th Battle Squadron."[53]

These quotations would have been more generous than the nagging footnote in reply to Lord Jellicoe's remarks.[54]

I will pass by the discourteous tone in which the replies to Lord Jellicoe's criticisms are framed, which must strike anyone who is accustomed to the traditions of official courtesy.

It is needless to dive further into the *Narrative* and produce more examples of inaccuracies. But it is interesting to inquire first who wrote the *Narrative,* and, secondly, to consider what useful purpose it can serve.

That it was not passed by the Board of Admiralty is evident, as it lacks the usual official notice to say that it is published with the approval of the Board. Yet My Lords express opinions in the footnotes to Appendix G. Why do My Lords speak in the footnotes and yet not approve the *Narrative*? It looks very much as if the Naval Staff prepared the *Narrative* expecting the Board to take the responsibility of acknowledging it, and that the Board refused to do so!

The *Narrative* as a literary production is poor; the writers rarely allow themselves to depart from a dull monotony of technical words. We were, however, cheered to find that this reserve was occasionally departed from, for we read:[55] "That in the lull hours (*sic*), between 5.10 and 5.40, Admiral Beatty may have found time to review the state of his force."

Again, just below: "Every minute, too, was bringing them nearer and nearer to the Grand Fleet, and the Vice-Admiral (Beatty) could look forward with confidence to a renewal of the action." These must have escaped the observation of My Lords Commissioners of the Admiralty, who we notice are, in their footnotes, particularly vigilant, and reprove any inference made by Lord Jellicoe by pointing out that the *Narrative* is a narrative of fact only.[56]

In conclusion, the *Narrative* serves no useful purpose. If intended as a serious Staff production, it brings discredit on the Naval Staff at the Admiralty. If intended as a popular narrative it fails equally, as it is quite unintelligible to the man-in-the-street. When compared with Sir Julian Corbett's account of the battle it fails in composition, in clearness, in interest, and in balance of judgment. Are we really to believe that the *Narrative* represents the best effort of our much-vaunted Naval Staff after nearly four years of labour?

There is, however, a serious side to the whole episode, namely, the effect the history of the publication has had in lowering the opinion of the Navy of its Admiralty. A narrative issued by the Admiralty should have been full, straightforward, and free from bias, outspoken and fully concurred in by all Flag Officers and Commodores on matters within their own knowledge, or the reasons for any divergence of views stated impartially. Admiralty work should be above cavil and suspicion.

Judged from these standards the *Narrative* fails miserably, and therefore the high status of the Admiralty with the Navy has been correspondingly compromised for the first time within the memory of man.

The only redeeming feature so far as the relations of the Admiralty with the *Narrative* are concerned is the apparent refusal of the Board to issue it under their authority and with their benediction. Admiral Wemyss's Board passed the original report; the present *Narrative* has not received Board sanction. It had been far better to have stopped its issue altogether and to have issued in its stead the original report of the independent committee set up by Admiral Sir Rosslyn Wemyss.

Chapter 11
The Origin of the Book

When the official narrative of the Battle of Jutland was issued the *Daily Express* published what purported to be a recent interview with Admiral Scheer, highly uncomplimentary to Lord Jellicoe, on which aspect of the interview the *Daily Express* Special Correspondent did not fail to enlarge.

ADMIRAL SCHEER'S BOMBSHELL

Unfortunately the *Daily Telegraph* of August 16th published a letter from Admiral Scheer to the *Berliner Zeitung am Mittag*, which stated:

> The account in the *Daily Express* published without my foreknowledge is a gross misrepresentation of a conversation which I had with an English correspondent in 1922.
>
> In his report the English correspondent does not completely suppress the explanation given by me, but in a not very gentlemanly manner has not hesitated to deceive the English reader by the misleading title, "How I Escaped at Jutland", and by a false date.

We consider it impossible to deal thoroughly with Mr. Filson Young's article – which was the cause of writing this book – without quoting it verbatim, as it is redolent of innuendo and inaccurate assertions.

However, for the moment we will content ourselves with quoting a few statements to indicate the nature of the whole article. We will commence with the following extract:

> Whereas no one can find a technical fault with Admiral Jellicoe's deployment, which was strictly according to the rules. The only trouble lay in the fact that at 6.15 in the evening, and in the midst of a battle, there is not always time to observe the rules of the parade ground. Opportunity

177

was there, but opportunity did not wait long enough for Admiral Jellicoe. The real moment flashed up and was gone while he was waiting for it still to come.

It is true that there would have been a quicker way had Lord Beatty at 6 p.m. been able to supply Lord Jellicoe with the exact position of the German Battlefleet. In the absence of this information Lord Jellicoe's method of deployment was absolutely the correct one.

He was waiting for Lord Beatty to tell him where the German Fleet was. The failure of the latter to do so nearly caused the moment to slip.

Later on we find: "The plan and the principle were, *not to risk the Grand fleet.*" The plan was to act sanely and not like a lunatic. Would any reasonable person risk losing eight battleships to save for a few minutes only 3,000 yards in range?

Again:

> With that risk he [Admiral Beatty] played throughout his marvellous fighting chase towards and return from the south-east at Jutland, when he brought back the whole German High Seas Fleet and laid it, as a cat brings you a mouse, at Jellicoe's feet.

This is delightful! The cat ran away from the mouse and lost sight of it in twenty minutes, and never saw it again. When asked where the mouse was the cat had to confess it didn't know!

Also:

> At 7 o'clock on the evening of Jutland, when Beatty led the German Fleet in a state of confusion into the jaws of a trap from which there should have been no escape, and out of which Admiral Scheer admits he did not expect to escape.

We must here halt to discuss the diagram which otherwise there would have been no reason to publish. But the mis-statement is so glaring and uncalled for that it needs stamping on.

By 7 p.m. Lord Jellicoe had manoeuvred the fleet between the enemy and his harbour. In this, Lord Beatty, a junior Admiral obeying the orders of his Commander-in-Chief, had no hand at all. At 6.50 Admiral Scheer turned his ships round and got the head of the line of his battleships and battle cruisers in the positions shown by X and W at 7.12. In the meantime our fleet, altering course to where the German Fleet was hidden in the mist, had got into the position marked T T T T T T.

Between 6.55 and 7.12 Admiral Beatty had been having a little circle-turning of his own at the place marked Z. If any confusion existed at all, it was not in the German fleet but in our own battle cruiser fleet, who waltzed

178

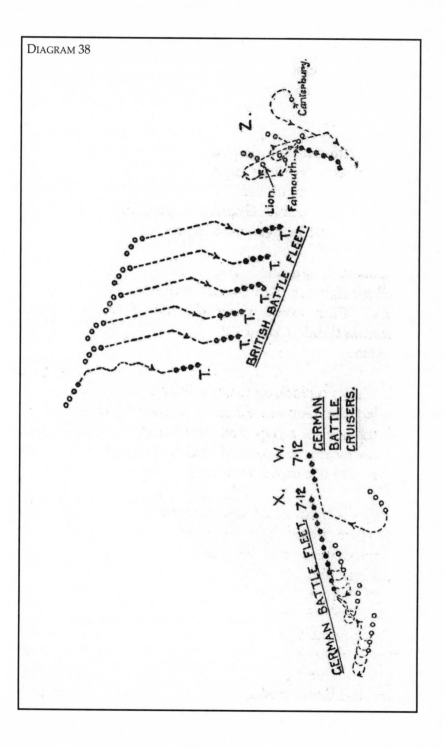

DIAGRAM 38

round like a kitten after its own tail. It is believed the reason for this excitement was a gyro compass that went wrong; but at all events Admiral Beatty, far from *leading the Germans into a trap from which there was no escape*, was busy trying to straighten up confusion among his cruisers.

We will end with the following:

> For that his glorious three thousand died. But if the judgment that made Admiral Jellicoe turn away from grasping the prize for fear that the Grand Fleet might be injured in the process was a right judgment, then the men of the *Queen Mary, Invincible,* and *Indefatigable* died in vain.

Let us be quite frank. The battle cruisers steamed at high speed away from the German Battlefleet and left the 5th Battle Squadron to fight them. The men of the *Queen Mary* and *Indefatigable* did not die in vain. But their loss was mainly caused by Admiral Beatty not bringing the 5th Battle Squadron into action until the *Indefatigable* had been sunk and only a few minutes before *the Queen Mary* was blown up.

The *Invincible* was not lost in the cruiser action, Phase I, but in Phase II of the battlefleet action by suddenly coming under fire of the German battleships as they emerged from the mist.

THE LEADING ARTICLE IN THE 'SUNDAY EXPRESS' OF THE SAME DATE

Admiral Scheer exploded a new Jutland bombshell in the columns of the *Daily Express*. He gave at last his own frank view of the most controversial fleet action in history. He went much further than he had gone in his published work, and declared roundly that Admiral Jellicoe had thrown away a chance of annihilating the German High Seas Fleet, giving chapter and verse for his assertion.

He shortly after exploded a second one under Mr. Filson Young and the editor of the Sunday Express *stating that the* Daily Express *correspondent had not hesitated to deceive the English reader by a misleading title and a false date.*

The Scheer bombshell has been the talk of England for four days. It has revived the whole controversy in an acute form and set the world wondering again. Admiral Jellicoe replied to Admiral Scheer

In spite of the controversy being revived, the Sunday Express *refused to print a reply to Mr. Filson Young's article.*

yesterday through the columns of the *Evening Standard*. He denies his assertions, declares that the German "turn all together" was made before the British "turn away", recalls familiar circumstances of the battle, and declares unequivocally that other tactics on his part would have exposed the Grand Fleet to possible or probable disaster. We publish on this page a striking article by Mr. Filson Young, who was specially equipped for understanding the minds of Lord Beatty and Lord Jellicoe, and who had seen in practice the very manoeuvre which, according to Lord Jellicoe's critics, lost us the chance of devastating victory. He gives us Lord Beatty's criticism of this manoeuvre. "If he does this when he meets the Germans he cannot win."

Lord Jellicoe did not win. Jutland – "the battle that was never fought", as Beatty described it – was inconclusive. The vindication of Lord Jellicoe is to be sought in the fact that the German High Sea Fleet never ventured out again, and that it came to humiliating surrender at Scapa Flow, where it still rots at the bottom of the seas it challenged. For the rest the controversy remains. One critic says one thing and one another. The belated official account of the battle eight years after it was fought has left the layman as bewildered as ever. The rival statements of Scheer and Jellicoe leave the conflict of evidence and opinion to be settled by personal inclination to one side or another.

I should doubt Mr. Filson Young's ability to understand Lord Jellicoe's mind.

This manoeuvre was used twice by Lord Beatty and both times wrongly.

The report was belated because the Admiralty suppressed the report of independent experts and issued one edited by the Admiralty.

What of the man in the street? He will read Mr. Filson Young's lucid article with vivid interest.

Yes, and owing to the action of the Sunday Express, he will now be able to read the reply to it.

He is inclined to think that the British Navy lost its golden hour of glorious opportunity.

Owing to misrepresentation of facts this has been his opinion.

Lord Jellicoe, himself a man of rare and splendid courage, was no doubt a victim. He was caught in the machine that he had fashioned, enveloped in the Admiralty red tape of which he had himself tied the knots, bound by his own rules.

He, with the assistance of his staff and admirals of experience, laid down certain rules to be followed in certain emergencies. It is this class of quiet thought before a battle that leads to success, and saves disaster.

He was in the midst of the indescribable carnage and chaos of a fleet action.

He was not. Owing to his fine tactic of crossing the enemy's T, the good training he had given to his battleships and their excellent shooting, there was no carnage in the Iron Duke, *and throughout the fleet there was no chaos.*

He was obsessed by the fear of risking the Grand Fleet.

He was obsessed by no fear. But he and every other admiral of experience knew that unless at certain times he performed certain manoeuvres he would be gambling away the chance of thrashing the enemy.

If he had lost it by recklessness which achieved no overwhelming triumph he would have been exe-crated and abhorred. He would have exposed us defenceless to invasion, and the war would have been lost to the Allies. He did not risk the Grand Fleet, we were not invaded, the war was won for the Allies, and the German Fleet scuppered itself in British waters after unconditional surrender.

We do not suppose such an idea entered Lord Jellicoe's head. An admiral or general rarely, if ever, during an operation thinks of himself or his reputation, but he does most earnestly consider the success of the business in hand. In Lord Jellicoe's case this was the sinking of the High Sea Fleet.

Yes. But if Beatty had been in

If Lord Beatty, an inexperienced

command? If we had closed the trap, taken the risks, fought to a finish? That is the "if" that sticks.

admiral, had been in command, what then?

The Grand Fleet would have suffered in its training. He would have turned away from a massed torpedo attack just as Lord Jellicoe did, or else he would have lost several battleships and seriously reduced the margin of strength of our fleet over that of the German fleet.

But the Battle Cruiser Fleet would have been under the command of an experienced admiral who might have sunk several of the German cruisers without the loss of the Indefatigable *and* Queen Mary, *and who would have given Lord Beatty, in command of the Grand Fleet, early information of the position of the German Fleet, and therefore he might have deployed as correctly as Lord Jellicoe did.*

Trafalgar might have been outdone by a naval victory more complete and as decisive.

This could not be the result of a modern sea fight. Lord Beatty could have done no more damage to the Germans than was done by Lord Jellicoe. No one has ever suggested in what way greater damage could have been inflicted.

In this I am, pedantically speaking, in error. Mr. Churchill has made suggestions to this effect, but they have been shown to be without any value.

The page of our naval history might have been illuminated as never before.

The page of our naval history might, on the other hand, have recorded a defeat owing to inexperience in organization, training and tactics.

The war might have been shortened.

No one has ever suggested how this could have been done.

There is no disposition to misunderstand Lord Jellicoe.

It is not a misunderstanding of Lord Jellicoe that is the cause of the trouble, but the utter inability of the writer to understand the fundamental elements of naval tactics or to appreciate what sea and fleet experience means to a man who is in command of a fleet.

That "if" still sticks.

That "if" is the handful of mud, some of which was sure to stick if thrown at Lord Jellicoe; hence this leader. However, sufficient has been written in this book to make that "if" to stick to some purpose in the mind of the nation, though not exactly in the manner hoped by the Sunday Express.

Undoubtedly the criticism to which Lord Jellicoe has been subjected sprang chiefly from the disappointment of the nation at large that the German Fleet had been fought and not annihilated. The disappointment was considerably augmented by the bald announcement made by the Admiralty as to the result of the action.

The position of the Admiralty was one of difficulty. They knew our own losses from Admiral Jellicoe, but neither they nor Admiral Jellicoe knew what damage had been done to the German Fleet. The Admiralty could not say more than they knew; they had at all costs to avoid exaggeration. Their announcement ran:

The Secretary of the Admiralty makes the following announcement:

On the afternoon of Wednesday, May 31st, a naval engagement took place off the coast of Jutland.

The British ships on which the brunt of the fighting fell were the Battle Cruiser Fleet, and some cruisers and light cruisers, supported by four fast battleships.

Among those the losses were heavy.

The German Battlefleet, aided by low visibility, avoided prolonged action with our main forces, and soon after these appeared on the scene the enemy returned to port, though not before receiving severe damage from our battleships.

The battle cruisers, *Queen Mary*, *Indefatigable*, *Invincible*, and the cruisers *Defence* and *Black Prince*, were sunk. The *Warrior* was disabled, and after being towed for some time had to be abandoned by her crew.

It is also known that the destroyers *Tipperary*, *Turbulent*, *Fortune*,

Sparrowhawk and *Ardent* were lost, and six others are not yet accounted for.

No British battleships or light cruisers were sunk.

The enemy's losses were serious.

At least one battle cruiser was destroyed and one severely damaged; one battleship reported sunk by our destroyers during a night attack; two light cruisers were disabled and probably sunk.

The exact number of enemy destroyers disposed of during the night attack cannot be ascertained with any certainty, but it must have been large.

Of course everyone jumped to the conclusion that this message covered a disaster, and that the Admiralty had not said all that they knew.

The only alternative to the Admiralty statement would have been one, on much the same lines, but with an addition to say that the engagement occurred too late in the day for a signal success to have been obtained, and that the enemy ran under shelter of darkness back to their harbour.

But it is doubtful if such a statement even would have allayed disappointment.

The Public had been convinced from the moment the war started that if the German Fleet was ever engaged by our battlefleet the majority of their ships would be sunk. A battle had been fought and they were not sunk: *ergo* someone was at fault. The man in the street did not trouble himself to learn the facts, or to grasp that an enemy who runs away cannot be overtaken unless the ships chasing him have greater speed and sufficient time in which to overtake him. He knew nothing about the Navy or modern fighting at sea; he looked on those matters as the business of the Navy which it was not necessary for him to understand. He knew little of sea fighting except what he had read had happened in the old days. Then Nelson sank French ship after French ship. Where was our Nelson?

Then rumour seized on the deployment on the tooth-of-the-comb furthest from the German Fleet. Shades of Nelson! Fancy not getting as near to the enemy as possible! It was never explained to him that deployment on the tooth nearest the enemy did not mean that the enemy would be sighted nearer to our fleet than when the deployment was carried out on the tooth furthest away from the enemy; or that such a deployment would not have helped to bring about a closer range action; that it merely meant the enemy would be sighted a quarter of an hour later; but in that quarter of an hour our fleet was able to attain a position of great advantage instead of being caught in one of disadvantage. None of these things was explained to the people of this country.

To turn away from the enemy during a fight simply because of an attack being made by puny destroyers carrying torpedoes again seemed to savour of undue caution and of a desire not to press the engagement. The man in the street was never told that the chances were that two out of every five torpedoes in such an attack would hit ships; that such a manoeuvre had been fully discussed and agreed to by all the admirals, and was used by every admiral who was confronted by such an attack throughout the war. He was never told that such a turn *away* was merely a swing for a few minutes and then a swing back; the counterpart of the step back of a boxer to avoid a blow.

Further, Admiral Beatty's signal to say that if the van of the battlefleet followed him he could cut off the enemy's fleet was interpreted to mean that, had Admiral Beatty commanded at the battle, the German Fleet would have been cut off from their harbours. It was never explained that the German Fleet had already been cut off from their harbours, that the ships the Vice-Admiral had sighted were part of the same division that were in sight at the same moment of Admiral Jellicoe and the ships near him, eleven miles off from Admiral Beatty.

"Why did not Jellicoe go right at the German Fleet?" was also asked. No one answered; so the nation grumbled and rumour passed from mouth to mouth. Jutland was condemned as a poor affair, and people thought, and said, that had Admiral Beatty commanded at Jutland things would have been very different and the German Fleet would have been annihilated.

No one wishes to pretend that Jutland was a glorious victory. It was not. No glorious victory was possible under the daylight conditions that prevailed on May 31st.

A victory was perhaps lost on the morning of 1st June by the failure of responsible subordinates during the previous night; but, so far as the actual battleship engagement is concerned, it is an action of which our nation and our battlefleet may well be proud.

The German tactics were in every case excellently adapted to serve the purpose that Admiral Scheer had in view; their fleet was out-fought and out-manoeuvred; it could not be annihilated. They scurried back to their harbours determined never to risk another action with our battlefleet. Strategically, for the remainder of the war they might as well have been at the bottom of the North Sea.

The two blots of magnitude were, first, the failure of Admiral Beatty to close up the Battle Cruiser Fleet and thus losing the chance of smashing up Admiral Hipper's squadron, and, secondly, the failure of the rear ships during the night to report the presence of German battleships. But so far as the daylight battlefleet action of the 31st May is concerned the battle is one that may well be looked on with pride, even though adverse conditions wrested from our fleet a more sweeping victory.

Let me add a few words about the relative efficiency of the battleship and the Battle Cruiser Fleets.

Of the qualities on which judgment can be based two are outstanding, namely, gunnery efficiency and signal efficiency.

Let us first take gunnery efficiency. There is little doubt that the battle cruisers were considerably inferior in merit as regards accurate gunnery. Admiral Jellicoe took the greatest trouble to enforce gunnery practices on the battleships. The gunnery practices of the 1st and 2nd Battle Cruiser Squadrons were under the Admiral commanding the Battle Cruiser Squadrons. The boast that the "battle cruisers did their gunnery practice in action", if true, fully accounted for their bad shooting in the Jutland battle.

Admiral Hipper, the Admiral commanding the German battle cruisers, reported to the Commander-in-Chief of the German High Sea Fleet after the battle, commenting adversely on the shooting of the battle cruisers and eulogistically on the shooting of the battleships.[57]

Again, Commander Georg von Hase, gunnery officer of the *Derfflinger* in his book, *Kiel and Jutland* (after forty five minutes' action with our battle cruisers), states:

> 4.50.   First part of battle cruiser action closed.
> *Derfflinger* had come out with fighting strength unimpaired.

Later on during twenty minutes engaged with our 5th Battle Squadron, he states:

> 6.25.   *Lutzow* heavily hit.
>
> 6.30.   Three hits on *Derfflinger.*
>
> 6.50.   *Derfflinger* was now a pretty sorry sight.

After another bout of ten minutes with our battlefleet.

> 7.55.   Salvo after salvo fell around us. Hit after hit struck the ship.

These quotations, coupled with the fact that six of our battle cruisers fought for three-quarters of an hour with five German battle cruisers and did them no serious damage, while we lost two ships, cannot but convict the battle cruisers of inferior shooting.

The next section of vital importance in fighting is the signal department. The signal department is all-important next to the engine-room and the gunnery officer departments. Here much was left to be desired. After every allowance has been made for disorganization caused by damage done in battle, the signal organization of the battle cruisers must stand convicted of want of efficiency.

The concentration of fire at the Dogger Bank was muddled, and also again in Jutland, Phase I.[58] Here a signal for concentration of fire was made, but the *Princess Royal*, the ship next astern of the *Lion*, was the only one to take in the signal. Why was the ordinary hard and fast routine when repeating signals not adhered to?

The result was that the *Derfflinger* was left for nearly ten minutes unfired at, which was a fatal mistake, as it is of the utmost importance that no ship of the enemy should be allowed full undisturbed exercise of her fire control. The signal was made before fire was opened, so we cannot look to the flurry of a fight for the excuse.

Again, Jutland, Phase I, the general signal at 2.32 to turn in succession to S.S.E. was not passed on to the 5th Battle Squadron.[59] At 3.5 the *Tiger* informed the *Lion* that the 2.32 signal and the signals made since had not been passed to the *Barham*. Yet again, at 4.40, when Admiral Beatty swung round away from the German Battlefleet, the signal made by flags could not be seen by Admiral Evan-Thomas, who was eight miles off.[60] So important a signal should have been passed by searchlight direct to the 5th Battle Squadron. That one was available is shown by it being used both before and also after this signal was made.[61] The result was that the 5th Battle Squadron held on for eight minutes towards the German Battlefleet, and consequently suffered considerable damage.

These signal matters may seem of small moment, but in reality they are not. The evidence afforded by these failures is that the signal departments of the battle cruisers, the medium for vital battle-intercommunication in the fleet, were slack and had been indifferently trained.

No mistakes in signalling seem to have occurred among the ships of the battlefleet.

Taking the gunnery and signal performance of the battle cruisers and of the battlefleet into consideration, we are forced to the conclusion that the training of the battle cruisers for battle was inferior to that of the battle-ships. Had Admiral Beatty therefore been in command of the Grand Fleet up to the date of the Battle of Jutland there is reason to assume that that fleet would have shown less efficiency than it did on the 31st May, 1916, the day that Jutland was fought.

If we take the whole of the above into quiet thought there is little doubt all will echo the short prayer: "Thank God that Lord Jellicoe commanded the Grand Fleet both before and at the Battle of Jutland."

Chapter 12

Remarks on Mr Churchill's Criticism of the Battle of Jutland Published in *The World Crisis*

We have seen that Admiral Beatty failed to close up his fleet on receipt of information that an enemy's vessel had been sighted, but wasted twelve minutes before he turned towards the direction of the enemy. These twelve minutes would have sufficed amply to close up his fleet.

Mr. Churchill treats this episode in an unsatisfactory manner. He writes, "Six minutes steaming away from the enemy might mean the loss of six thousand yards in pursuit." Evidently the "six minutes steaming away from the enemy" refers to the description given in Appendix A, of the earlier editions of this book, of the most rapid way in which the Battle Cruiser Fleet could have been closed up; viz. by Admiral Beatty turning and steaming for six minutes towards the *Barham*.

This matter can be simply explained. If, when the signal that the enemy had been sighted was received (see Diagram 39), the *Lion* had turned, say,

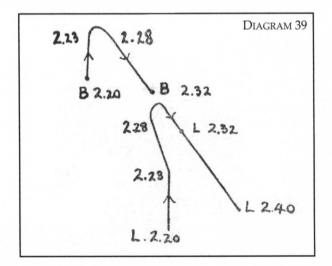

DIAGRAM 39

at 2.23, towards the *Barham* (the Flagship of Admiral Evan-Thomas) and steamed for five minutes to 2.28 and then back again for the same time, she would, allowing two minutes for the turn, have been back again in the twelve minutes to the position 2.32, or approximately to the place from which she had started. If, as she turned towards the *Barham*, she had signalled with the searchlight to that ship to close; then, if we allow three minutes for the *Barham* to have taken in the signal and to have turned, that ship would have had nine minutes in which to close the *Lion*. This was a sufficient time to bring her into her proper station behind the sixth or rear battle cruiser at 2.32. The main object of the turn *towards* would have been to allow all the ships to work up to full speed while the 5th Battle Squadron was closing up.

This swing "towards and away" *so as to work up to full speed while awaiting a concentration* is a commonplace to a tactical mind. Mr. Churchill, by dismissing this manoeuvre in the curt way that he has done, leads us to doubt whether he is in any way familiar with the niceties of naval tactics.

The diagrams 40 41 and 42 show the matter clearly. Diagram 39 shows a "swing towards" which has just been described. The net result would have been the fleet closed up arid steaming 23 knots at 2.40.

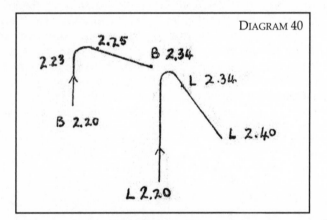

Diagram 40 shows what would have happened if *Barham* had been told to close at 2.20. Net result, the fleet closed up and steaming 20 knots at 2.40.

Diagram 41 shows what actually happened through nothing being done for twelve minutes and then the searchlight not being used to make the turning signal. Net result, *Barham* left ten miles behind.

Diagram 42 shows the gain in the chase by employing No.1 method over No.2 method; that is, by turning "towards and away". Net result, a gain of one and a half miles.

In the above, five minutes have been allowed for *Lion* to signal, for *Barham* to take in the signal and then to turn. This is a reasonable allowance.

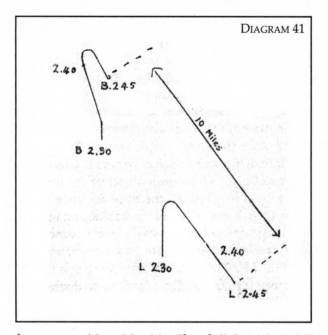

Now the reason adduced by Mr. Churchill for Admiral Beatty not closing up his fleet before commencing his action with the enemy's battle cruisers, although he had a whole hour in which to do it, is that which might be put forward as an excuse by a youngster in charge, for the first time, of a torpedo flotilla, or a raw subaltern temporarily in command of a company. Let us quote Mr. Churchill:

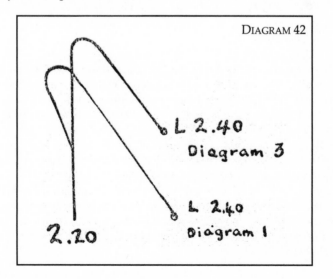

The doctrine that after sufficient force has been concentrated an admiral should delay and, at the risk of losing the whole opportunity, gather a still larger force, was one which could only be doubtfully applied even to the battlefleet.[62]

This is an excellent piece of special pleading; the fallacy of its application is shown, first by the fact that the force with which Admiral Beatty rushed to meet the enemy proved to be *insufficient*, and, secondly, that he would have incurred no delay by closing up his ships.

It is not by trusting to luck, but by doing the correct thing, that unforeseen eventualities are forestalled. The history of the past, experience in the past, and the study of tactics, all teach the primary necessities of closing up a fighting force before commencing an action. This was not done, and Mr. Churchill seeks further to excuse it in the following sentence:

All that impulse, all that ardour gives was no doubt present in the Admiral's mind; but these were joined by all that the coldest science of war and the longest view of naval history proclaimed.[63]

This is Mr. Churchill's considered opinion in spite of the fact that Admiral Beatty was led into a trap by the utter disregard by the elementary axioms of tactics and by the waste of twelve minutes.

Mr. Churchill, however, recants, for later on we find a naive confession[64] which completely upsets his previous special pleading that Admiral Beatty had collected a sufficient force:

... the enemy whom he could not defeat with six ships to five are now five ships to four. Far away, all five German battle cruisers – grey smudges changing momentarily into rippling sheets of flame – are still intact and seemingly invulnerable.

It surely must occur to every reader, taking these paragraphs together, that, after all, the teaching of naval experience in the old wars, which insists on an admiral concentrating all the force possible in order to guard against the many unforeseen contingencies of a naval action, was the real and true "longest view of naval history", and that the disregard of such teaching cooled Admiral Beatty's "cold science" down to the not too useful temperature of absolute zero. In short, common sense is bound to admit that the "cold science of war" impelled the closing up of the 5th Battle Squadron immediately the enemy was sighted by our light cruisers instead of Admiral Beatty wasting twelve minutes before turning towards the enemy; or, at all events closing that squadron up to the battle cruisers during the three-quarters of an hour that elapsed before the enemy's battle cruisers were sighted by him.

We will now turn to Mr. Churchill's apportionment of blame, between Admiral Beatty and Admiral Evan-Thomas, for the delay in closing up the 5th Battle Squadron.

The *Barham*, the flagship of the 5th Battle Squadron, was unable to read the signal to alter course made at 2.32 p.m. owing to it having been made with flags instead of by searchlight; smoke and want of wind militated against a clear view of the flags.[65] For the loss of these eight minutes, for which the signal staff of Admiral Beatty's flagship and not Admiral Evan-Thomas must be held responsible, the latter is blamed by Mr. Churchill in thunderous periods, while Admiral Beatty, for the loss of the twelve minutes between 2.20 and 2.32 for no reason at all, receives unstinted adulation.

Let us look closely into Mr. Churchill's statements.

Admiral Evan-Thomas was stationed five miles from Admiral Beatty's flagship. The reason for this, as has already been pointed out, was that Admiral Beatty was expecting shortly to sight our battlefleet. The 5th Battle Squadron would, by this stationing, have been the exact distance from the battle cruisers which was laid down in the Grand Fleet Battle Orders.[66]

The formation of the Battle Cruiser Fleet was therefore what is called "peace cruising" formation; that is, one for convenience and not for fighting. Yet we find:

> Admiral Evan-Thomas' general and dominant orders were to keep supporting station five miles from the line.[67]

This is not a fact. There was nothing in the signal that was made at the time when the 5th Battle Squadron was stationed which gave either *general* or *dominant* orders to its admiral to keep *supporting* station. No one conversant with naval tactics, or with North Sea conditions during the war, would imagine that a squadron stationed five miles on the *English-shore-side* of a faster squadron had *dominant orders* to support that squadron when it was ordered there merely by an ordinary everyday disposing signal. That they did afford a minor support to the battle cruisers is true, but only in the same sense that the main battlefleet, although out of sight, was supporting the battle cruisers; or that any two squadrons in proximity, *de facto*, give some form of support to one another.

No. Admiral Evan-Thomas was, by the signal that was made, stationed, in all probability, for the purely utilitarian purpose of being in a convenient position for taking up his station on the battlefleet when it was sighted.

The next thing to note is that, having once been definitely stationed on a given bearing, and at a given distance from his senior officer, Admiral Evan-Thomas had no right to leave that post unless circumstances arose which prevented his senior officer communicating a new order, or unless some information came to him, suddenly and unexpectedly, which was unknown to his senior officer.

Neither of these two eventualities had occurred. He knew, from the signal that Admiral Beatty had made to the destroyers to form a screen on a S.S.E. course, that his senior officer meditated turning his cruisers to this course; but, as no signal came to him to "close" or to alter course, he remained quite in the dark as to that officer's intention regarding the 5th Battle Squadron. He has stated his dilemma as follows:

> The only way that I could account for no signal having been received by me was that the Vice-Admiral (Admiral Beatty) was going to signal another course to the 5th Battle Squadron, possibly to get the enemy's light cruisers between us. Anyway, if he wished us to turn, the searchlight would have done it in a moment. *It was not until the Tiger asked Lion by wireless whether the signal to turn was to be made to the Barham* that the Vice-Admiral seemed to realize the situation.[68]

This frank statement points to the fact that Admiral Beatty, undoubtedly obsessed with thoughts of the enemy, did not observe that the 5th Battle Squadron had not altered course until his attention was called to the matter by the *Tiger*; and then, instead of slowing down to allow that squadron to close, he rushed on and left it ten miles astern.

For three-quarters of an hour Admiral Beatty steamed with his fleet straggled out, in spite of the fact that three minutes after turning at 2.32, the Commodore Alexander-Sinclair in the *Galatea* signalled:

> Have sighted large amount of smoke as though from a fleet bearing E.N.E.

At 2.45 again:

> Smoke seems to be seven vessels besides destroyers and cruisers. They have turned north.

Mr. Churchill does not mention these signals; but, on the other hand, he excuses Admiral Beatty under the plea that

> ... the impression that every minute counted was dominant in his mind.

How about the twelve minutes wasted between 2.20 and 2.32? Did they not count?

It may be thought that this one episode has been treated at too great a length; this, perhaps, might be so if it were not for the blame cast by Mr. Churchill on the late Admiral Evan-Thomas for Admiral Beatty's shortcomings. That Admiral Evan-Thomas should be made a scapegoat is cruelly unfair, and the matter is one which called for the fullest investigation.

We will now quote Mr. Churchill's crowning effort to clear Admiral Beatty at the expense of Admiral Evan-Thomas:

> If only they [the 5th Battle Squadron] had been five thousand yards closer the defeat, if not the destruction, of Hipper's squadron was inevitable. That they were not five thousand yards closer was due entirely to their slowness in grasping the situation when the first contact was made with the enemy.

A statement more at variance with the official records could hardly have been made; especially when we remember that the first contact with the enemy was made at 2.20 and that Admiral Beatty did nothing till 2.32p.m. and during this interval had ample time to close up his fleet.

Mr. Churchill's naive confession made in a previous volume of *The World Crisis* flashes vividly back to the mind; and we recognize in this laboured defence of Admiral Beatty[69] the same blindness to naval requirements and exigencies that led him to appoint that Admiral to the command of the Battle Cruiser Squadron "over the heads of all against the advice of his technical advisers", apparently because he viewed naval matters as a military and not a naval officer, and hunted and played polo.

We will close this episode with examples of some of the literary red herrings employed by Mr. Churchill.[70]

> The *Galatea*'s message at 2.20 and the sound of her guns at 2.28 were sufficient for Admiral Beatty. German warships were at sea. At 2.32 the *Lion*, having warned her consorts of her intentions, turned about again.

Let us note, first of all, that the news at 2.20 should have been sufficient without the guns at 2.28 for Admiral Beatty to turn. There was no reason to wait to hear guns before turning; he knew German warships were at sea. But the insertion of this gratuitous piece of information about the gun fire might well cause the casual reader to reduce the apparent time of Admiral Beatty's inaction from twelve minutes to four minutes!

Again we find that:

> But the facts, when, at 2.32 Beatty *decided that the enemy was present in sufficient strength* to justify turning his heavy ships about, made it his clear duty to steam at once and at the utmost speed in their direction.[71]

It is here inferred that Admiral Beatty received information at, or immediately before, 2.32, in addition to that which he had at 2.20, which determined him to take action. What was this information? It could not have been the *Galatea*'s guns, for those told him no more than he already knew about the enemy's strength. In fact nothing had occurred to make any difference between what was known concerning the enemy at 2.20 and what was known at 2.32. So that if it was Admiral Beatty's "plain duty to steam at once and at the utmost speed" in the enemy's direction at 2.32, it was equally his plain duty to have done so twelve minutes earlier. This paragraph is a good example of the literary "red herring".

Surely Mr. Churchill would have been on safer grounds if he had been content to argue that Admiral Beatty was a fine, impulsive fighter; that in the preliminary action he was obsessed with a desire to come to grips with the enemy who had escaped him in the Dogger Bank Action; that he was confident that his battle cruisers could deal with the German battle cruisers without the assistance of the 5th Battle Squadron, and that it was for this reason that he did not wait to close them up. Unfortunately his conviction as regards the result of an action between two battle cruiser divisions was upset, and soon after the action had commenced he had sore need of the assistance of the ships of the 5th Battle Squadron which was not forthcoming owing to his precipitous rush into battle.

If such a frank statement of the case had been made there would have been little to criticize, for the nation loves a bold leader and welcomes a Rupert in battle, although such a leader may in the end prove to be somewhat expensive. But it is distinctly unfair to pass blame on to the shoulders of a junior Admiral in trying to prove that Admiral Beatty was a cautious as well as a gallant fighter. Lord Beatty's shoulders are strong enough to stand the racket of his own actions. Why should Mr. Churchill attempt to implicate another officer?

Mr. Churchill's description of the crisis of the battle cruiser action is vivid, but it loses much of its historical value when its fascinating and sonorous periods receive a douche of cold common sense. Take the following excerpt:

> But the movements of these blind, inanimate castles of steel were governed at the moment by the spirit of a single man. Had he faltered, had he taken less than a conqueror's view of the British fighting chances, all these great engines of sea power would have wobbled off in meaningless disarray.[72]

This, let us remember, is applied to the period of an action in which four British battle cruisers and four superb British battleships were pitted against only five German battle cruisers! What would the country, the Navy, and the world, and even Mr. Churchill himself, have said if the Admiral in command of such an overwhelming force had faltered and allowed his ships to "wobble off" in the middle of such an action?

This paragraph is a direct insult to the fighting spirit of the British Navy.

We will now move on to the time when the German High Sea Fleet was sighted by the scouts of the Battle Cruiser Fleet; then Admiral Scheer's trap was at once disclosed, and it became forthwith necessary for the Battle Cruiser Fleet to retreat to the northward and join the battlefleet, reporting fully, on the way, the movements of the enemy.

As soon as Admiral Beatty received news from the *Galatea* that the enemy's battlefleet was in sight, and had himself made out the approaching vessels, he signalled to his fleet to alter course to the northward. There are two things to be noted about the manner in which the turn was ordered and carried out:

    (1) The signal that was made to the 5th Battle Squadron was not the one best adapted to turn all the ships away from the danger that was threatening and which was every minute growing greater.

    (2) The 5th Battle Squadron was still steaming to the southward towards the enemy after the *Lion* had turned to the northward. The order for the Battle Squadron to turn was given far too late; in fact not until it had passed the *Lion* and was still steering towards the enemy.

The hoisting of a signal warns all ships of the Admiral's *intention*. It is improper to carry out the order conveyed until the signal is *hauled down*. "Hauling down" is the executive order from the Admiral to execute the signal. A signal is frequently hoisted by the Admiral *before the moment of its execution is due* in order to convey a warning of his intentions, and he hauls it down only when in his opinion the moment for its execution has arrived.

The signal for the 5th Battle Squadron to turn could therefore not be obeyed by Admiral Evan-Thomas until it was hauled down on board the *Lion*. It would have been highly improper for him to have complied with the order before the signal had been hauled down, especially as he was steaming towards the enemy.

It has been necessary to clear up this point before examining the remarks made by Mr. Churchill on this period of the fight. His statement is here divided, for convenience, into paragraphs; in the book they run concurrently:[73]

    (1) On sighting the main German Fleet, Beatty had *turned about so swiftly* that his ships soon passed the 5th Battle Squadron coming up at full speed and still on their southerly course.

    (2) As the two squadrons *ran past each other* on opposite courses the *Lion* signalled to the *Barham* (Admiral Evan-Thomas's flagship) to *turn about in succession*.

    (3) The *Lion's signal of recall* was flown at 4.48. She passed the *Barham* with the signal still flying at 4.53 and Rear-Admiral Evan-Thomas responded to the signal *three or four minutes later*.

    (4) Perhaps the Rear-Admiral having been slow in coming into action was inclined to be slow in coming out.

(5) Brief as was the interval, it was sufficient at the speed at which all the ships were moving to expose the 5th Battle Squadron to action with the van of the German Fleet.

(6) The van was formed by the German 3rd Squadron comprising the *Königs* and the *Kaisers*, the strongest and the newest vessels in the German Navy. The four *Queen Elizabeths* were now subjected to a tremendous fire concentrated on the point where each turned in succession.

If the English language means anything, the impression that must be conveyed by paragraphs (3) and (4) is that the damage done to the 5th Battle Squadron was owing to Admiral Evan-Thomas' delay in obeying Admiral Beatty's signal.

Now for the facts which probably are not apparent to the general reader. To begin with, Admiral Beatty made the wrong signal. He should have turned all the ships of the 5th Battle Squadron *together*, either at B^I or B^{II} (see

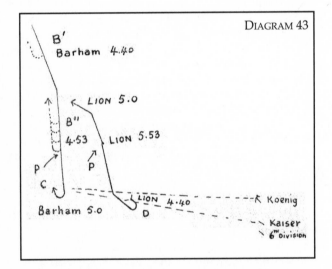

DIAGRAM 43

Lion at D 4.40 turns well out of range of the German Battlefleet. The 5th B.S. should have been turned by signal at B^I, or at the latest all the ships should have been turned together at B^{II}.

Instead of either of these two turns being ordered, each ship of the 5th B.S. was turned in succession round the point C under fire from the German Battlefleet.

The *Barham* passed the *Lion* when the two ships were at P P. The signal for the 5th B.S. to turn was not hauled down until after the two ships had passed each other.

Diagram 43), in the same way that Admiral Scheer, later on, turned his fleet, to escape from our battlefleet.

Instead of turning all his ships *together* (the manoeuvre that later on is belauded by Mr. Churchill when adopted by Admiral Scheer), Admiral Beatty first turned his cruisers "in succession" round a pivot (position D),[74] and then, by the signal he made caused the 5th Battle Squadron similarly to turn round a point C, on which the fire of the German van was concentrated.

Moreover, Mr. Churchill states that the signal to the *Barham* was *kept flying* until after she had passed Admiral Beatty's cruisers; but he does not mention at what time the signal was *hauled down*, or that Admiral Evan-Thomas obeyed the signal as soon as it was hauled down. In paragraph (3) of his statement above he remarks that:

> She passed the *Barham* with the signal still flying at 4.53, and Rear-Admiral Evan-Thomas responded to the signal three or four minutes later.

What he fails, however, to state is that this delay was due to the signal not being hauled down on board the *Lion*.

The average civilian would probably not appreciate that a signal is not obeyed until it is hauled down; he would naturally, therefore, read Mr. Churchill's incomplete statement as meaning that Admiral Evan-Thomas did not immediately obey the signal but wasted three or four minutes.

As a matter of history, when the draft of the *Official Narrative*, which had been compiled by the Naval Staff when Lord Beatty was Chief of the Staff, was sent to Admiral Evan-Thomas for his remarks, he pointed out the above facts and the reason for the delay of the 5th Battle Squadron to turn. It was the refusal of the Admiralty to make the necessary corrections in the *Narrative* that caused Admiral Jellicoe to make a strong protest. This important correction, however, when forced on the Admiralty, was merely inserted as a footnote in that publication.

Note also, how, by carelessly calling the signal "the signal to turn" in one case, and the "signal of recall" immediately afterwards, the uninitiated might imagine that two signals were made, and the fact that "the signal to turn" was left flying until after the *Barham* had passed the *Lion* is liable to be overlooked by the casual reader. Moreover, as the "general recall" is acted on and obeyed as soon as it is *seen*, and the signal "to turn" is not complied with until after it has been *hauled down*, the professional reader even, unless on his guard, might be betrayed into the belief that Admiral Evan-Thomas did not obey a general recall (which was never made) as promptly as he should have done.

The remark in paragraph (4) is uncalled for and undeserved.

From this sifting of Mr. Churchill's "facts" it has become clear that the blame for any damage done to the 5th Battle Squadron by the van of the German Battlefleet must be placed entirely on Admiral Beatty's shoulders. Mr. Churchill's attempt to implicate Admiral Evan-Thomas merely shows his want of knowledge of signalling in the Navy and insight into naval tactics, and reflects on his judgment on these matters.

Phase III

We confess to feeling considerable regret that Mr. Churchill did not treat, in that vivid prose of which he is such a consummate master, the dramatic change in role that came over the Battle Cruiser Fleet the instant the German High Sea Fleet was sighted at 4.33 p.m.

In the flash of a second the duties and functions of the Battle Cruiser Fleet underwent a complete change. One second before that momentous event they were an independent fleet fighting the enemy to the death, with no other preoccupation than, at all hazards, to sink and destroy. One second after the news that the German High Sea Fleet had been sighted was flashed to the Admiral they became merely the scouting force of the battlefleet, and there was one object only for their existence: namely to give the Commander-in-Chief of that fleet all the information possible so as to ensure that when he met the enemy's battlefleet he should do so under the most favourable conditions. Admiral Beatty was no longer a Commander-in-Chief; he became the Admiral of the Scouting Squadron, to whom fighting was but a subsidiary function to be indulged in merely to prevent the enemy's cruisers sighting our fleet, or so long as it did not interfere with the primary duty of scouting.

Of this sudden transformation nothing, unfortunately, is said. We are told, however, that: "Beatty tried to lead Hipper and the German Fleet up to Jellicoe."

Let us examine this assertion in the light of facts. What actually did Admiral Beatty do?

He ran back to the battle-fleet out of sight of the German High Sea Fleet, carrying on a desultory game of long bowls with the German battle cruisers. If his first object had been, as Mr. Churchill states, "to lead the German High Sea Fleet up to Jellicoe", he would surely, at all costs, have remained in sight of them, acting as a bait to draw them on. What actually happened was that the 5th Battle Squadron formed the bait, and this only because, at maximum speed, they could not sufficiently outpace the fast battleships of the enemy. As a matter of fact the German Battlefleet required no leading. They chased our battle cruisers with a will.

Let us now pass to the junction of the battle cruisers and the Grand Battlefleet. It is well here to repeat clearly and emphatically that Admiral Beatty, after sighting the German Battlefleet, had become the Admiral commanding the main scouting force of the Grand Fleet.

It was his duty to convey exact information to his Commander-in-Chief. But this is precisely what he failed to do. He arrived in sight of the *Iron Duke* (Admiral Jellicoe's flagship), having lost sight of the German High Sea fleet.

Admiral Jellicoe signalled at 6.01 p.m.: "Where is the enemy's battlefleet?"

Admiral Beatty did not know. He had, so to speak, mislaid them. He could give no reply.

Although he had thirteen light cruisers under his command, he had not thrown out any of these to form connecting links to pass, by visual signals, to his Commander-in-Chief information regarding the movements of the German Battlefleet.

For a *whole quarter of an hour* Admiral Jellicoe could get no answer from Admiral Beatty except that "the German battle cruisers bore S.E." As if it mattered a brass farthing to Admiral Jellicoe how the German battle *cruisers* bore! What Admiral Jellicoe wanted to know, and what he should have been able to learn from Admiral Beatty, was where the German Battle *Fleet* was. As a matter of fact they were on a totally different bearing from that of their battle cruisers.

In this manner the valuable quarter of an hour which should have been available to Admiral Jellicoe to swing the columns of the battlefleet so as to deploy to the best advantage to meet the enemy was lost through Admiral Beatty failing to realize the functions for which his cruiser fleet mainly existed.

Now how does Mr. Churchill deal with this matter?

In a most barefaced manner he attempts to take the onus for scouting off the shoulders of the scouting Admiral and put it on to those of the Commander-in-Chief.

Let us quote Mr. Churchill's views of what Admiral Jellicoe should have done. These, being lengthy, are divided into paragraphs for simplicity of treatment:

(1) Apart from the fourteen light cruisers detached with Admiral Beatty's advance force, Jellicoe had reserved, for his own special use, *four* of the very latest *Caroline* class of light cruiser.

(2) He had, besides, the eight armoured cruisers of the pre-dreadnought era. At the first alarm he ordered these old vessels to increase to full speed and cover his front, but as they could not steam more than *twenty knots*, and he was himself making eighteen and rising twenty, they did not appreciably draw ahead of him in these important two hours.

(3) In two hours the *Carolines*, in a fan formation, could easily have gained fifteen miles from the *Iron Duke* in the general direction of the enemy. The *Carolines* themselves, at this time, could see at least seven miles. Then the *Commander-in-Chief, had he so wished*, could have had more than twenty miles accurate notice by visual signal of the position and line advance of the German Fleet.[75]

We will take these paragraphs *seriatim* and show the errors they contain:

(1) There were five *Carolines* with Admiral Jellicoe, not four as stated.

(2) The armoured cruisers could steam twenty-two and a half and twenty-three knots. Not twenty as stated; they were, therefore, at least from four and a half to two and a half knots faster than the speed at which the battlefleet was steaming during the two hours in question. The true reason why they did not reach the position assigned to them was, not because their speed was as slow as Mr. Churchill imagined it to have been, but because, after 4 p.m., the weather thickened and the ships had to close one another to keep visual touch. This meant that the wing ships had to "close in" on diagonal courses and so the "advance" of the whole screen was delayed.

(3) Even if the speed of the armoured cruisers had been as low as that on which Mr. Churchill bases his argument, there still was no reason for sending the *Carolines* ahead at 3.10 instead of the armoured cruisers, for the simple fact, which he appears to have overlooked, that at that time the 3rd Battle Cruiser Squadron with two light cruisers was stationed twenty miles ahead of the battlefleet, in the very position to which Mr. Churchill suggests that Admiral Jellicoe should have sent the *Carolines*. It is obvious, therefore, that it would have been useless from every point of view to have sent the *Carolines* ahead, especially as the only enemy reported at sea at 3.10 (the time that the armoured cruisers were sent ahead) was a German Light Cruiser Force, with which the armoured cruisers and the two light cruisers were perfectly able to deal.

It is often difficult to follow Mr. Churchill's arguments because of the inaccuracies they contain; the above is an example, for there are no fewer than three in the quoted paragraphs, namely: the speed of the armoured cruisers is incorrect; the number of *Carolines* under Admiral Jellicoe is mis-stated; the time at which the armoured cruisers were sent forward was not "at the first alarm", but fifty minutes after the first alarm. But the really important point that emerges is that the whole of Mr. Churchill's elaborate argument as to what the Commander-in-Chief of the Grand Fleet should have done is based on an inaccurate estimate of the speed of the armoured cruisers and an oversight as to the position of the 3rd Battle Cruiser Squadron at 3.10 p.m.

We must remember further, that the Admiralty had informed Admiral Jellicoe at noon that the German High Sea Fleet was still in the Jade. If the *Carolines* had been sent ahead at 4.38, when for the first time it was known, or even suspected, that the German High Sea Fleet was at sea, they could only have arrived ten to twelve miles ahead of our battlefleet.

The visibility for signalling purposes at that time was only five miles, so that, as a matter of fact, the westernmost *Caroline* would only have been in the position then occupied by the *Black Prince*, one of the armoured cruisers. Moreover, as events turned out, Admiral Beatty had failed to keep in touch with the German Battlefleet; so, even if the *Carolines* had, by some miraculous impossibility, sighted the *Lion*, they could not have obtained any useful information from her. Their queries might, however, have awakened Admiral Beatty to a sense of his scouting responsibilities.

As regards paragraph (3), no reader can fail to regret Mr. Churchill's insinuation contained in the words "had he so wished", incompetence is the very least that this could imply.

To sum up, Mr. Churchill absolves the scouting Admiral for his failure to fulfil his scouting duties; and, in order to clear him, tries to throw the blame on the Commander-in-Chief of the battlefleet, quite failing to appreciate that even if he could show that the Commander-in-Chief could have assisted Admiral Beatty to pass important news of the exact position of the enemy's fleet, this did not in any way relieve the latter of his responsibilities as Admiral in command of the scouting forces of the Grand Fleet.

Further, in instructing the world as to what the Commander-in-Chief should have done, he bases his theory on incorrect data and fails to appreciate the effect that the rapidly thickening haze had on the disposition of the outposts of the battlefleet.

This is a good example of the errors into which an amateur is liable to drop when attempting to deal with naval tactics. We shall, however, see worse later on.

Why, again, could not Mr. Churchill look on this episode in a common-sense way? He could have pointed out that Admiral Beatty allowed his fighting instincts to dull his appreciation of the scouting duties of his fleet. His attention was undoubtedly fixed on his old enemy, the German Battle Cruiser Squadron, and so the scouting suffered. Everyone would recognize that with an impulsive fighter the meticulous care of a more stable temperament is apt to be lost; it is rare to find both qualities evenly balanced. This could be well understood, but to try to persuade the people of this country that the Commander-in-Chief of the battlefleet was responsible for the scouting failure of his scouting Admiral is merely to tax their patience and over-estimate their credulity.

Mr. Churchill now leaves cruiser tactics and, taking on the role of naval battle-tactician, lays down an alternative tactic that should have been used in the deployment of the battlefleet, and, at the same time, expresses astonishment that Admiral Jellicoe should

> never have attempted to deal with this alternative in any of his accounts
> and explanations of his actions.

How naïve! Did it never occur to Mr. Churchill that it was never worthy even of the terse comment passed on it by the authors of the German *Official History of the War*? But I am anticipating.

The battlefleet is now about to deploy, and we have the option either of visiting Mr. Churchill as he sits in an armchair in his well-lighted and commodious library, with all the many charts of Jutland showing the positions of both fleets and all their auxiliaries spread out before him, the result of the labour of many brains during several years of post-war work. Here, with pencil, compasses, protractor and eraser, he satisfies himself as to what Admiral Churchill would have done had he commanded the British Fleet eleven years earlier. Or we can, in spirit, stand with Admiral Jellicoe on the bridge of the *Iron Duke* in the mist and haze of the North Sea, with the guns of the enemy heard but difficult to locate, with his scouting battle cruisers having steamed into sight on a bearing quite different from that which was expected, and their Admiral unable to supply him with the much-needed information of the enemy's position.

All is haze and uncertainty; seconds are ticking by, and no information is forthcoming as to the exact position of the enemy's battlefleet. Deploy he must, but how? How best to act so as with advantage to meet the enemy of whose exact position he should have been, but has not been, informed?

The two positions are so different that we must, in turn, visit both. Let us, to begin with, take the comfortable library.

The British Battlefleet was steaming down fast to the southward in six parallel lines, the teeth of a comb formation, each tooth being composed of a division of four ships. The total distance between the extreme right-and left-hand tooth was five miles. In order to form line-of-battle any one of the six divisions could have been told to steam straight on, and the other divisions ordered to form astern of it. Considerable controversy has raged round the question as to which was the best division on which to "form". Mr. Churchill advocates a division which does not commend itself to the naval officer.

If we turn to page 137 [of Volume III], we find the situation accurately summarized:

> He [Admiral Scheer] had no intention of fighting a battle against the whole British Fleet. He was under no illusions about the relative strength of the rival batteries. Nothing could be more clownish than to draw up his fleet on parallel courses with an opponent firing twice his weight of metal and manned by a personnel whose science, seamanship and fortitude commanded his sincere respect. *He had not come out with any idea of fighting a pitched battle*. He had never intended to fight at a hopeless disadvantage.

With this statement of the case everyone will agree. Let us see how it bears on the advantages or disadvantages of any special form of deployment.

The main points to keep in mind are: (1) That Admiral Scheer had no intention of fighting a pitched battle, so the moment he sighted our battlefleet he intended to turn and flee unless, by any chance at that moment, he found himself in a position of considerable tactical advantage[76];

and (2) he would have sighted our battlefleet at the same distance off whichever column Admiral Jellicoe selected for the Grand Fleet to deploy on, since the range of visibility was unaffected by deployment. It did not matter in the slightest if Admiral Scheer sighted the leading battleships of our fleet right ahead or on his bow; in either case he would have turned and run straight away from them.

Let this be thoroughly understood, as it is a point that all the many lay tacticians have missed.

Look at Diagram 44. If Admiral Jellicoe had deployed on the division R, the leading ship of that division would have been sighted by Admiral Scheer at A, when he (Scheer) was at X.

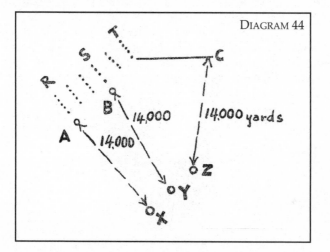

DIAGRAM 44

If the deployment had been, as Mr. Churchill suggests, on the division S, Admiral Scheer would have sighted the leading ships at B, when he was at Y. The deployment actually took place on the division T, and he sighted the ships of our battlefleet at C, when he was at Z.

The distance at which he would have sighted the ships in the first two cases would, of course, have been exactly the same as that at which he did actually sight our fleet in the third case, namely about 14,000 yards.

He would, without doubt, have turned had he sighted our fleet at Y, for exactly the same reason that he did at Z; namely to run *straight* away from our fleet. At the moment that he turned our fleet would have been *no nearer* to him had it deployed on R or S than it was when it deployed on T.

Yet Mr. Churchill states as regards the deployment on S, which is the one he recommends:

This deployment would have placed the British line about 4,000 yards nearer the German Fleet.[77]

205

It would have done nothing of the sort. The visibility obtaining at that time in the North Sea could not have been affected however the manoeuvre might have been performed.

He even becomes more grasping and, at the same time, more obscure; for he claims for his manoeuvre, which he modestly calls the "sure, prudent, glorious and middle course", that

> he [Jellicoe] would have had three miles and ten minutes more to spare
> if he had deployed on the wing towards the enemy.[78]

We confess to not grasping what *"three miles and ten minutes more to spare"* means. But if we understand him at all, his claim has risen from 4,000 yards to three miles, which is equivalent to 6,000 yards. Perhaps the "ten minutes" means ten minutes earlier contact with the German Fleet.

Now since not one of these three methods of deployment ensured our fleet being nearer to the enemy's fleet than either of the other two, what was the virtue of any one deployment over another? Let us look at Diagram 45.

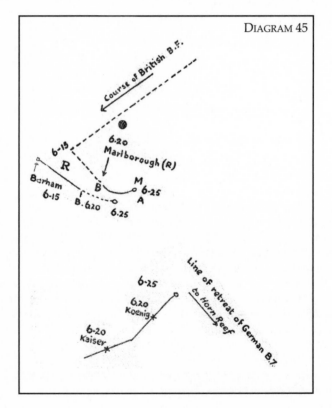

DIAGRAM 45

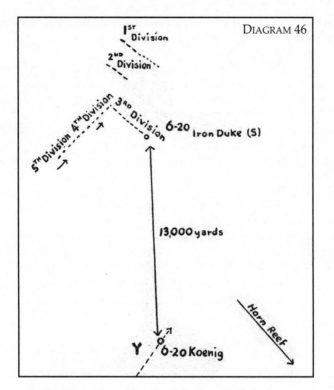

DIAGRAM 46

Mr. Churchill's "sure, prudent, glorious and middle course".
Fleets sight each other at 6.20.
Line of retreat to Horn Reef open.
British Fleet badly bunched.
Honours divided so far as crossing the T was concerned.

In the case of deployment on the division R there was a great danger of the German Fleet overlapping the head of our line (crossing its T), which is the one position of real disadvantage in which a fleet can be placed. If this comes to pass, the leading ship of the line that is advancing along the upright stroke of the T comes under the fire of the broadsides of all the ships steaming along the top bar of the T, while she herself is only able to reply with her right-ahead fire. She is forced to turn parallel to the crossbar (as the *Marlborough* would have had to do at A), and as every succeeding ship turned, each is unmercifully strafed at the pivot between B and A, a place of which the enemy has obtained the exact range.

The "sure, prudent, and glorious middle course" of deploying on S presented no advantage to either side as regards "crossing the T" (see Diagram 46). Both fleets could have used their broadside guns.

207

The deployment on the division T reversed the advantage described in the deployment on R; we thereby crossed the enemy's T, and strafed them with considerable effect (see Diagram 47).

But there was yet another great advantage which was gained by deploying on the division T (Diagram 44). This was, that when Admiral Scheer, at Z, turned and ran *straight away* from our Fleet, the *"straight away"*[79] led him, as Mr. Churchill points out, towards *England*. At either X or Y the course *straight away* from our fleet was the direct course for the German coast. If he had sighted our ships at X or Y he would have turned and run straight away to his harbour, which he could have entered at night and been no more seen.

Admiral Jellicoe naturally dismissed Mr. Churchill's "sure, prudent, glorious and middle course", since, while offering no advantage, it would merely have "bunched" the fleet badly in case of torpedo attack. He therefore deployed on the division T, with the result that he drove the German Fleet away from their own shores.[80] He brought his fleet just as *near* to the German Fleet as would have been the case in any other method of deployment, and by not deploying on the R (or *Marlborough*) division he

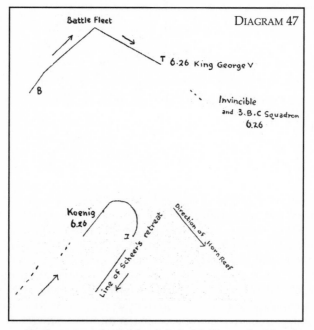

DIAGRAM 47

Deployment adopted by Admiral Jellicoe whereby the German T was crossed. Admiral Scheer mistook the *Invincible* for the head of our Battlefleet and did not dare to retreat to the Horn Reef; so turned dead away from our Fleet.

saved that division, the succeeding division, and the 5th Battle Squadron from a severe handling by the *König* and *Kaiser* dreadnoughts.

It is very easy for anyone dealing for the first time with problems of naval tactics to drop into mistakes like the above, over which Mr. Churchill has so unfortunately come to grief.

But inaccuracies on this matter of deployment do not stop here. We find further on:

> Our present knowledge leads to the conclusion that he [Jellicoe] could have deployed on the starboard wing without misadventure.[81]

Our present knowledge shows that such a deployment would have caused considerable risk to the *Marlborough* division, as the Germans were virtually across the *Marlborough*'s T (see Diagram 4).

He then continues:

> The 5th Battle Squadron, with its unequalled guns, armour and speed, was, in fact, *about* to take the van ahead of the *Marlborough*.

About to take is a very different thing from *having taken*. The 5th Battle Squadron would have had to steam, under fire, for at least ten minutes before it could have arrived into station ahead of the *Marlborough*; and, during the whole of that time, its ships would have masked the fire of the guns of the *Marlborough* division and been subjected to a heavy concentration of fire from practically the whole of the *König* and *Kaiser* divisions of seven ships.

In conclusion, surely a telling argument against the deployment on the starboard, or R, division so dear to the amateur tactician, is the verdict of the German Naval Staff in their *Official History of the War*. These officers had no axes to grind, and their considered opinion, which is free from all bias, is as follows:

> One must agree with the British leader [Jellicoe] that had he acted in this way [i.e. deploying on the starboard wing division] he would in fact have led his ships into a position which would have been only too welcome to the German Fleet.

As regards Mr. Churchill's "sure, prudent, glorious and middle course", the same high authority sweeps this aside for a reason which, from knowledge of the efficiency in manoeuvring of our battlefleet, I prefer not to advance, namely that it was too complicated a manoeuvre to have been undertaken in the presence of an enemy. Perhaps Mr. Churchill might feel inclined also, in turn, to sweep aside this verdict, and, with pardonable prejudice in favour of all things British, say: "Oh yes, but the German officers were not so highly trained as ours and might, therefore, naturally shirk a manoeuvre which was well within the capacity of our Fleet."

In case this might be his reply we would point out that later on he glorifies the training of the High Sea Fleet at the expense of the Grand Fleet under Admiral Jellicoe, and remarks:

> The Germans, following the Army system of command, had foreseen before the war that the intelligent co-operation of subordinates, who know thoroughly the views and spirit of the Chief, must be substituted in a fleet action for a rigid and centralized control.[82]

The manoeuvre recommended by Mr. Churchill was essentially one in which *the intelligent co-operation of subordinates was substituted for a rigid and centralized control*, since at least two Divisional Commanders might well have taken charge and manoeuvred their divisions by signal. The German Naval Authorities, therefore, according to his own showing, should have been thoroughly good judges of the manoeuvre, yet their verdict is unhesitatingly adverse to it.

Our naval officers do not condemn it on the same grounds to the same extent; but there is no doubt that it is a manoeuvre that any admiral would hesitate to order in close proximity to an enemy, unless it held out at the moment far greater advantages than were on this occasion likely to accrue.

A glance at Diagram 46 will show that the ships of our battlefleet would have been "bunched" up and very vulnerable to torpedo attack had one been launched against them during twelve of the eighteen minutes, or so, that it would have taken to carry out the deployment on the column that he has advocated.

Mr. Churchill now proceeds to tell us what the Commander-in-Chief should alternatively have ordered the 5th Battle Squadron to do while the fleet was deploying. Here he gets completely out of his depth. We find:

> His [Jellicoe's] cautious deployment on the outer wing made it more imperative to make sure of the enemy being brought to action. To do this he had *only* to tell the four *Queen Elizabeths* of the 5th Battle Squadron ... to attack separately on the disengaged side of the enemy. ... They were eight or nine knots faster than Scheer's fleet as *long as it remained* united.[83]

First of all let us note that there were only three of the 5th Battle Squadron left at 6.20. *Warspite* was out of action.

If Mr. Churchill had used his compasses he would have discovered that Admiral Jellicoe was more than three thousand yards out of sight of the German Fleet when he made the signal to deploy. He was hardly, therefore, in a position to order one of his divisions to attack an enemy whom he could not see, and of whose exact position he was in doubt. Moreover, as the ships of the 5th Battle Squadron were at that time on the *engaged* side of the enemy it would have been impossible for them to get through the German Fleet to its disengaged side. If they had attempted to go round it they would have had to steam some forty miles; and had they ever arrived at so impossible a position as the one Mr. Churchill suggests, they would have had, during their journey, the broadsides of the whole of the German Dreadnought Fleet to contend with (see Diagram 48)!

So we find that Mr. Churchill, in reality, suggests that Admiral Jellicoe should have ordered one of his divisions, whose strength is wrongly stated, to attack the disengaged side of an enemy whom he could not see, whose

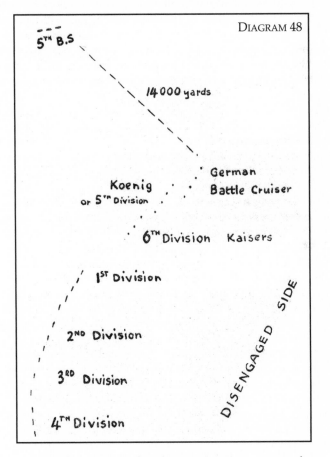

Problem: How was the 5th Battle Squadron to get to the
disengaged side of the enemy as Mr. Churchill suggests?

position he did not know, and whose disengaged side it was impossible to get at.

But with Mr. Churchill, unjustifiable assumption follows fast on the heels of impossible suggestion. For further on he assigns still further duties to the 5th Battle Squadron. We read:

> They [the 5th Battle Squadron] could, at any moment if too hard pressed, break off the action. Thus assured, what could be easier than for them to swoop round on the old *Deutschland* squadron and cripple or destroy two or three of these ships in a few minutes?

Thus Mr. Churchill wrote from his armchair in the clear atmosphere of his library, with the post-war charts spread on the table. It never seems to have struck him, seeing, as he did, the whole of the German dispositions laid out before him, that neither Admiral Jellicoe, nor Admiral Evan-Thomas, nor anyone else in the Grand Fleet, had any knowledge where exactly the *Deutschlands* were. None of the enemy battleships except the leading division of the German dreadnoughts could be seen by Admiral Evan-Thomas, still less by Admiral Jellicoe, who, at that moment, could see none of the enemy's ships, nor had any except these few ships been seen by anyone in the battlefleet.

What sort of a naval idiot would Admiral Evan-Thomas have been thought and Admiral Jellicoe have been accused of being, if, without knowing where the *Deutschlands* were, either of them had ordered a wild-goose chase on the part of the 5th Battle Squadron past the flank of sixteen German dreadnoughts to attack ships which they could not see, and incidentally in so doing have separated that squadron several miles from the main Fleet?

If, before criticizing the actions of the Commander-in-Chief of the Grand Fleet at any particular phase of the action, Mr. Churchill had enlisted the services of some competent person to prepare a chart, which chart excluded all the enemy's forces except those that were visible to the Commander-in-Chief at the particular moment in question, he would have been less likely to have fallen into errors of the same class as those with which we have been dealing. He would then not have pored over a post-war chart that set forth the whole dispositions of the enemy, and based his criticisms on the assumption that the Commander-in-Chief was blessed with eyes that could penetrate more than five miles beyond normal human vision.

We will next turn to Mr. Churchill's argument in favour of independent action on the part of the various units of the fleet. Let us quote him on this matter:

> Neither admiration nor agreement can adhere to the system and training which he [Admiral Jellicoe] had developed in his fleet. Everything was

centralized in the flagship, and all initiative, except in avoiding torpedo attack, was denied to the leaders of squadrons and divisions.[84]

Neither admiration nor agreement can adhere to this statement in the light of the following extracts from the Grand Fleet Battle Orders which Mr. Churchill should have consulted. There is nothing in these extracts which can in any way be looked on as confidential.

The opening paragraphs of these orders, which were in force at the Battle of Jutland, read as follows:

> The Commander-in-Chief controls the whole battlefleet *before* deployment and *on* deployment except in the case of low visibility.
>
> He cannot be certain *after* deployment of being able to control the movements of three battle squadrons when steaming fast and making much funnel smoke: with the noise and smoke of battle added, the practicability of exercising general control will be still further reduced.
>
> It therefore becomes necessary *to decentralize command to the fullest extent possible*, and the Vice-Admirals commanding squadrons have discretionary power to manoeuvre their squadrons independently while conforming generally to the movements of the Commander-in-Chief and complying with his known intentions. As the Commander-in-Chief is in the centre, he will ordinarily control the movements of the 4th Battle Squadron should separate action by that squadron become necessary; but, as the fleet is manoeuvred by divisions in the fifth organization after deployment, the Vice-Admiral 4th Battle Squadron will control the movements of his division, conforming generally to the movements of the division led by the Commander-in-Chief, unless any contrary directions are given. Similarly the Rear-Admirals 1st and 2nd Battle Squadrons control the movements of their divisions unless they receive directions from the Commander-in-Chief or the Vice-Admirals of their squadrons.

Although paragraph (3) states that

> the ruling principle is that the Dreadnought Fleet as a whole keeps together, attempted attacks by a division or squadron on a portion of the enemy line being avoided as being liable to lead to the isolation of the ships which attempt the movement,

this did not deny initiative in other respects, as the following paragraphs show:

> There are several conditions which may cause a separate action on the part of commanders of squadrons and divisions.

213

Among the conditions was

> a movement of one of the enemy's divisions necessitating a counter on
> our part, such as, an attack on the rear or attempt to close for the purpose
> of firing torpedoes, etc.

There were also certain instructions as to dealing with the German Battlefleet if it divided, which mentioned that commanders of squadrons and divisions might have to act independently. It was stated that the 3rd Battle Squadron (which, however, was detached before the battle) was to be manoeuvred by the Vice-Admiral commanding independently of the Dreadnought Fleet.

A final paragraph laid down that whenever junior flag officers or captains find themselves without special directions during an action, either from inability to make out or receive the Admiral's signals or from unforeseen circumstances rendering previous orders inapplicable, they are to act as their judgment shall dictate in making every effort to damage the enemy.

It is difficult to see how Admiral Jellicoe could have given wider discretionary freedom to his juniors without a general action developing into a number of small engagements swayed by the idiosyncrasies and varying temperaments of the commanders of the divisions. How was it possible for Mr. Churchill to be so misinformed as to make a statement so palpably at variance with fact? Mr. Churchill has indeed been badly served by his naval advisers, who should have pointed out to him these very obvious mistakes. He was kind in not mentioning their names in the preface to his volumes.[85]

But the above is by no means his only erroneous statement on the matter of organization. We find:

> A ceaseless stream of signals from the flagship was therefore required to
> regulate the movements and the distribution of the fire.[8]

This, was not so. Between 6.15, after the signal to deploy had been made, up to 9.11, when the fleet turned to a southerly course for the night (apart from sixteen signals giving the course and speed of the flagship, which would still have been necessary if the fleet had been divided into separate manoeuvring squadrons), twenty-four signals only were made giving orders for the movements of the fleet. The distribution of fire was left to the admirals commanding the divisions. Twenty-four signals in approximately three hours, or two signals every quarter of an hour, can scarcely be called a "ceaseless stream".

Mr. Churchill continues:

> These signals prescribed the course and speed of every ship as well as
> every manoeuvring turn.

Anyone reading this would surely imagine that the whole of the twenty-seven battleships had a ceaseless stream of signals made to each of them prescribing their courses. Needless to say, Mr. Churchill meant nothing of the sort. What he intended to convey was, that a single three-flag signal would order all the leaders of divisions to turn in a certain direction; the ships behind them would follow their leaders round. A single three-flag signal would control the whole movement.

This is what Mr. Churchill must have meant. It is a pity, therefore, that he, who at times can be so explicit, should apparently at other times be so careless as to the impression his writings cannot fail to convey to a public who are mainly ignorant of naval matters.

A little later, when he wishes to convey the impression that the German system of fleet control was superior to that of the Grand Fleet, we read in support of the argument:

> At this moment [*the approach of the two fleets before sighting each other*] the line in which they were approaching was, in fact, three self-contained, independently moving squadrons following one another.[87]

As a matter of fact this was not so. As we have already seen, during the run north after 4.33 p.m. Admiral Scheer had chased the 5th Battle Squadron; that is, he had taken his ships along at their utmost speed. This inevitably led to his squadrons gradually opening out from each other, since while each squadron was composed of ships of approximately the same speed, each squadron varied in speed from the other two. The result was that certain gaps developed between the squadrons, but they still remained units of a combined fleet. Indeed, Mr. Churchill himself confirms this:

> He [Scheer] therefore at 6.35, with the utmost promptitude, turned his whole fleet about, every ship turning simultaneously.[88]

If this was not control of the fleet by one man, nothing in this world can come under that definition. Had the fleet been made up of "independently moving squadrons". Admiral Scheer would perforce have signalled his intention to turn and then each of the leaders would have signalled to their squadron to turn. Nothing of the sort was done; he *turned his whole fleet, every ship turning simultaneously.*

We must now pass to the contact between the two battlefleets which took place at 6.25.   In the opening paragraph,[89] where Mr. Churchill deals with this encounter, he makes an inexcusable statement. He describes the hasty retreat of von Scheer's battleships and adds:

> Jellicoe, threatened by the torpedo stream, turned away according to his long resolved policy.

Neither at this time, nor even approximately at this time, did Admiral Jellicoe turn away from a torpedo attack; for from the *Iron Duke* no attack by destroyers appeared to be in course of preparation. On the other hand, two turns were made *towards* the enemy, one at 6.44 to S.E. and a second at 6.55 to S. It is regrettable that so erroneous a statement should have been made by a responsible narrator, for it discloses a profound ignorance of one of the leading features of the battle.

It was now that the crossing of the German T by our battlefleet woke Admiral Scheer out of a fool's paradise; here was the British Fleet right across his path. He turned and fled towards the English coast. Admiral Jellicoe, unaware of his turn away, and thinking that his disappearance was only a momentary manoeuvre due to the mist, and that he would shortly come again into sight, circled his fleet gradually round, expecting every minute to sight him again.

Till at 7.10 Admiral Scheer, while trying to cut across the stern of our fleet, found himself again with the British Fleet across his T. This was brought about by Jellicoe's gradually circling round while feeling for his enemy.

After describing this attempt on the part of Admiral Scheer, Mr. Churchill states, rather disparagingly:

> Jellicoe's fleet was no doubt somewhat inconveniently arranged. He was steaming south with his divisions in echelon. In fact he now, at 7.12 p.m., was in the very position he had so disliked before his original deployment.[90]

Here the innocence of the amateur again peeps out, for, since the leaders of the divisions were on their proper bearing to re-form into line ahead at right angles to the line of bearing of the enemy, the disposition in echelon did not matter, and was no inconvenience at all. The fact that the bearing of the leaders of his divisions from each other was not at right angles to *the bearing of the enemy* was what Admiral Jellicoe "disliked before his original deployment". He continues:

> But nevertheless in practice no serious difficulty arose.

Of course no difficulty arose. There was absolutely no reason why one should have arisen. The point is of little interest except to the professional tactician, but it is well to correct the disparaging impression that Admiral Jellicoe was caught in an inferior tactical formation.

Mr. Churchill ends his description of the short, sharp encounter between the two fleets as follows:

> (1) Here at any rate was a moment when, as a *glance* at the map will show, it would have been quite easy to divide the British Fleet with the 5th

Battle Squadron leading the starboard division and so take the
enemy between two fires.
(2) But the British Commander-in-Chief was *absorbed in avoiding* torpedo
attack by turning away. The range opened, the fleets separated, and
Scheer vanished again from Jellicoe's view – this time for ever.[91]

The mistakes made by Mr. Churchill in his tactical suggestions come,
perhaps, largely from *glancing* at a map. Considerable *study* of a map is, as
a rule, necessary before a considered opinion can be given on any tactical
point.

It is obviously an axiom that at least two fast squadrons are necessary to
envelop an enemy's fleet, one to steam up on his starboard side and one on
his port side. But, unfortunately for Mr. Churchill, only one squadron, and
that only of three ships, viz. the 5th Battle Squadron, was available for his
enveloping movement. Now the information that anyone will gather from
a careful study of Diagrams 49, 50 and 51 is that, although the three ships
of the 5th Battle Squadron could have drawn ahead and engaged the
German dreadnoughts on their starboard quarter, we had no ships fast
enough to support them or even to get within range of the enemy on his
port quarter.

Diagram 49 shows the 7.20 p.m. position of the leading divisions of the
two fleets. Diagram 51 shows what would have been their position at 8.20
p.m. after one hour's hard steaming. Diagram 50 shows what would have
been their position at 7.50 p.m. There can be no doubt about these positions,
provided that our fleet was not forced further astern than is shown owing
to a torpedo attack being launched by the Germans.[92]

What Mr. Churchill and the majority of the critics have overlooked is
that the fast *Königs* (which were faster than any of our dreadnoughts, except
the 5th Battle Squadron) were leading the German advance at 7.12 p.m.,

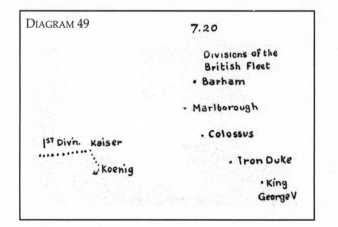

DIAGRAM 49   7.20

Divisions of the
British Fleet
• Barham

· Marlborough

. Colossus

1ST Divn. Kaiser
....
ُ Koenig

• Iron Duke

• King
George V

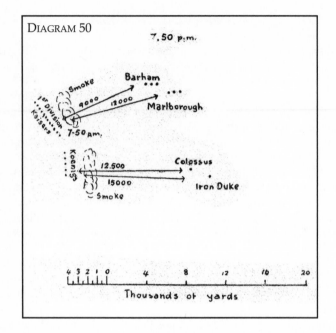

DIAGRAM 50

and therefore were nearer our battleships than were the slower German dreadnoughts, whose steaming speed was approximately equal to that of our battleships and nearer still than the old *Deutschlands*. The whole German Fleet was turned "together" the moment the *Königs* sighted our battleships.

The result was that, since the whole fleet was turned at the same moment *together* away from our fleet, their fastest ships were now in the rear of the retreat and could easily walk away from our dreadnoughts as they steamed back towards the other divisions. The slower German dreadnoughts, which were out of sight from our battleships, could, speaking generally, maintain the same distance that they were away from our fleet after they had turned. The older *Deutschlands* were yet further away, in fact so far off that even the 5th Battle Squadron could not possibly have overhauled them before dark.

Mr. Churchill's tactics would inevitably have led to the three ships of the 5th Battle Squadron being exposed, unsupported, to the murderous fire of six German dreadnoughts.

If, therefore, Admiral Jellicoe had ordered a general chase, no useful purpose would have been served, as only a little over one hour of daylight remained, during which time it would have been impossible to overhaul any vessels of the German Battlefleet. But at nightfall our battle-fleet would have been a disorganized armada, with its vessels widely separated, in which condition safe night-cruising would have been impossible.

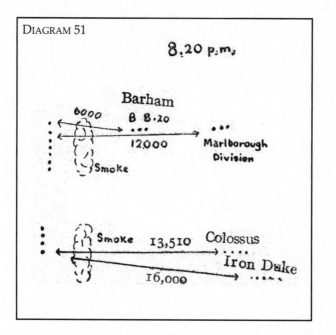

If the *Barham* division had been sighted through the smoke the fire of twelve German ships would have been concentrated on three British.

There were many other points that were not brought home to Mr. Churchill in his library, but which were most important to Admiral Jellicoe on the bridge of the *Iron Duke*. To commence with, it was possible to obtain only a very meagre view of the German Fleet as it emerged from the mist. The visibility grew rapidly less and less, owing, chiefly, to the smoke from the guns and funnels, and the North Sea mist. This made it difficult to estimate the number of the German ships or their formation. They could only be glimpsed in the intervals between the opaque patches of smoke poured out from our own guns, and then they were nearly obscured by the funnel and cordite smoke of the German vessels. Immediately our fleet was glimpsed by the German Admiral, his destroyers were ordered to advance and make a smoke-screen, and it was behind this screen that the German Fleet turned and, quite properly, ran away.

Let us put ourselves in Admiral Jellicoe's place. The first glimpse of the enemy showed that his ships were steaming almost straight towards the *Iron Duke*. Splendid! If they continued on that line they would have the head of their line smashed to atoms. Then it was seen that the leading ships had turned parallel to our lines; again excellent! A broadside action with our fleet closing rapidly was the best thing that could happen so far as we were concerned. Then, suddenly, the ships were lost sight of behind a screen of smoke. What did this mean? Admiral Jellicoe knew perfectly well that it heralded a massed attack with torpedoes by the destroyer flotillas. The very manoeuvre that he had been warned that the Germans intended to carry out. A deadly scheme, the intention of which was to incapacitate a number of our battleships and then to fight a battlefleet action with approximately equal numbers on each side, or, perhaps, with the advantage in their favour. All the necessary factors to the success of the scheme were present: thick weather, failing light, a broadside action, and a smokescreen – just what were required to ensure the success of a massed attack by destroyers.

We can therefore well appreciate that the problem Admiral Jellicoe had to solve appeared to him in a very different light – when viewed by him through the smoke and haze of that fast darkening evening – from what it seemed to Mr. Churchill as he threw a glance at his post-war chart, lit up either by broad daylight or strong electric lamps. The essential difficulties of the moment that faced Admiral Jellicoe were: (1) The complete blotting out of the German Fleet by smoke, and his consequent inability to observe their alteration in course; and (2) The immediate danger which threatened his battleships from torpedo attack.

Since the war many trials have been carried out by firing torpedoes, without explosive charges, at a line of ships. The results are well known to all interested, and show conclusively that it is futile to trust to ships individually trying to avoid torpedoes by attempting to steer clear of the track they leave behind them as they run through the water.

The actual figures cannot be quoted, since they, rightly, are looked on as confidential; but there can be no harm in stating – what must now be common knowledge – that these trials lead to the belief that the chances were that at least seven of the Grand Fleet battleships would have been put out of action if Admiral Jellicoe had not turned his fleet away from the attack; further, that he would have incurred a very grave risk had he turned his ships *towards* the direction of attack. The latest information at Admiral Jellicoe's disposal showed that he might have had to deal with eighty-eight German destroyers in a fleet action. That is, taking a very extreme case, four waves of attack of sixty-six torpedoes each.

Is there any sane unbiased person living who, had he been in Admiral Jellicoe's place, would have said: "I don't care a farthing for the threat of a torpedo attack. I will throw all caution to the winds and act as if torpedoes do not exist"? I venture to say that no responsible person would have followed such a course in actual war, however much they may bluster and criticize in peace-time.

Before this short digression we left Admiral Jellicoe on the bridge of the *Iron Duke* faced by the menace of torpedo attack. He quite properly turned his fleet four points "away" and saved, probably, some six or seven ships from being incapacitated or sunk. Mr. Churchill, however, does not hesitate to pooh-pooh the risks. On page 113, after quoting some views expressed by Admiral Custance, he says:

> Again and again I have heard him contend that the torpedo would play only a very unimportant part in a great sea battle, and that the issue would be decided by a combination of gun fire and manoeuvre. The results of Jutland seem to vindicate this unfashionable opinion.

Here Mr. Churchill hardly gives fair prominence to the fact that the reason why the torpedo was ineffective in the battlefleet action was because it was defeated by Admiral Jellicoe's unpopular tactic of turning away from the attack. The main advocates of the torpedo have always recognized that it was not a "deciding factor" in determining a fleet battle; but they have insisted that it imposed certain limitations on the free action of the opposing fleet, and would demand on certain occasions action on their part. In the case in point, the massed attack, compelled Admiral Jellicoe to turn his ships away; it therefore relieved the immediate pressure on the German battleships. Exactly the class of inconvenient compulsion that had been foreseen.

Most of the critics who have had the temerity to criticize the action of the Commander-in-Chief of the Grand Fleet have advocated that at this juncture he should have paid no attention to the threat of the torpedoes, but turned straight at the German Fleet. Not so Mr. Churchill, who, though still apparently not caring a fig for torpedoes, proposes an eccentric solution of the difficulty, namely that of dividing the fleet into two portions with a view to enveloping the enemy. This he advocates in spite of the fact that only three of our ships were able to steam faster than the leading division of the enemy's fleet, and the remainder of our fleet could not get within range of the slower German battleships before darkness set in. Further, that had such a manoeuvre been attempted, those three fast ships would, for the last half hour before dark, have been left unsupported while fighting six or more German dreadnoughts.

It is now necessary to point out a gross mis-statement that is made on page 153, which again is paragraphed for simplicity of analysis:

(1) Between 6 and 7.30 the German flotillas had delivered no fewer than seven attacks upon the British Battlefleet.

(2) The true answer to these attacks was the counter-attack of the British flotillas and Light Cruiser Squadrons, of which latter two were available and close at hand. These should have been ordered to advance and break up the enemy's torpedo craft, as they were fully capable of doing. Instead of using this aggressive parry Jellicoe turned his battleships away on each occasion and contact with the enemy ceased.

Why, we wonder, does Mr. Churchill choose the times 6 till 7.30? The two battlefleets were not in contact till 6.25. Moreover, no general attack was made by the enemy's destroyers until 7.10 p.m., although one or two torpedoes were sighted by the ships of the 1st Battle Squadron earlier, one of which struck the *Marlborough*, and was probably fired by the disabled *Wiesbaden*.

Only three separate attacks were delivered between 7.10 and 7.30, and a fourth attack by the German 3rd and 5th Flotillas was commenced; but, as the battleships had turned away, they sighted nothing but our 11th Flotilla, so they retired without firing their torpedoes.

These inaccuracies are of little moment, however, compared with what his statement conveys (but which it is barely conceivable that it was intended to convey), namely that *seven* different attacks were made between 6 and 7.30, and that Admiral Jellicoe turned away *seven* times.

As a matter of fact, Admiral Jellicoe turned away from one attack, and one attack only, this turn taking place at 7.22 p.m., and by so doing he probably saved seven of our battleships.

Since Mr. Churchill has no experience of fleet work he may be forgiven many of the errors of which he has been guilty, but a statement so carelessly worded as the one that we have just quoted, and one so apt to mislead the general reader, is inexcusable on the part of a serious historian.

As regards (2), the 4th Light Cruiser Squadron *was* ordered to attack and break up the attempt of the enemy's destroyers; it did this in company with the 11th Destroyer Flotilla. But it is not so easy, in real warfare, to break up an attack, made by brave and desperate men, as compass measurements on a chart might lead Mr. Churchill to suppose. The forces mentioned *checked* the attack, but they were powerless to prevent the enemy's destroyers firing their torpedoes within range of the battlefleet.

It may also be remarked that the Grand Fleet Battle Orders had assigned the very duty to the Light Cruiser Squadrons that Mr. Churchill has suggested should have been entrusted to them. The order as regards destroyers is worth quoting as an example of the decentralized control that existed in the Grand Fleet:

> Take up the best position that you can for offensive action for operating against both the German Battlefleet and its destroyers, having always in view the relative number of destroyers present on both sides.

Other orders laid down that, as the first defence against torpedo attack on the battlefleet, the light cruisers and destroyers were to adopt a vigorous offensive against enemy vessels of similar class.

Another mistake most misleading to the casual reader will be found on the chart showing "Admiral Scheer's second turn away". Here we find entered the remark: "Three boats of 3rd Flotilla 7.15 fired three torpedoes."

No mention is made of the other thirty that were fired, although the 7.20 positions of the ships and destroyers are clearly shown. The inevitable inference to be drawn from careless charting and wording is that Admiral Jellicoe ran away seven times from an attack of three torpedoes only.

We now pass to the last paragraph on page 153: "Beatty, however, still sought to renew the action."

This is an innuendo that Admiral Jellicoe did not wish to renew the action. A distinct, untrue, and unworthy suggestion. Innuendoes, it has been said, resemble the buttons placed in the collection plate in church: spurious in value, deceptive in purpose, and easy to disown.

We have now to follow Mr. Churchill very closely in a remarkable attempt to show that Admiral Jellicoe deserted Admiral Beatty, and left him to engage the enemy unsupported; we will quote the essential portions of this covert accusation:

> At 7.45 he [Admiral Beatty] signalled the bearing of the enemy through the leading battleship, and at 7.45 sent the much-discussed message to the Commander-in-Chief: "Submit that the van of the battleships follow me; we can then cut off the enemy's fleet." Almost immediately after he altered course to close the enemy.

The first thing to note is that the enemy were already "cut off" from the only place from which they could be cut off, namely their home ports. The signal therefore only showed that Admiral Beatty had mistaken the strategical as distinct from the tactical situation. It is a pity that Mr. Churchill did not lift his eye from the tactical diagram to glance at the strategical map of the North Sea with the position of the two fleets marked on it.

In order to explain clearly what the message Mr. Churchill has quoted conveyed to Admiral Jellicoe, and the difficulty in which it placed him, it is necessary to cite the five signals made between 7.30 and 8 p.m.

At 7.40 p.m. Admiral Jellicoe ordered the following signal, which was despatched at 7.43:

(1) C.-in-C. to *Lion* by W/T.   Present course of Fleet S.W.

Immediately after sending this, he received from the *Lion* the following signal:

(2) *Lion* to C.-in-C. by W/T.   Enemy bears from me N.W. by W. 10 to 11miles. My position lat. 56° 56′ N., long. 6° 16′ E. Course S.W., 18 knots.

A further signal was received in *Iron Duke* at 7.59 p.m., which had been made by the *Lion*:

(3) *Lion* to S.O. – 2nd Cruiser Squadron by searchlight.

Pass to leading battleship. Leading enemy battleship bears N.W. by W. Course about S.W.

At 8 p.m. the Commander-in-Chief ordered the fleet to alter course to west by the following signal:

C.-in-C. general flags and W/T.

Divisions separately alter course in succession to W. preserving their formation. Speed 17 knots.

Then immediately afterwards Admiral Beatty's signal, the one quoted by Mr. Churchill, was handed to Admiral Jellicoe:

Lion to C.-in.-C. by W/T.

Urgent. Submit van of battleships follows battle cruisers. We can then cut off whole of enemy's battlefleet.

Comparing these signals with one another, two points at once become clear regarding the information of which Admiral Jellicoe was in possession when the signal from Admiral Beatty, quoted by Mr. Churchill, was handed to him:

(a) The course of the *Lion* as last signalled by Admiral Beatty was southwest. Admiral Jellicoe had just altered course of the battlefleet to west. He was therefore steering with the battlefleet four points more *towards* the enemy than was the *Lion* by her last signal.

The battle cruisers did not alter from their south-west course until 8.10 p.m., and then only steered W.S.W. two points *less* towards the enemy than the battlefleet was steering. This point, which is one of great importance, is not mentioned by Mr. Churchill.

(b) The signal (1) as worded was incorrect, as the *Lion* was at that time thirteen and a half miles from any German battleship, and eighteen and a half miles from the leading one.

In these circumstances it is not to be wondered at that Admiral Jellicoe should have taken a minute or two to consider what Admiral Beatty's signal was intended to convey, for, first of all, message (3) put the German Battlefleet in a different position to that in which Admiral Jellicoe knew it to be.

Secondly, the No.4 signal, made seven minutes later, contained a proposal to "cut off" that fleet, when it had already been cut off from the only place from which it could have been cut off.

Lastly, as it did not include the course of the *Lion*, the presumption (a correct one) was that she was steering the same course as that given in her last signal, namely S.W., which was four points further in direction from the enemy than the west course that the battlefleet was steering!

After a few minutes' consideration, Admiral Jellicoe ordered the leading division of battleships to follow Admiral Beatty, but, as the *Lion* was out of sight to the south-westward, that division was unable to comply with the order before darkness set in.

As a matter of fact the British Battlefleet was closing the German Battlefleet more rapidly than were the battle cruisers; so that, had Admiral Jellicoe complied with Admiral Beatty's request to follow the *Lion*, the battleships would have steered further away from the enemy than they were actually steering.

Now to finish the quotation of Mr. Churchill's summary:

> A quarter of an hour was allowed to elapse after Jellicoe received Beatty's signal before he sent the necessary order, and in no urgent terms, to the 2nd Battle Squadron.

As a matter of fact the signal was received in the *Iron Duke* at 7.54 p.m., so Admiral Jellicoe would have seen it shortly after 8 p.m. He had just signalled to Admiral Beatty that the course of the battlefleet was west; and, about 8.5, he told the *King George V* to follow Admiral Beatty. This time is fixed by being logged in the log of the *King George V* as received at 8.7 p.m. It appears, therefore, that the quarter of an hour that Mr. Churchill alleges that Admiral Jellicoe took to make up his mind was nearer five minutes; not a very long while, considering the complexity of the data which he had before him.

We will now pass to Mr. Churchill's description of the night of May 31st. His commencement is most telling. The difficulties met with in night fighting and the disabilities imposed on the various arms are well and tersely put; but, unfortunately, soon, for want of sea-going experience, he is unable to interpret the markings on his chart. We find on page 156:

> They [*the British and German mine-fields*] were marked as clearly as rocks or shoals, and could be avoided with almost equal certainty.

Mr. Churchill forgets that shoals and rocks are charted by careful observation in daytime; the British mine-fields were laid always at night, mostly by mine-layers and a few by destroyer leaders, after steaming some two hundred and fifty miles. The mines might easily therefore have been any distance from five to ten miles different from their charted position. In all cases of uncertain charting, the maximum possible error in position has to be allowed for when navigating a fleet.

In discussing the possible routes that the German Fleet might have taken to make their way home we find:

> Retreat into the Baltic by the Kattegat gave Scheer no security against being brought to battle in daylight. It involved a voyage of nearly three hundred and fifty miles, giving the faster British a long day to chase in the open sea. Jellicoe could have provided for this route by the simple process (which he did not, however, adopt) of sending a few light cruisers to watch the area and thus ensure timely information at dawn.

We are beginning to be cautious when we read *of simple and easy* courses which have been discovered by Mr. Churchill and which the Commander-in-Chief of the Grand Fleet did not adopt. This particular *simple* course would have been a futile one.

Had Admiral Scheer attempted the Kattegat route he would, steaming at sixteen knots, have been about one hundred and fifty miles from the Grand Fleet at dawn. It certainly would have required a long day to allow the Grand Fleet to have overtaken him in daylight. A day longer even than the one when "the sun stood still upon Gideon and the moon in the valley of Ajalon". Joshua only required twenty-four hours for his battle; Mr. Churchill, graspingly, demands some thirty-eight hours of daylight on the 1st of June.

Another point that Mr. Churchill has missed is, that the *Official History* states that Admiral Jellicoe was sent the *general direction* of the routes. This is a very different thing to the full information entered on post-war charts which were at Mr. Churchill's disposal.

Mr. Churchill dismisses the probability that Admiral Scheer would take the Ems route, by saying that as it was long and roundabout it might be dismissed as improbable.

Doubtless this may be dismissed now that we know that the German Fleet did not make use of it; but at 9 p.m. on May 31st, 1916, Admiral Jellicoe would have been ill-advised to have disposed so easily of the possibility of its use by Admiral Scheer.

The distance to the Ems channel was one hundred and eighty miles; half of this could have been covered in the dark, leaving only a little less than six hours' steaming for the German Fleet in the daylight. If, as Mr. Churchill suggests he should have done, Admiral Jellicoe had steamed for a point ten miles to the south-westward of the Horn Reef, the Ems passage would have been uncovered. This he calls a good movement. In view of present knowledge this may be true; but viewed in the light of the facts which were at the moment before Admiral Jellicoe, this was not the case.

What were the facts as they appeared to the Admiral?

Take, first of all, the sound of gun firing when the 4th German Scouting Group came into contact with the British 2nd Light Cruiser Squadron. Mr. Churchill remarks:

Firing in this quarter, though it was no proof, at least suggested that the enemy was seeking to pass astern of the British Fleet on the way to the Horn Reef. But confirmation of a decisive character was at hand.

The firing heard was that of light calibre guns. Why should Admiral Jellicoe or Admiral Beatty, both of whom were well able to locate approximately the direction of the firing, come to any other conclusion than the one at which they did arrive (which incidentally was the correct one), that our light cruisers and destroyers were engaging some of the lighter German vessels? The fact of two light cruiser squadrons engaging at night was no evidence that the German battleships were passing astern of our fleet. That the German light cruisers were likely to be at some distance from their battleships was so probable as to almost to amount to a certainty. That our destroyers should have come into contact with a German light cruiser division and its destroyers, which were groping in the dark looking for our battleships with a view to making a torpedo attack, was a far more probable assumption than that the German light cruisers were close ahead of their battle-fleet. None of the other ships of our battlefleet which were nearer to the firing drew the inference that the German battlefleet was crossing behind our fleet.

Mr. Churchill continues as follows:

At 10.41 the *Iron Duke*, and at about 11.30, after it had been decoded, Sir John Jellicoe received the following electrifying message: "German Battlefleet ordered home at 9.14 p.m. Battle cruisers in rear. Course S.S.E. ¾. E. Speed 16 knots." If this message could be trusted it meant, and could only mean, that the Germans were returning by the Horn Reef.

Later Mr. Churchill asks:

But could the Admiralty message be trusted?

This latter is the really important point to be considered. The major signals received by Admiral Jellicoe were:

(1) The Admiralty signal, time of origin 9.58 p.m., received by him at about 10.45 p.m. This message was obviously incorrect, since it placed the rear ship of the German Fleet at 9 p.m. eight miles to the southward of (that is approximately ahead of) the position occupied by the *King George V*, which was the leading ship of our battlefleet at that time. This, not unnaturally, tended to create a mistrust of signals intercepted and deciphered by the Admiralty.

(2) The second Admiralty message quoted above, which would probably have been accepted had it not been for the reports from Commodore Goodenough and the *Birmingham*, given in (3) and (4).

(3) The message from the Commodore at 10.15 p.m. received in *Iron Duke* at 11.38 p.m., which placed the German 4th Scouting Squadron to the westward of the line of advance of the British Battlefleet.

(4) The message from the *Birmingham* at 11.30 p.m., which placed the German battle cruisers thirty miles to the northward (nearly right astern of our battle-fleet), steering a southerly course (i.e. following our fleet).

It was impossible, if the Admiralty message was correct, that the German Commander-in-Chief had altered course S.S.E. ¾. E. at 9.15 p.m. and that the German battle cruisers could yet be astern of our fleet and steering a similar course at 11.30 p.m.

Which evidence was to be trusted by Admiral Jellicoe at 11.30 p.m.? A signal intercepted by the Admiralty two hours previously, or the information just received from one of his cruisers?

It is easy to be wise in the light of present knowledge; but, at the moment, matters were not at all clear. Admiral Jellicoe decided to act on the report of his own cruisers. Mr. Churchill, however, remarks:

> It is difficult to feel that this decision was not contrary to the main weight of evidence. Certain it is that if Sir John Jellicoe had acted in accordance with the Admiralty message he would have had, even if that message had proved erroneous, a justification for his action which could never have been impugned.

But is this so? Let us suppose that the German Fleet had made the Ems Channel and arrived safely in port. Could not Mr. Churchill have marshalled the facts against Admiral Jellicoe somewhat as follows?

> *Firing astern! What of that? Surely the Admiral was expecting some of his destroyers to be engaged, else why had he stationed them in that position? The error in the first Admiralty signal should have made him cautious in accepting a second one from the same source when the reports from two of his own ships, from ocular evidence, positively proved the enemy to be in a position which was impossible if the Admiralty signal was correct. Surely much could have happened between 9.15 p.m. and 11.30 p.m. to have caused the German Admiral to alter his mind. If Sir John Jellicoe had acted in accordance with the evidence of his own cruisers he would have had – even if that information was incorrect – a justification for his action which could never have been impugned.*

The whole truth of the matter is that unless the German Fleet had been met and stopped, whatever action Admiral Jellicoe had taken was bound to be open to subsequent criticism.

The Admiralty at 10.10 had Admiral Scheer's message to the airship detachment requesting early air reconnaissance off the Horn Reef. This as well as some other signals were never passed to Admiral Jellicoe. If this had been done the extra evidence, one hour later than the first signal, would have caused him to believe that Admiral Scheer would choose the Horn Reef route. Why this was never passed has never been made public. Let us hope that the Admiralty will in the near future explain this matter.

One further remark. The evidence which was before Admiral Jellicoe was also in the possession of Admiral Beatty. He likewise believed in the Ems route, as is shown by the following signal, made at 4.4 a.m. on June 1st, to Admiral Jellicoe when the latter ordered the fleet to turn for the Horn Reef:

> When last seen enemy was to the westward steering south-west and proceeding slowly. Zeppelin has passed astern of me steering west. Submit I may sweep south-west to locate enemy.

If both Admiral Beatty and Admiral Jellicoe gave a similar interpretation, at the time, to the signals and happenings of the night, we are inclined to believe that Mr. Churchill's opinion must be somewhat tinged by knowledge that came only after the event.

Here we leave that portion of *The World Crisis* that claims to be a record of the Battle of Jutland, which, though plausible to the casual reader, is historically unreliable, both because of the inaccuracy of many of the statements regarding the details of the fight, and also because of the deductions drawn from them by Mr. Churchill.

Lately, Major Claude Wallace has published a book which contains an "eye-witness" account of the Battle of Jutland. Personal narratives are always interesting, but criticisms of a naval battle, based on the limited view vouchsafed to a single observer in a battlefleet of twenty-four ships, is bound to be untrustworthy. Such a publication would not have merited notice had it not been that publicity has been given to the account in the Press without pointing out the errors into which the author has dropped.

The fundamental absurdity of the criticism lies in the fact that the writer is not versed in the intricacies of a naval battle, nor conversant with the speeds of the various battleship units. Major Wallace might smile if a naval officer had expressed wonder at a general allowing a squadron of cavalry to escape by not sending a battalion of infantry to capture them. Surely naval officers may smile when they read that Major Wallace wonders why Admiral Jellicoe did not chase twenty-three knot German battleships and annihilate them with his eighteen knot fleet.

Chapter 13
Postscript to Chapter Twelve

Here are Mr Churchill's reasons for appointing Admiral Beatty to the command of the battle cruisers:[93]

A few weeks after my arrival at the Admiralty I was told that among several officers of Flag rank that wished to see me was Rear-Admiral Beatty. I had never met him before, but I had the following impressions about him.

First, that he was the youngest Flag officer in the fleet. Second, that he had commanded the white gunboat which had come up the Nile as close as possible to support the 21st Lancers when we made the charge at Omdurman. Third, that he had seen a lot of fighting on land with the army, and consequently he had military as well as naval experience. Fourth, that he came of a hard-riding stock. His father had been in my own regiment, the 4th Hussars, and I often heard him talked of when I first joined. The Admiral, I knew, was a very fine horseman, with what is called 'an eye for country'. Fifth, that there was much talk in naval circles of his having been pushed on too fast. Such were the impressions aroused in my mind by the name of this officer, and I record them with minuteness because the decisions which I had the honour of taking in regard to him were most serviceable to the Royal Navy and to the British arms.

I was, however, advised about him at the Admiralty in a decisively adverse sense. He had got on too fast he had many interests ashore. His heart, it was said was not wholly in the service. He had been offered an appointment in the Atlantic Fleet suited to his rank as Rear-Admiral. He had declined this appointment – a very serious step for a naval officer to take when appointments were few in proportion to candidates – and he should in consequence not be offered any further employment. It would be contrary to precedent to make a further offer. He had already been unemployed for eighteen months, and would probably be retired in the ordinary course at the expiration of the full three years unemployment.

230

But my first meeting with the Admiral induced me immediately to disregard this unfortunate advice. He became at once my Naval Secretary (or Private Secretary, as the appointment was then styled). Working thus side by side, in rooms which communicated, we perpetually discussed during the next fifteen months the problems of a naval war with Germany. It became increasingly clear to me that he viewed questions of naval strategy and tactics in a different light to an average naval officer; he approached them, as it seemed to me, much more as a soldier would. His war experiences on land had illuminated the facts he had acquired in his naval training. He was no mere instrumentalist. He did not think of 'matériel' as an end in itself, but only as a means. He thought of war problems in their unity by land, sea and air. His mind had been rendered quick and subtle by the situations of polo and the hunting field, and enriched by varied experiences against the enemy on Nile gunboats and ashore. It was with equal pleasure and profit that I discussed with him our naval problem, now from this angle, now from that; and I was increasingly struck with the shrewd and profound sagacity of his comments expressed in language singularly free from technical jargon.

I had no doubts whatever when the command of the Battle Cruiser Squadron fell vacant in the spring of 1913 in appointing him over the heads of all to this incomparable command, the nucleus as it proved to be of the famous Battle Cruiser Fleet – the strategic cavalry of the Navy – that supreme combination of speed and power to which the thoughts of the Admiralty were continuously directed.

Appendix I

The Dogger Bank Action

I have included this account of the Dogger Bank Action as Admiral Sir Gordon Wilson Moore has suffered for the mistake made by Admiral Beatty. Diagram 52 shows the critical time of the fight.

The *Lion* was steaming E. b S., along the dotted line, damaged and unable to keep up. At 10.45 Admiral Beatty sighted, or thought he sighted, which amounts to the same thing in action, the wash of a periscope two points on his starboard bow. The *Lion* had then dropped a mile and a half behind the remainder of the ships.

Instead of making the warning signal that a submarine had been sighted, letting the other ships go on and turning the *Lion* *towards* the submarine, Admiral Beatty signalled to the whole Battle Cruiser Fleet to turn eight points away from the submarine to a N. b E. course. As no submarine warning flag was hoisted, no one in the fleet could guess the motive for the manoeuvre. No sooner had he done this than he made a signal to turn back again three points to N.E., and then, wishing to get our cruisers once more to attack the German cruisers, he hoisted "Engage the enemy's rear"; but *as the N.E. compass signal was still flying* before the latter signal was hauled down, all the ships read it correctly as an order to attack

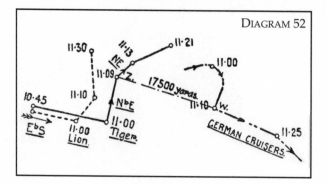

DIAGRAM 52

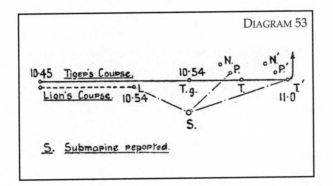

the enemy bearing N.E., which was the *Blücher*, which ship was already disabled and was drifting astern of her squadron. This they all proceeded to do, and the result was that the German cruisers escaped.

Now let us see in greater detail what led to the confusion. At 10.45, when the *Lion* was at L (Diagram 53), Admiral Beatty saw what appeared to him to be the wash of a periscope two points on the starboard bow. The *Tiger* was at Tg, one and a half miles ahead of the *Lion*.

The wash of a periscope could hardly have been sighted by Admiral Beatty further than a mile; but let us increase this even up to a mile and a half. Even at such a distance, there would have been no possibility of any turning signal helping the *Tiger* and the other cruisers, who were steaming at 25 knots.

Even supposing that such a signal could have been made, received and acted on in three minutes – a phenomenally short time; for, as a matter of fact, in reality it took six minutes; but let us take a possible three minutes – the *Tiger* and her consorts would by that time have been as shown at T P N. The submarine would have been 50 degrees abaft the beam of the centre ship, the *Princess Royal*, while the *New Zealand*, N, the rear ship, would have been perfectly well able to look after herself.

An eight-point turn was in any case ridiculous, as it brought the sterns of the ships *past the bearing of the submarine* and opened their port sides to attack.

As a matter of fact, when at 11 o'clock the turn was actually made at the position shown at T"P"N", the ships were as safe as if the submarine had been in the Atlantic.

It was absolutely useless to signal a turn to the cruisers; they should have been allowed to go on with their action. All that was necessary for Admiral Beatty to do was, first, to hoist the submarine warning signal, then to turn the *Lion towards* the submarine, and then to signal to his next in command to take over the command of the fleet. Had these simple things been done there is a very good chance that we might have bagged all the German cruisers.

Now, had an admiral of experience been in command of the battle cruisers, and, without in any way wishing to be invidious, we might, as examples, name two out of the several who come under that category and who were serving in the Grand Fleet, viz. Vice-Admiral Charles Madden or Vice-Admiral Doveton Sturdee – had any such admiral experienced in fleet work and naval weapons, commanded at the Dogger Bank, we would in all probability have scooped up all the German battle cruisers. What had the Admiral to do? Simply nothing except to fight a straightforward chasing action in clear weather, in broad daylight; and, thank goodness, we have many admirals dogged enough not to let go when once they have their teeth into an enemy; and, secondly, when an emergency arose, instinctively, from experience, to do the right thing. Emergencies arose when a submarine was reported, and when the flagship, the *Lion*, was disabled.

To appreciate (1) that it was impossible to turn, by signal, ships that were 3,000 yards ahead, and steaming at 25 knots, in time to avoid attack from a submarine whose wash had been sighted two points on his bow; and (2) that the submarine warning signal would have caused a searching look-out to have been kept abaft the beam of all the ships, would have been mere commonplace inferences to a practised brain. Moreover, the differentiation between a massed long-range destroyer attack, and isolated short-range submarine attack would have been accomplished mentally weeks beforehand in quiet thought. Nor would an admiral of experience have failed to express his wishes clearly to his fleet; nor, when his flagship had been disabled, have failed to turn over the command to his next in seniority, nor left that unfortunate officer without any knowledge as to when his Commander-in-Chief had ended giving orders and therefore he himself free to take command.

But let us return to 11.9 a.m., when the course was altered to N.E. This could not cut the *Blücher* off from the rest of her squadron (as suggested in the *Official History of the War*, Vol II, p.93). A course nothing to the northward of E. b N. would have been required for this. The turn to N.E. is inexplicable except on the grounds that the *Blücher* was the target intended.

The result of the action was decided at 11.14. Let us see why.

Had Admiral Moore then assumed command, disobeyed the signal to attack the *Blücher* and turned the ships to chase the German cruisers, at least two minutes would have elapsed before the ships would have taken in the signal and have commenced to turn, and at least the equivalent of two more minutes would have elapsed due to turning and consequent loss of speed. The position would then have been as shown in Diagram 54. Our cruiser admiral would have had the choice of two alternatives.

(1) To chase for three-quarters of an hour[94] until he again got within range, and then use his bow armament only. But at this period of the action it was essential to inflict the maximum damage as time was short, *for owing*

234

to geographical reasons the action could not be carried on for more than another two hours; or:

(2) To try and get into a position to use the whole of the armament of each ship; which he could not have done for nearly an hour and a half.

As a matter of fact, he would at first have hauled out on the port side of the enemy's ships as shown in Diagram 54, because he was already on their port side; and then at 11.25, as they altered course for Wilhelmshaven, he would have been obliged to turn to starboard and haul out on their starboard side. If he had originally started to haul out on the starboard side they would probably have kept on for Heligoland.

It all comes back to the same hard fact, namely, that the eight-point turn – quite needlessly undertaken – allowed the German cruisers to escape.

Let us look a little more closely into the signalling.

The *Lion* had only two signal halyards left, but a lot can be done with two halyards and a daylight signal lamp.

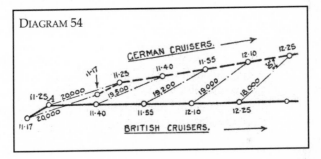

DIAGRAM 54

Admiral Beatty used the *Blue* pendant for the eight-point turn to N. b E. This meant that all the ships were to turn at the same moment. This was correct. But when he turned back the three points to N.E., instead of using the *Blue* pendant again, like any experienced admiral would have done, he used the *compass* pendant, which either signifies a course to be steered; or, if hoisted with another signal, it shows the bearing of the object talked about in the signal. As this pendant was flying at the same time as the signal to engage the enemy's rear, not one ship only, but all the ships, understood it to mean "attack the ship bearing N.E.", namely the *Blücher*. Had the *Blue* pendant been used there could have been no such confusion. Inexperience again.

Now the *Lion* was dropping fast, and Admiral Beatty had got the cruisers going full speed on an errand which he did not want; so, in hope of heading them off, he made "Keep closer to the enemy". Which enemy? Whether the *Blücher* or the other cruisers was not specified; but as no one saw the signal it made no difference to the action.

Now, had he done what any admiral whose brain had been prepared for emergencies would have done, he would at 11 have made no signal at all except to his second-in-command to take charge. At that time he had the *Aurora* and *Arethusa* close to him, either of which could have communicated his signal to the fleet if the *Lion* was unable to do so. By failing to do this, his second-in-command was put in a very awkward position.

In the first place Admiral Beatty did not make the usual signal indicating that a submarine had been sighted. Hence the Admiral second-in-command and all the Captains of the other cruisers were absolutely in the dark as to why the eight-point turn, which headed the ships away from the German Battle Cruiser Squadron and toward the *Blücher*, had been made. No one had the slightest idea what was the meaning of the manoeuvre. Had Admiral Beatty hoisted the recognized signal for submarine attack, he would have at once placed everyone *au courant* with his reasons for the turn.

Now the signal to "engage the rear of the enemy bearing N.E." was not hauled down by the *Tiger* repeating to the *New Zealand* till 11.14. Admiral Moore in the *New Zealand*, therefore, up to 11.14, was acting directly under Admiral Beatty's orders. When was Admiral Moore to take over in default of his Commander-in-Chief delegating the command to him by signal?

He could not do so until Admiral Beatty gave up the command, which he never did. His orders as conveyed by the signal were to attack the *Blücher*. He had to obey, and after this had been done the German cruisers had gained so much distance that it was practically hopeless to expect to overhaul them. Yet, to the world at large, Admiral Moore has been unfairly held to blame for their escape.

Appendix II
Synopsis of Losses in British and German Fleets

PHASE I: CRUISER ACTION

	British Losses	German Losses
Battle cruiser	*Indefatigable*	Nil
Battle cruiser	*Queen Mary*	Nil
Destroyer	*Nestor*	*V 27*
Destroyer	*Nomad*	*V 29*

PHASE II: ADVANCED CRUISER ACTION

Battle cruiser	*Invincible*	Nil
Armoured cruiser	*Defence*	Nil
Armoured cruiser	*Warrior*	Nil
Light cruiser	Nil	*Wiesbaden*
Destroyer	*Shark*	Nil

PHASE III: BATTLEFLEET ACTION

Battle cruiser	Nil	*Lutzow*
Destroyer	Nil	*S 24*
Battleship	Nil	*Pommern*
Light cruiser	Nil	*Frauenlob*
Light cruiser	Nil	*Rostock*
Light cruiser	Nil	*Elbing*
Flotilla leader	*Tipperary*	Nil
Destroyer	*Ardent*	*V4*
Destroyer	*Fortune*	*V4*
Destroyer	*Sparrowhawk*	Nil
Destroyer	*Turbulent*	Nil

The British losses were mainly in the Cruiser Action, Phase I, the reasons for which have been discussed; and in the Advanced Cruiser Action, Phase II, owing to the armoured cruisers and the *Invincible* coming under the concentrated fire of the German battleships and battle cruisers as they emerged from the mist.

Phase III, the battlefleet action: our fleet sank one battle cruiser and one destroyer, and lost nothing.

Phase IV, the Night Action: the destroyers did well, sinking one battleship, three light cruisers and two destroyers for the loss of one flotilla leader and four destroyers.

Notes and References

PART I: The Truth About Jutland

1 House of Commons, 29 October 1919.
2 House of Commons, 11 April 1923.
3 The words 'report', 'narrative' and 'record' were used indiscriminately when referring to my Official Record. It was a 'record' and not a 'report', which latter word implies comment.
4 It will be noted that the Record has now "almost reached completion", whereas on 29 October 1919 it had "been completed".
5 House of Commons, 15 December 1920.
6 Between 15.35 hours and 22.00 hours on 31 May, thirty reports of enemy submarines were made by our ships. Of these two were reported as seen on the surface, two were reported as being sighted breaking the surface and two were believed to have been rammed, although not actually seen at the moment. Of the remainder, some stated that a periscope had been sighted, one remarking that the alleged periscope was undoubtedly a dummy. Beatty in his report states, at about 16.00 hours: "It would appear at this time that we were passing through a screen of enemy submarines."
7 See Appendix for details.
8 *Ibid.*
9 *Ibid.*
10 The "Long Forties" extend for some 110 miles from the coast of Aberdeenshire.
11 The figures at the end of a message indicate the time of origin of that message, or in other words the actual time, expressed in the four-figure notation, at which the message was written. The instructions contained in this message were, therefore, actually given by the Commander-in-Chief at 19.30 hours. The time of origin gives little indication of the time of *receipt* of the message by the person to whom it is addressed. This depends partly on the method used to transmit the message. In the case of cipher messages sent by Wireless Telegraphy it depends to even a greater extent on the time taken to decipher the message. It is clear, therefore, that instructions contained in any signal message, by whatever method it is transmitted, cannot be acted on by the recipient until, at least, some minutes after the time at which the actual

239

instructions were given. The delay in the case of visual messages, sent in plain language, should be very small as compared with that of cipher messages sent by wireless. No time of origin is appended to signals made by Flags, in this case the time of receipt of the instructions should be practically identical with the time the signal is hoisted.

12   See the chapter "Under-Water Attack".

13   *Official History of the War – Naval Operations*, Vol. III, p.315.

14   The seaplane-carrier *Campania,* attached to the fleet at Scapa Flow, was some hours late in leaving, owing to a misapprehension as to the time the battle fleet was sailing. She could not have overtaken the fleet in time for her machines to be of any use for reconnaissance purposes; so, at 04.21 hours, she was ordered by Jellicoe to return to harbour. This obviated the necessity of detaching destroyers to act as a screen for this ship alone.

15   *Official History of the War – Naval Operations*, Vol. III, p.376.

16   "I observed a salvo pitch abreast 'Q' turret of *Queen Mary* (this was the first time I had seen *Queen Mary* hit) and almost instantaneously there was a terrific upheaval and a dense cloud of smoke. This could not altogether be avoided as *Tiger* was close up (about 2 cables) from *Queen Mary.* As *Tiger* passed through the cloud there was a heavy fall of material on her decks, but no sign whatever could be seen of the *Queen Mary.* She must have sunk instantaneously." (Extract from Report of Captain of HMS *Tiger*.)

17   A few examples will illustrate the necessity of continuous reports being received if any tangible result is to be obtained by striking an average. At 15.38hours the *Falmouth* reported her position, and at the same time reported that *Galatea* bore N.N.E. 2 miles from her. But at 15.35 hours the *Galatea* in a report gave her own position, which was over 8 miles from that reported by *Falmouth.*

The *Lion* reported her position at 15.35 hours and again at 15.50 hours. The distance between these reported positions was 1½ miles, whereas the ship actually travelled 6.2 miles in the fifteen minutes' interval between these reports.

The positions of *Southampton* given in the signals made from that ship at 16.30 hours and at 16.38 hours indicated that she travelled 8 miles in eight minutes. A wireless message from the Admiralty which was sent at 17.00 hours gave the position, course and speed of the enemy battle fleet at 16.09 hours; and a second message, sent at 17.45 hours, gave the position, course and speed of the enemy main force at 16.30 hours. The position of the enemy given in these messages from the Admiralty was some 17 miles to the westward of that deduced from the *Southampton*'s message and some 8 miles to the westward of that deduced from a message from the *Lion* at 16.45 hours.

In each case it is estimated that the enemy was sighted at a distance of about 10 miles. It will be seen, therefore, that the position of the enemy differed by about 9 miles, according to which reckoning was taken as correct, *Lion*'s or *Southampton*'s. As a fact, the positions given in the Admiralty messages were approximately correct, but only one was received in time to be of use. Greater reliance would naturally, at this date, have been placed on positions given by ships in actual contact with the enemy than on positions obtained by directional wireless on shore, then in its infancy. Reciprocal directional wireless between ships did not then exist.

18   Investigations made in 1919 led to the belief that, as stated previously, both the *Iron Duke* and the *Lion* were somewhat out in their reckoning. It was therefore decided to locate, and fix the position of, the wreck of the *Invincible*; this wreck being a definite point in the battle area. Ascertaining the position of this wreck would once and for all determine the exact geographical position of the action, and would enable the position of any other ship to be deduced with considerable accuracy at any stage of the action. The wreck was, therefore, searched for, located, and the position fixed.

19   The next day the two halves had subsided, and no sign of the wreck was visible on the surface of the water.

20   An element of mystery has always been made about this turn, though why the battle-cruisers should not turn through 360°, if so desired, is not clear. They were not in action. No possible danger of any collision would be involved. With the firm belief that submarines were about, evidenced by a wireless report made by Beatty at 18.54 hours, one minute before the turn was commenced, that one had been sighted, it would naturally be undesirable to reduce speed to any great extent. To get within visual touch of the battle fleet without delay would have necessitated a very large reduction in the speed, unless course was also altered. What more natural, therefore, than to turn and, having turned nearly 180° before realizing that there was no necessity to continue any farther to the northward, to resume the original course as quickly as possible? The quickest method of doing this, having turned nearly 180°, would obviously be to continue the turn through 360°. This matter is not one which can be swept aside as of no importance, if accuracy in plotting the ship's tracks is required. The *Lion*, having turned through 360°, was, after about eleven minutes, in the same position as when the turn was commenced, whereas if she had made any other form of turn the position would not have been the same.

   Referring to Battle of Jutland – Official Despatches (Comd. 1068), we find, in Plate 10, Track of *Lion*, which is signed by the Vice-Admiral commanding battle-cruiser fleet himself, this turn shown as a circle. Again, in Plate 31, showing the track of the *New Zealand*, it is conspicuously shown. In the report of the Captain of the *Lion* it is stated that "ship continued to circle to starboard", and in the report from *New Zealand* we find, "commenced to circle to starboard" and "gradually circling round to starboard". In the *Official History*, Sir J. Corbett, who had, besides the above evidence, the evidence of the ships' logs at his disposal, states definitely that the turn was made. It is common knowledge that a good deal of discussion among those concerned took place on this point shortly after the battle, and also at other, more recent, times.

   In view of this overwhelming weight of evidence it is difficult to understand the reason for showing this turn on Chart 8a – Official Despatches – as a turn to starboard followed by a turn to port. This chart, which is also signed by Admiral Beatty, is stated to be of a date 17 July 1916. It is, however, of little value as evidence owing to the obvious errors it contains. The geographical positions of the *Lion* do not agree with those given in her cipher messages reporting the position of the enemy, and the ranges of the enemy are at

241

variance with those given in the gunnery records of the battle-cruisers. The position of the *Lion* at 19.15 hours, for example, is shown as about 5,000 yards on the starboard bow of the *Iron Duke*, that is, nearer the enemy, whereas, in reality, she was about 8,000 yards on the *Iron Duke*'s port bow, or farther from the enemy.

21   The three submarines sent to positions in the Horns Reef Passage did not, as it transpired, act as a menace to the safe return of the High Seas Fleet by this route. Their stations were assigned to them before it was known that the present operation was being undertaken. Their instructions were to lie on the bottom until 2 June. The sudden change in the situation was not transmitted to them before leaving Harwich, at 19.00 hours on 30 May, although there seems no reason why this should not have been done. They, therefore, carried out their original orders and remained quietly below the surface, thereby missing a good opportunity of inflicting severe damage on the retreating enemy.

22   The possibility of the enemy crossing astern of the fleet and, although detected, not being reported would not, of course, occur to anyone.

23   See Appendix for details.

24   In this connection it should be noted that, during the hours of darkness, even the enemy capital ships would be using their secondary armament, rather than their more ponderous turret guns. There would, therefore, be little to distinguish between the firing of battleships and light cruisers so far as flash and glare were concerned.

25   The *Warspite* had fallen out and was on her way back to harbour.

26   *Official Despatches*, p.474.

27   *Official History*, Vol. III, pp.413, 415.

28   *The World Crisis*, Vol. II, p. 87.

29   *Narrative of the Battle of Jutland*, p.106, Note 1.

30   *Ibid*, p.113, Note 6.

31   *Narrative of the Battle of Jutland*, p.34.

32   *Ibid*, p.24.

33   *The Battle of Jutland*, p.134.

34   *Battleships in Action*, Vol. II, p.135

35   *Ibid*, p.136.

36   *The World Crisis* (1916-1918), p.122.

37   House of Commons, 14 March 1927.

38   *The World Crisis* (1916-1918), p.123.

39   *Ibid*, p.125.

40   *Narrative of the Battle of Jutland*, p.21.

41   *The Fighting Forces*, January 1927, p.556.

42   *Ibid*, p.20.

43   Royal United Services Institute Journal, No.485, p.34.

44   *The World Crisis* (1916-1918), p.130.

45   *Ibid*, p.132.

46   *Ibid*, p.129.

47   *The Battle of Jutland*, p.139.

48   *The Navy in Battle*, p.338.

49   *Battleships in Action*, Vol. II, p.150.

50   *Ibid*, Vol. II, p.152.
51   *Ibid*, p.157.
52   *Ibid*, Vol. II, p.191.
53   German Official History, Vol. V, pp.283-4.
54   *The Battle of Jutland*, p.184.
55   *Ibid*, p.292.
56   *Ibid*, p.188.
57   *Ibid*, p.262.
58   *Battleships in Action*, Vol. II, p.159.
59   *The World Crisis* (1916-1918), p.152.
60   *Official Despatches*, pp.459-62:
        6.23.   Course of Fleet S.E. by E.
        6.26.   Speed 14 knots.
        6.33.   Speed 17 knots.
        6.44.   Course of Fleet S.E.
        6.54.   Course of Fleet South.
        7.5.   Alter Course 3 points to starboard.
        i.e. between 6.23 and 7.5 the course of the battle fleet was altered 90 degrees *towards* the enemy.
61   *The Battle of Jutland*, p.187.
62   *Ibid*, p.41.
63   Vide Chapter II, p.32.
64   *The World Crisis* (1916-1918), p.153.
65   *Narrative of the Battle of Jutland*, pp.68-9.
66   *Ibid*, p.73.
67   *Ibid*, p.72.
68   *Ibid*, p.74.
69   *Ibid*, p.76.
70   *Naval Operations*, Vol. III, pp.413-5.
71   *Battle of Jutland*, p.221.
72   *Ibid*, p.222.
73   *The Times*, 19 February 1920.
74   If it had been it would, or should, have been equally received by Beatty, but he makes no allusion to it.
75   *Battle of Jutland*, p.220.
76   *Ibid*, p.223.
77   *Battleships in Action*, Vol. II, pp.164-5.
78   *Ibid*, Vol. II, p.165.
79   *The Battle of Jutland*, pp.235-6.
80   *The World Crisis* (1916-1918).
81   *Ibid*, pp.156-7.
82   *Ibid*, p.157.
83   *Ibid*, p.161.
84   German Official History.

PART II: The Jutland Scandal

1   Mahon, *Influence of Sea Power Upon the French Revolution*, Vol. I, p.57.
2   The distance from the bow of the leading ship to the bow of the last ship would be 23 times 500 yards, but the length of the last ship has to be added to this. Moreover, a line of ships is always a little longer than the exact mathematical length.
3   Corbett, Julian, *The Official History of the War – Naval Operations* (Longmans & Co., London), Vol. III, p.323.
4   *Official Despatches*, p.443.
5   *Ibid*, p.444. Flag signals from *Lion* were always difficult to see at a distance owing to clear view being interfered with by her fore control position.
6   Corbett, p.331.
7   *Ibid*, p.328.
8   *Ibid*, p.336.
9   *Ibid*, p.334.
10   *Ibid*, p.336.
11   *Ibid*, p.337.
12   *Ibid*, p.338.
13   *Ibid*, p.340.
14   *Ibid*; see plans 26, 27, 28, 29, 30.
15   *Official Despatches*, p.449.
16   *Ibid*, pp.445-6.
17   Viscount Jellicoe of Scapa, *The Grand Fleet* (Cassell, London), p.329.
18   Corbett, p.353.
19   Viscount Jellicoe of Scapa, p.353.
20   Corbett, p.355.
21   *Ibid*.
22   *Ibid*, p.356.
23   *Ibid*, p.361.
24   *Ibid*, Frontispiece.
25   *Ibid*, p.372.
26   Viscount Jellicoe of Scapa, pp.310-3; *Brassey's Naval Annual 1913*.
27   Commander Georg von Hase, *Kiel and Jutland*, p.125.
28   Viscount Jellicoe of Scapa, p.361.
29   Corbett, plans.
30   *Ibid*, p.383.
31   *Ibid, footnote*.
32   *Ibid*, p.395. This is not borne out by the German *Official History*.
33   A similar incident happened to me in the 1906 manoeuvres when trying to break through Admiral Sir Assheton Curzon-Howe's fleet. I was fortunate enough to intercept the challenge and reply which enabled me to steam for a whole hour in company with the enemy's fleet until I got an opportunity of breaking through.
34   Corbett, p.403.
35   *Ibid*, p.402.
36   *Ibid*, pp.401-2.

37   *Ibid*, p.410.
38   Viscount Jellicoe of Scapa, p.385.
39   Corbett, p.414.
40   *Ibid*, p.397.
41   *Ibid*, p.398.
42   In reality the battleship *Nassau*.
43   *Ibid*, p.399.
44   *Ibid*.
45   *Ibid*, p.342.
46   *Ibid*, p.405.
47   *Ibid*, p.414.
48   *Admiralty Narrative*, p.42.
49   Corbett, plan No.41.
50   *Official Despatches*, p.195.
51   *Ibid*, p.67.
52   *Ibid*, p.134; *Admiralty Narrative*, p.107.
53   *Official Despatches*, p.141.
54   *Admiralty Narrative*, p.107, footnote.
55   *Ibid*, p.22.
56   *Ibid*, p.106, footnote 2, and p.113, footnotes 3 and 6.
57   Admiral Scheer's *High Sea Fleet*, p.144.
58   Corbett, p.334.
59   *Ibid*, p.331 footnote 2.
60   *Ibid*, p.340.
61   *Official Despatches*, 1608-1745.
62   Winston Churchill, *The World Crisis*, Vol III, p.125.
63   *Ibid*.
64   *Ibid*, p.129.
65   It was well known that the fighting top of *Lion* was apt to obscure signals.
66   *Admiralty Narrative*, p.46, diagram.
67   Winston Churchill, Vol III, p.124.
68   Letter to *The Times*, February 1927.
69   Winston Churchill, Vol II, p.124. Also see postscript to this Chapter.
70   Winston Churchill, Vol III, p.122.
71   *Ibid*, p.125.
72   *Ibid*, p.129.
73   *Ibid*, p.133.
74   As there was plenty of time in hand, there was no reason why the battle cruisers should not have been turned in *succession*. The fact that this was done is merely recorded here.
75   Winston Churchill, Vol III, p.142.
76   In an article in the *Fortnightly*, Admiral Scheer clearly states the fact that he would have fought if he could have placed his fleet in a position of advantage, but not otherwise.
77   Winston Churchill, Vol III, p.141.
78   *Ibid*, p.148.
79   *Ibid*, p.151.

80   The *Invincible*, ahead of our battlefleet, was believed by Admiral Scheer to be leading our line of battleships, which again headed him away from his own ports.
81   Winston Churchill, Vol III, p.147.
82   *Ibid*, p.136.
83   *Ibid*, p.149.
84   *Ibid*, p.136.
85   See the preface to Winston Churchill, *The World Crisis*, Vol III.
86   Winston Churchill, Vol III, p.136.
87   *Ibid*.
88   *Ibid*, p.151.
89   *Ibid*, p.152.
90   *Ibid*.
91   *Ibid*, p.153.
92   There can be no ambiguity as regards the plotting of these diagrams as Admiral Scheer would have had no alternative but to run away as soon as he found that our fleet was following him. Every advantage lies with the fleet which is being chased during a stern chase. Moreover, though steering a safe course away from our fleet, they would at 8.40 p.m. have been only five miles further from the Horn Reef than they actually were at the time.
93   Winston Churchill, Vol II, p.87.
94   This gives the British ships one knot speed over the Germans, after the *Blücher* had fallen out.

Index

Mines, 12, 42, 51, 62, 77, 111, 121, 225
Moore, Admiral Sir Gordon Wilson, KCB, 96, 232, 234, 236,
Moray Firth, 15

Napoleon I, Emperor of the French, 102
Nelson, Admiral Horatio Lord, xi, 98, 102-10, 111, 185
Nile, Battle of, 98, 109, 110, 161, 230, 231

Official History of the War - Naval Operations, 4, 57, 64, 76, 93, 143, 146, 152, 159, 173, 203, 209, 226, 234
Orkney Islands, 16

Paschen, Commander, 70
Pollen, A.H., 65, 71, 95

Rosyth, 15-19, 139
Royal Marines, 26
Royal Navy,
First Battle Squadron, 16, 79, 86, 213, 222
Second Battle Squadron, 16, 17, 52, 85, 174, 213, 225
Third Battle Squadron, 170, 214
Fourth Battle Squadron, 16, 85, 213
Fifth Battle Squadron, 16, 17, 20-2, 24, 26-8, 30, 33, 55-8, 68-72, 75, 78, 82, 134, 140-4, 148, 175, 180, 187-8, 190, 192-200, 209-12, 215-18
First Battle-Cruiser Squadron, 17, 87, 148, 187
Second Battle-Cruiser Squadron, 17, 87, 148, 187
Third Battle-Cruiser Squadron, 16, 28, 36, 38, 40, 86, 148, 202
First Cruiser Squadron, 16, 19, 86
Second Cruiser Squadron, 16, 19, 86
First Light Cruiser Squadron, 17, 46, 47, 88
Second Light Cruiser Squadron, 17, 27, 53, 88, 146, 226
Third Light Cruiser Squadron, 17, 46, 47, 88

Fourth Light Cruiser Squadron, 16, 44, 51, 86, 173, 222
First Torpedo-Boat Destroyer Flotilla, 17, 88
Fourth Torpedo-Boat Destroyer Flotilla, 16, 53, 87
Ninth Torpedo-Boat Destroyer Flotilla, 17, 79, 88, 143
Tenth Torpedo-Boat Destroyer Flotilla, 17, 79, 88
Eleventh Torpedo-Boat Destroyer Flotilla, 16, 51, 53, 87, 222
Twelfth Torpedo-Boat Destroyer Flotilla, 16, 55, 58, 87, 165
Thirteenth Torpedo-Boat Destroyer Flotilla, 17, 88, 142, 169
Vessels,
Abdiel, 51, 62, 86
Acasta, 87, 147
Achates, 87
Acheron, 88
Active, 86
Agincourt, 86
Ajax, 85
Ambuscade, 87
Ardent, 87, 167, 185, 237
Arethusa, 236
Ariel, 88
Attack, 88
Aurora, 236
Badger, 88
Barham, 24, 27-8, 55-7, 68-9, 87, 142, 175, 188, 189-90, 193-4, 197-9, 219
Bellerophon, 85
Bellona, 86
Benbow, 85
Birkenhead, 88
Birmingham, 54, 55, 88, 164, 165, 227, 228
Black Prince, 58, 86, 184, 202
Blanche, 86
Boadicea, 86
Broke, 53, 54, 87, 168
Calliope, 47, 86, 173
Canada, 85
Canterbury, 17, 28, 86
Captain, 105

249